# Seducing Souls

# Seducing Souls

## Education and the Experience of Human Well-Being

### Karl D. Hostetler

continuum

2011

**The Continuum International Publishing Group**
80 Maiden Lane, New York, NY 10038
The Tower Building, 11 York Road, London SE1 7NX

www.continuumbooks.com

© 2011 Karl D. Hostetler

**Library of Congress Cataloging-in-Publication Data**
Hostetler, Karl D., 1954–
Seducing souls: education and the experience of human well-being / Karl D. Hostetler.
    p. cm.
  Includes bibliographical references and index.
  ISBN-13: 978-1-4411-2618-4 (hardcover: alk. paper)
  ISBN-10: 1-4411-2618-X (hardcover: alk. paper)
  ISBN-13: 978-1-4411-4960-2 (pbk.: alk. paper)
  ISBN-10: 1-4411-4960-0 (pbk.: alk. paper)
  1. Transformative learning. 2. Well-being. 3. Education—Philosophy. I. Title.
  LC1100.H67 2011
  370.11'5—dc22              2010048876

ISBN:    978-1-4411-2618-4 (hardcover)
         978-1-4411-4960-2 (paperback)

Typeset by Pindar NZ, Auckland, New Zealand
Printed and bound in the United States of America

*For my parents*

# Contents

# Acknowledgments

Many professional colleagues have contributed directly or indirectly to the work that has led up to this book. They are too many to name individually, but I hope they will know who they are and understand my appreciation. Some content in Chapters 6, 7, and 8 I adapt from two papers I have published previously: "Making a Place for the Good in Educational Deliberations," in Randall Curren, ed., *Philosophy of Education 1999* (Champaign, IL: Philosophy of Education Society, 2000), pp. 57–65; and "Toward a Perfectionist Response to Ethical Conflict," *Studies in Philosophy and Education* 17, (4), (1998): 295–302. Some material from Chapter 9 was published previously in "In Praise of Passivity in Teaching: An Essay on Life in Classrooms," *Journal of Instructional Psychology* 20, (1), (1993): 40–8. I am grateful for permission to use that material here.

There are some individuals who deserve my special thanks. David Barker, editor at Continuum, guided this book to its completion. Dr. Jonas Soltis has been mentor and friend ever since he was my doctoral advisor way back when. Doctoral students Brad Baurain, Eric Evans, Di Kitterer, and Brooke Koliha participated in a seminar in which I used my manuscript. I benefited from their thoughtful discussion and criticism. Tom Kraft, Margaret Macintyre Latta, and Loukia Sarroub are wonderful colleagues whose conversation and support have been invaluable. Mary Sawicki read parts of the manuscript and gave me feedback and encouragement. Finally, inadequate as it is, in some small recognition of all I owe them, I dedicate this book to my parents, Wayne and Carolyn.

# Introduction

Aristotle proposes that, without a doubt, living well or doing well is the highest of practical goods and the aim of politics.[1] I'm not sure there's no room for doubt there, but in this book I argue that as a practical and political endeavor, the fundamental aim of education should be to serve people's well-being, to help them live well. Educators have no greater obligation than to serve the welfare of students, themselves, colleagues, and the broader community and world.

That might seem to be a strikingly unremarkable proposition. After all, would anyone deny that people should be better-off through education rather than worse-off? I hope not, but the obviousness of the point is one reason why well-being merits our attention. While there are occasional references to well-being in education literature and policy, typically there is a lot more assuming than careful thinking going on. The meaning and value of human welfare might appear so obvious that it escapes critical scrutiny and philosophical conceptualization. In education, well-being has not been granted the importance and attention it needs, with the result that too often conceptions of education are "flattened and narrowed,"[2] offering people educational experiences that, if not downright harmful, do little to help them live lives that are fulfilling. Genuine concern for well-being requires us to explore the most basic aspects of the human condition: What constitutes a worthwhile life for a human being?

"Seducing souls" might seem an odd way to characterize the aim of education for human well-being. Seduction suggests manipulation and exploitation, which are not good things, by and large. I choose the title in part to be provocative but also to indicate the extent to which we must rethink education if education is to help people live worthwhile lives. We must engage body, emotion, and spirit, as well as minds. We must release the urge to control and allow

1

ourselves to be seized by, seduced into, meaningful experiences. Education for human well-being might necessitate some amount of deception — Socrates provides one example — but the ultimate aim is not to manipulate people, but to draw their whole being into experiences where their selves can be elevated and transformed, where their vision can become broader, deeper, and more perspicuous, and their lives enriched.

## WHY THINK ABOUT WELL-BEING?

Why get into the question of well-being now? The question is always relevant, and its neglect is one motivation for this book. But there are some current conditions that make the question of well-being especially pressing. I believe the welfare of students and teachers is under attack right now, especially in public education, and needs defense. Such attacks are not new, but recently they have been especially strident and dangerous. As I write this, I think it's fair to say that elementary and secondary education in the United States is dominated by the legacy of No Child Left Behind, with its emphasis on high-stakes testing, a narrow curriculum, particular sorts of education research, and punishing "underperforming" schools and teachers. I might as well admit that I am motivated to write a response to what I consider a terribly ill-conceived piece of legislation.[3] By and large, the response to the perceived crisis[4] in education has not been to raise and meaningfully debate fundamental questions but to retrench in the comfort of "high standards" and self-righteous condemnation of students, schools, and teachers who "fail."

There is nothing new about bad education policy and some aspects of No Child Left Behind.[5] What might be new, or if not new then rising to prominence, is a sense of uncertainty, even fear, as to the future of the United States and the world. Terrorism, dangers to the environment, and an unpredictable economic future are some of the things that are especially distressing right now and are likely to be for some years to come. Our increasingly multicultural society, with concomitant value pluralism, prompts some people to fear we are losing track of "traditional values" as we slide into "relativism."[6]

The uncertainty can be disconcerting, but it also provides an opportunity. Richard Bernstein writes:

> When individuals sense that they are living through a period of crisis, when foundations seem to be cracking and orthodoxies breaking up, then a public space is created in which basic questions about the human condition can be raised anew ... primary questions have been raised about the nature of human beings, what

constitutes knowledge of society and politics, how this knowledge can affect the ways in which we shape our lives, and what is and ought to be the relation between theory and practice.[7]

Bernstein discerns these primary questions being raised in philosophy and social and political theory. Education, as a philosophical, social, and political activity, can benefit from the advances he identifies, which open up space for exploring essential questions of education and life. Foundations and orthodoxies are cracking, and that can help create a space for critical public deliberation about basic questions of the human condition. I hope this book will be an example of philosophical work that might contribute to meaningful debate about those questions.

However, while crumbling orthodoxies might help create a dynamic public space, the opposite can happen as well. When people feel threatened and uncertain they can dig in their heels and cling desperately to old dogmas and conventions. They can find comforting certainty in making a clear division between friend and foe, dividing people rather than seeking common ground.

I worry that that is exactly what is happening in education today. Of course, not everything is rosy in schooling, but if there is a crisis in education it lies in the failure to acknowledge and explore the sort of primary questions Bernstein identifies. Perhaps "crisis" is not the right word; a problem that has persisted for a couple of centuries isn't exactly a crisis; it's more like a long-term malady. "Crises" come and go. Every now and again education as a whole goes through spasms of perceived crisis, conscience, angst, and/or ideological attack that prompt reform attempts of one sort or another. So, we go through periods when we think a bit about education. The real problem is that rarely, if ever, is the thinking more than superficial; we neither reach nor try to reach the fundamental questions that must be explored if any sort of meaningful progress or adaptation in education is to be achieved.

Human well-being is such a fundamental issue. Well-being might be an uncontroversial aim in some sense, but it can be radical in its import for education. I mean "radical" in a couple of ways (in addition to the rather radical notion of "seducing souls"). For one thing, well-being provides an ideal for facilitating a thoroughgoing critique of all aspects of education. If human welfare is an obvious end, we still face the task of specifying its meaning and educational implications. We should ask of any proposal for curriculum, instruction, discipline, research, or whatever: "How does this contribute, if at all, to making life worthwhile for human beings?" I suspect that the majority of people would have trouble articulating a cogent answer to that question, one that went beyond mere platitudes. A cogent response to the question of well-being requires us to look at education very differently than is the case commonly.

Good work has been done regarding well-being and issues relevant to it. At the same time, there is a lot of poor thinking out there, and it is not confined to any one political orientation. Just consider the bipartisan congressional support for No Child Left Behind. I aim to be radical by proposing we should ask of any perspective on education — liberal, conservative, and in-between; modern, premodern, and postmodern — "Does this perspective provide helpful insight into the question of well-being?" We need to get beyond simplistic and divisive labels. The aim should be to help people live good lives, not merely espouse and defend some ideology.

Perhaps I'm being too harsh. Giving education reformers the benefit of the doubt, let's suppose that they honestly believe their reforms benefit people (academic excellence, global economic competitiveness, accountability, and critical awareness are examples of popular reform goals), and that they put some real thought into their reforms and don't endorse them merely because it is politically or ideologically expedient to do so. But are the necessary questions being asked? What's meant by "academic excellence," for instance, and why is it worthwhile? What sort of academics and what sort of excellence? Who really benefits from "academic excellence"? Students? All students? Teachers? Society? What sort of benefit, if any? Admission to college? A job? A meaningful life? Enjoyment? When I charge inattention to ends, I mean lack of vigor and depth in exploration of such questions.

This book identifies and explores basic questions about our human condition and offers some suggestions for how to respond to those questions and conceive an education that serves human well-being. However, in the passage quoted earlier, Bernstein identifies other fundamental questions, concerning knowledge, politics, theory, and practice. As he says, this knowledge affects how we think about our lives. In line with Bernstein's point, this book is about more than well-being. If we are to come up with a plausible conception of well-being and helpful ideas for how education can aid people in achieving well-being, we have to think broadly about how human beings understand and live in their world and with one another.

For example, if we are to serve well-being, we must broaden our conception of knowledge beyond the boundaries of science, into "unscientific" areas, where notions such as soul, spirituality, seduction, reverence, and being are key elements of living and understanding. We have to challenge the dominance of instrumental thinking, which emphasizes "what works" to the detriment of attention to the merits of the ends sought. Returning to Bernstein, he says:

We are coming to realize that human rationality cannot be limited to technical and instrumental reason; that human beings can engage in rational argumentation in which there is a commitment to the critical evaluation of the quality of human life; that we can cultivate theoretical discourse in which there is a rational discussion of the conflict of critical interpretations, and practical discourse in which human beings try not simply to manipulate and control one another, but to understand one another genuinely and work toward practical — not technical — ends.[8]

Human beings can inquire rationally into the quality of human lives, and they must do so. This is a moral obligation for educators who inevitably affect the quality of people's lives. It is a moral imperative for any human being; in failing to pursue such inquiry "we will surely become less than fully human."[9]

But there are obstacles. In education, theoretical discourse is often devalued compared with instrumental thinking, dismissed in favor of "practical" applications. But theory is supremely practical because with it we can critically evaluate different options for human lives, our own lives and these of others. Techniques have little value if we lack an adequate sense for what aims are worth pursuing.

Bernstein claims that human beings can engage in argumentation that looks beyond manipulation and control for the sake of achieving a sound understanding of human welfare. To accomplish that we have to challenge subjectivism in ethics, the idea that questions of the good and well-being are matters of "opinion" only, where justification for one's values goes no further than statements such as "That's just what I believe" or "I feel strongly about that." The belief that ethics is irrational or nonrational is abetted by the dominance of technical and instrumental reasoning. Such reasoning is concerned for determining effective and efficient means — techniques and instruments — for achieving particular ends. In itself, such reasoning is legitimate and valuable. The problem arises when it dominates, when people go to the extreme of believing that only technical questions are subject to rational scrutiny and determination, that theory, especially moral theory, is irrelevant to any critical understanding of our human condition. Without a rational basis, beliefs can only be expressed and influenced via exercise of power, manipulation, and control.

A central aim of this book is to challenge the dominance of instrumental reason and subjectivism in ethics and present an alternative for understanding human beings and their welfare. Educators need to be more than effective enactors of techniques and strategies. We can deliberate rationally, sensitively, and cooperatively about what makes a human life worthwhile and take actions that serve human well-being. We must if we are to be fully human and humane.

## CHAPTER SKETCHES

Part One is devoted to developing a conception of human well-being. I will not try to summarize all of my argument here, but I will alert you to several central points. The issues might be discussed in more than one chapter, but I note chapters that emphasize particular ideas.

Chapter 1 explores some fundamentals of well-being, including subject-relativity, happiness, and the role of meaning in human life and welfare. Subject-relativity is a particularly troublesome idea. The basic point is that well-being is not only about determining what things are good but also about what things have "prudential" value, what things are good for particular individuals' actual lives.[10] The prudential value of something depends on who the particular individual is (and other context-dependent factors). The chapter also presents some initial points about well-being as an experience. A principal theme in succeeding chapters is to understand the nature and importance of experience for well-being.

Chapter 2 compares and contrasts my conception of well-being as experience with another prominent theory: well-being as satisfaction of desires. The chapter seeks to establish the importance of experience generally considered. However, the experience needed must be specified; not all experience is conducive to well-being. In Chapter 3 I begin to go into detail about my conception of well-being and experience. Of central concern is the question of how human beings are in relation to their world. I develop the idea of "attunement" to the world.

Of special interest is how human beings come to value things, how they can experience value in the world, rather than believe that value is something human beings merely create or choose. And in valuing the aim is not just to value things but also to see their value correctly. If people are living well it is not just because they think they are, but because their lives really are good. Chapter 4 examines that issue.

One conclusion reached in Chapter 4 is that the values by which one leads a worthwhile life cannot be arranged in a hierarchy of importance. Leading a worthwhile life is too complicated for that. The question then is how any sort of structure can be achieved in one's values, beliefs, and actions so that those things aren't just haphazard. In Chapter 5 I argue that a legitimate and helpful structure can be attained, but it needs to be thought of as a "constellation" of values.

With a conception of well-being in hand, Part Two explores implications for the politics of education and for classroom teaching. Again, I will note only a few basics.

In Chapter 6 we return to the issue of subjectivity, because even if individual well-being is subject-relative it doesn't follow that, in order to properly serve well-being, schools must provide unique curriculum and instruction for every student. For practical and prudential reasons, we look for values that serve everyone's, or nearly everyone's, well-being. "Human capabilities" are the values proposed.

Even with human capabilities as a basis, we face complex and controversial issues of how to encourage those capabilities and other aspects of well-being through education. I offer some suggestions for education (for example, in Chapter 9, how teachers can appropriately "seduce" students), but I emphasize that I offer suggestions. Because of the subject-relativity of well-being and other factors, detailed, decontextualized prescriptions for education have limited value. So, I emphasize the importance of public deliberation. The answers to difficult questions of education and well-being need to be worked out publicly and not dictated by me or some other sage.

Public deliberation about the good and well-being is controversial for a couple of principal reasons, though: doubts about the extent to which those issues are within the proper purview of state agencies, such as public schools; and doubts about the extent to which deliberation is possible and desirable if people differ in their conceptions of good and well-being. In Chapter 7 I address those issues and argue that fair, meaningful deliberation is possible.

However, if we are to do more than talk about well-being, people have to be ready to discriminate between lives that are good and lives that are not, between activities that have "higher" or "lower" value, which surely is a difficult and controversial task. Chapter 8 argues that legitimate judgments can be made and actions taken.

Educators need to guide youth toward good lives, but that presents the issue of how to exercise that guidance. Chapter 9 considers the classroom interactions needed if students and teachers are to discern prudential values and lead satisfying lives. Prominent ideas will be dialogue, spiritual exercises, and seduction. We will have to consider how, in those classroom interactions, teachers can provoke and guide without violating parents' and students' freedom of self-determination.

To conclude the book, in the Epilogue I propose that the discussion of well-being and education suggests philosophy as a way of life for educators and other people. Well-being can take any number of forms. Yet one desirable constant is a way of being in the world where people are sensitive to and capable of dealing with life situations that confront them with issues of their welfare and that of others. That doesn't mean that people are doing well only if they constantly ponder their well-being. However, people need to be ready and able to deal with issues of well-being even if they cannot, and should not, constantly dwell on them. So, if education cannot always serve people's well-being directly or make them practically wise, it can help people become philosophers competent to conceptualize and live satisfying lives.

## REMARKS ON APPROACH

To conclude this Introduction I wish to clarify and explain several aspects of the approach I take in this book.

I consider this a book on education, although many of my statements and examples are directed specifically at teachers in public elementary and secondary schools, which constitute only part of education. I have special concern for those people and settings, because I deem them to be at particular risk due to current education policies. However, although I do not offer an argument for it, I suggest that at least the basics of my argument apply to other educational contexts and agencies — higher education, private schools, libraries, and mass media, for example.[11] Even if their particular roles and means differ to some degree, all these agencies of education should share the aim of serving people's welfare. Education can take place in a variety of contexts, but that does not change the fundamental ways human beings experience the world. Education is about life, ultimately. The lives of young children might be different than the lives of teenagers or senior citizens in some ways, but to think that these people therefore are radically different in the requirements for their humanity is to make a grievous error.

As I have mentioned, I conclude the book with a claim about philosophy as a way of life. I hope this book presents a helpful example of philosophical thinking. Although I anticipate that educators will be my principal audience, many readers might be unfamiliar with academic philosophy. However, good philosophy need not be "academic" in the traditional sense. I'm not saying people cannot learn good things from professional philosophers, but the philosophy I encourage is philosophical primarily because of the questions with which it is concerned, questions of good human lives. Those questions can be meaningfully explored in a number of ways, such as through popular films, which I use in my discussions.

Still, I am aware that I try to walk a rather fine line, offering an argument that is philosophically interesting, substantial, and sound, but that is also accessible and useful to readers who lack background in academic philosophy. In walking my line, I probably tend toward one side of it, where philosophical rigor is the concern; I do not advocate "pop" philosophy.[12] Educators need to be careful thinkers, knowledgeable and skillful in confronting the philosophical aspects of their work. To take well-being seriously we have to delve into the complexities of that aim and not avoid them. I present some of those complexities, although I try to steer clear of overly technical language and place some of the more technical discussions in endnotes. Nonetheless, I can imagine some readers getting impatient with what might seem to be picayune points. I'll risk that in an attempt to show how this sort of thinking and writing has value.

Part of what I deem important is confronting views that challenge mine. I can imagine how this could be frustrating to readers, who might think, "Why don't you just tell us what your point is?" But trying to do justice to "the opposition," besides being a scholarly imperative, is an ethical imperative, implying a particular attitude toward people who might not see eye to eye with you that is crucial if public deliberation is to be dialogical rather than adversarial.[13] I can't say I do a perfect job of responding to differing views, but perhaps readers can get some sense that the approach has merit.

Finally, I want to say more about why I focus on teaching. I do not subscribe to the idea that "It's the teachers, stupid"[14] — that it is teachers who control whether students succeed or fail. There are many reasons why schools and teachers might succeed or struggle or fail, but while it can be expedient to put the onus solely on teachers, it is disingenuous and unfair.[15]

I focus on teachers, not to focus blame on them, but to offer a conception of their work that can help make that work rewarding and meaningful for them and students, compared with other conceptions predominant currently. Teaching is noble work; teachers deserve that work to be meaningful and satisfying. In terms of students' welfare, teachers cannot always overcome the obstacles placed in their and their students' paths, but as the people who work most closely with youth they can take advantage of opportunities to benefit students and at least ameliorate the damage done when those opportunities are lacking due to bad education policy and other factors. Sympathy and compassion can go a long way. Nel Noddings points out, "Allowing a child to express his misery over a conflict between the needs inferred by adults and his own wants is important for emotional health."[16] In education, we might want to institutionalize regret.[17]

The theory (if it deserves to be called that) and policy that dominate education have utterly failed to take up the commitment to which Bernstein refers, the commitment to evaluating and promoting the quality of human lives. Hence my purpose in writing this book: to persuade people who do not see the point of the commitment, and to confirm and support the people who do.

PART ONE

# Developing a Conception of Human Well-Being

*Chapter 1*

# Basics of Well-Being: Subjectivity, Satisfaction, and Experience

I will begin with a simple statement of my conception of well-being: well-being consists of satisfying experiences. Perhaps the basic idea is sensible enough. How fine wine contributes to my well-being depends on my experience with it and not merely on the quality of the wine. Regardless of how fine the wine is, if my tastes are plebeian my experience of the wine will be unremarkable. Similarly, a student's well-being depends on her experience with school activities and not merely on the quality of those activities. It seems sensible to suppose that a life of enjoyable or satisfying experiences is better than one filled with sadness or suffering.

However, once we move beyond those broad points and probe more carefully, the idea that well-being is obtained through satisfying experience presents a number of questions. For instance, regarding the idea of "satisfying" experience, that might seem to be a very mediocre aim. When people think about well-being they commonly think in terms of things like happiness; well-being is about doing well, not just satisfactorily. Regarding experience, we will encounter arguments that experience is not required for well-being. For example, isn't my life good if my children are doing well, even if I don't know they are, and so I don't "experience" that goodness? So, we have to consider whether "experience" is broad enough to capture all that contributes to well-being.

On the other hand, perhaps "experience" is too broad, for it is difficult to see how some satisfying experiences contribute to people's well-being. Drug use and cruelty might be satisfying to some people, but do those things really do them any good? Less extreme, imagine a chemistry teacher's complaint that his students don't get all they should from their chemistry labs; they just go through the motions. The students might have experiences but, again, they seem not to be the sort we want. We might have to narrow down "experience" to particular sorts that serve well-being.

Part One will confront such questions and begin to explain and justify the claim that well-being consists of satisfying experience, and consider what my claim implies for the pursuit of human well-being. The remainder of this chapter gets into some basics.

## THE SUBJECT-RELATIVITY OF WELL-BEING

Conceiving well-being in terms of the individual's experience has the advantage of accounting for the subject-relativity of individual well-being.[1] The ultimate concern is what makes a life worthwhile for the person living it. There is a difference between a good or worthy life and a life that is worth living, a life the individual finds worthwhile, satisfying, or fulfilling. That is, there is a difference between something's prudential value, its value for an individual's welfare, and other sorts of value the thing might have.[2] All of us have experiences of this difference. Fine wine might be genuinely better than Ripple, but the difference is lost on me. It is possible to say correctly of a person's life that it is ethically good, characterized by generosity, achievement, and other good things, while the person experiences it as frustrating, disappointing, mistaken, or otherwise unsatisfying. A subject-relative conception of well-being is needed, and experience provides the connection between values and the quality of life for a person.

However, making well-being "subjective" presents a number of questions. One problem is that people can be unwise or mistaken or misled about the way they live their lives. Consider, for example, the disturbing depiction of "contented" slaves in *Gone with the Wind*. Beliefs and attitudes can be constrained, deformed, and manipulated. For that reason, we might be suspicious that a subject-relative approach to welfare takes us in the wrong direction, that the central issue is not whether an individual is satisfied but what she is able to do and be.[3] We will see whether the subject-relative conception of well-being I offer has an adequate response to this concern for normativity. At this point, I use the objection as an opportunity to further clarify the position I am proposing.

My conception of well-being is subjective in the sense that it makes well-being logically dependent on people's attitudes of favor and disfavor.[4] So far as what well-being requires, I maintain that a person's satisfaction *is* central, although what we can or should *do* to serve others' well-being is a different question.[5] For example, as I argue in Chapter 6, education policy cannot ensure that everyone will be satisfied, but we can provide education that enables people to live a satisfying life.

Also, subject-relativity of well-being does not imply subject-relativity in other domains of value. When I say that Ripple is just as good as fine wine *for me* I do not contend that there is no real difference in the quality of wines. It may be that ethical, aesthetic, and other values — duty, honesty, courage, caring, beauty, spirituality — are objective in the sense that their value does not depend on an individual's attitude toward them, that sources and horizons of value exist for people independent of their attitudes. So, whatever contented slaves might believe, their lives are structured by violations of basic human rights of dignity, justice, and self-determination that limit what they can do and be. That fact provides reasons to question whether they are living well. So, the conception of well-being I propose is not subjective in the sense that a person's attitudes of favor and disfavor toward her life are all that matter for her well-being.

To make the individual's attitudes central to her well-being does not mean we have to just accept her beliefs regarding her well-being. Sumner argues, "the best strategy here is to treat subjects' reports of their level of life satisfaction as defeasible — that is, authoritative unless there is evidence they are non-autonomous."[6] For contented slaves there are reasons to think their attitudes are not autonomous. We need to respect individuals' judgments about their lives, but that is consistent with taking steps to change their attitudes and their situations.

Of course, different individuals will have different legitimate ideas about what their welfare entails, but the explanation for the variety is not that well-being is only a matter of personal opinion but that the objectivity of values is consistent with a variety of good ways to live. In this sense, my conception of prudential value is pluralistic, not subjective. The reason people see the world differently is not because they live in different worlds and see different things when looking at some object or event, but rather because they attend to different parts of the world, give those parts differing emphases, and see some things more clearly than other things.[7] Nonetheless, the subject-relativity of well-being does make the individual the ultimate authority regarding his well-being. He is the one who must live his life. We might have good grounds for believing he is making a mistake; nonetheless, ultimately, what counts for *him* for *his* well-being are his own attitudes of favor and disfavor toward his life.

There are dangers in taking this view. Imagine a successful criminal. He steals and lies. He hurts other people. Yet he is never caught and enjoys "the good life." He has a very favorable attitude toward his life. Less dramatic, imagine a couch potato who doesn't hurt anyone but is content to do little that is productive. In both cases, we would probably say that their lives aren't particularly good; maybe the couch potato's life isn't exactly bad, but it's not exactly good, either.

Even more disturbing is the case of the contented slave. Likely we are even more reluctant to accept the slave's attitude, for, more clearly than with the criminal or couch potato, the slave's attitude would seem to not be of his making. As we should be cautious not to usurp the authority a person has over his life, we should be cautious not to abjure our ethical responsibility to be aware, critical, and helpful.

Perhaps these examples should prompt us to wonder whether individuals, especially when it comes to children, really should be the ultimate authority on their well-being. Should ethical or other "objective" values be authoritative? There are problems with that approach, too. If a life lacking ethical quality should concern us, we should also be concerned about lives that are too "ethical." As Griffin suggests, "it is sometimes better to fail morally and stay alive than not to fail and thereby lose one's life."[8] And we can imagine examples that are not life-and-death. Imagine a student who strives very hard and successfully to do all the "right" things — getting good grades, handing in homework on time, serving on the student council — but is burdened down by this or feels that she is always doing what others expect of her and never considers what she should expect or want for herself. In the movie *Fried Green Tomatoes* the character Evelyn Couch tried to be "good" — visiting her husband's aged aunt, being polite to people, cooking her husband's favorite meals — but she finally got fed up, because her efforts were never appreciated or personally satisfying. So, one day she repeatedly rammed the car of two rude teenage girls (after the girls got out of the car) who sped past her into a parking spot she had been waiting for. This was liberating for Evelyn. Even if she acted unethically, it seemed to do her a lot of good. (We'll spend more time with Evelyn later.)

"Objective" moral sources and other values must have some important role in individuals understanding their well-being and living fulfilling lives. The question is what that role should be. Even if things are good or bad in an ethical sense or some other sense, it does not follow that embodying or pursuing them will contribute or should be expected to contribute to an individual's welfare. Objectivity in prudential value is contextual. There might be things that really are good, but still we need an account of how those good things make a *life* good for the person *living* it. The basic issue is the relationship between values and a person's well-being.

We can respond in one of two ways. We could argue that, despite their current attitudes, the criminal, couch potato, and contented slave are not living well just because their lives are not good ethically or in other ways. Or, we could grant that their attitudes are authoritative (yet defeasible) but see values providing standards and limits of other sorts. I take the latter approach.[9] We can accept (reluctantly perhaps) that the criminal is living well yet still put him in jail despite its blow to his well-being. We can sanction the couch potato if he neglects his responsibilities to co-workers, family, and others. Evelyn Couch might get sued or have her insurance rates increased. Even if a slave insists he is content, we have an ethical responsibility to help him better understand his situation and work to eradicate slavery.

We have to remember that it is the individual's well-being we are concerned about. We could deem a person's life bad, but that person still has to live her life. While changes in a person's life might bring real benefits, rarely if ever do benefits come without some sort of cost. A focus on individuals' well-being should keep us aware of the pain even beneficial changes can bring. Rorty proposes, "the best way to cause people long-lasting pain is to humiliate them by making things that seemed most important to them look futile, obsolete, and powerless."[10] It can be difficult for persons to realize they have been deluded about the quality of their lives. They might see themselves as stupid or gullible. Of course, for many things, the pain might be a small price to pay. Still, it is a price we should be aware of, an awareness often lacking.

Finally, a subject-relative conception of well-being embodies a fundamental practical point. People are going to have their own ideas about their well-being. Those ideas might be mistaken, but insisting that they are likely will not get us far if our aim is to help people see their lives differently. It is one thing to state the truth to people; persuading them is another. If persuasion is the educators' aim, as I will argue it is, then it makes sense to meet others on their own turf, to suppose that when someone sees their life as good we must think how that might really be so.

I have been talking about criminals, couch potatoes, and slaves, but many students find themselves in situations that are not all that different. They find themselves largely creatures of others' will — parents, teachers, policymakers, and others. They might feel content, but are they content with a life they have determined or one that has been determined for them? We expect them to endure painful things on the promise that it will be worth it somehow. The situation is similar for many educators. They are, or at least feel, under the control of superiors, policies, and other conditions, like mere functionaries in a system.

To this point I have tried to clarify what I mean by a subject-relative conception of well-being and anticipate some of the questions that might be raised about it. The key issue is the problem of normativity. The problem is that a life worth living is not just anything one believes it to be; there are norms or standards for well-being. People can be mistaken about their well-being. To be authoritative regarding one's life is not to be infallible.

What, if any, norms are possible within a subject-relative conception of well-being? As I have hinted, a subject-relative conception has responses to this question. But these responses become necessary because a subject-relative conception makes individuals ultimate authorities regarding their welfare. The problem would seem to go away if norms for well-being exist independently of people's attitudes. Before continuing to develop my subject-relative conception and its responses to the normativity issue and other issues, let us consider whether an "objective" approach might be more promising.

## OBJECTIVITY IN WELL-BEING

"Objective," like "subjective," is a complicated notion. It is unclear whether the subjective–objective distinction is very helpful at all. Be that as it may, I will begin from Sumner's definition of objective theories of well-being: they "exclude all reference to the subject's attitudes or concerns."[11] I'm not sure there are theories of welfare that exclude all reference to the subject's attitudes or concerns. Probably, it is more helpful to think of a continuum; theories will reference the subject's particular attitudes more or less directly. The issue is what sort of reference is made, and clearly it is possible to emphasize goods that make no *immediate* reference to a *particular* individual's *particular* interests, attitudes, and so on. An obvious and common example is "needs." Basically, the idea is that even if every individual has different abilities and ambitions, there are some things that everyone needs.

Needs surely have a place in well-being, but one problem is that it is difficult to identify needs. For instance, around education these days, a great deal of emphasis is put on supposed literacy "needs." There could be some real need there. For example, autistic people have difficulty with language; it is in their interest to develop some ability to communicate. But as Temple Grandin insists, too much emphasis is placed on the "deficits" autistic persons have and not enough on developing their abilities.[12] The more immediate need could be to allow autistic people (and others) opportunity to follow the interests that give them satisfaction.

Also, well-being requires much more than meeting needs. It is difficult to see how people "need" to take the family on picnics, pinstripe their cars, sculpt the *David*, or stop and smell the roses. Yet such things add quality and satisfaction to many people's lives.

We might argue that such things do satisfy needs — Michelangelo "needed" to sculpt; his life would have been unfulfilled if he hadn't. That argument makes sense, but if we go that route we lose what an appeal to needs is supposed to provide; namely, a way to identify what is clearly important for all or nearly all people. Perhaps we could say that Michelangelo was satisfying a basic need, a need to create, albeit in his own particular way, which is important for all or nearly all people. There is a point there, too, but it is not obvious that creativity is a need. Some people seem to get along very well without being especially creative. At least, if we take the proposed route we are compelled to see needs as complex and involving some dimension of subject-relativity.

We might persist, though. Maybe there are ways to rank needs. Maybe Michelangelo needed to sculpt, but that isn't the same as his need for food. Perhaps some needs are basic or essential needs — say, because we would not survive if they were not satisfied — compared with other things that are not vital to brute survival. This appears to be the tack taken by people who emphasize "the basics" in education. Few people would argue that math knowledge is sufficient for a good life, but many would argue it is a basic necessity, in contrast to something "impractical" such as the arts. However, we have examples that complicate attempts to rank needs. Many artists are willing to sacrifice a good deal for the sake of their art. Perhaps they don't starve, but they might come close to it. At least, they seem willing to accept a good deal of hardship for what the proposed scheme would deem nonessential. Yet I imagine we would be reluctant to say the artist was making a mistake. If we guaranteed her survival while denying her the opportunity to create her art, we could imagine her replying that life would not be worth living under those circumstances.

There are other examples where survival is ranked below seemingly nonessential interests. In public policy there are examples where "extraneous" things are pursued even at the cost of people's lives. Griffin notes:

> The French government knows that each year several drivers lose their lives because of the beautiful roadside avenues of trees, yet they do not cut them down. Even aesthetic pleasure is (rightly) allowed to outrank a certain number of human lives.[13]

So, we have to question just how basic even "basic" needs are. In addition, there is the question of what truly is basic. In *The Republic*, Plato argues that gymnastics and music are the basics of education.[14] Noddings, while agreeing that basic knowledge in language, arithmetic, and other academics is important, emphasizes what may be even more basic — caring about ideas, things, and people.[15] For what is the value of being able to read if one does not care about reading and the ideas thus encountered?

There is another common "needs" approach to try. We might grant that it is difficult to identify specific needs vital to every person's well-being yet argue that there are certain opportunities all people need to have. For instance, it might turn out that a person will not need mathematics in his career or otherwise rank it highly in his later life, but he should learn math so that he has the opportunity to be successful in a career that requires math, just to keep his career options open. This might be backed up by appeal to the need for equity; there is a history of some students being denied equitable educational opportunities.

As Noddings shows, though, concern for equality presents a host of questions. We can agree that inequality exists, but in mathematics, for example, rather than try to remedy that by requiring similar math preparation for all students, Noddings argues that we should

> consider other more generous ways of alleviating the inequity that has historically been associated with mathematics. For example, why not abandon the requirement that all college-bound students, regardless of their interests and abilities, present academic credits in mathematics? Why not consider ways to improve non-college courses so that the mathematics actually needed is taught sensitively and practically within those courses? Why decide that the road to equity is established by coercing everyone into becoming proficient in mathematics? A thorough discussion of aims might lead in a different direction.[16]

Also, if equal opportunities for career preparation are important, and if we follow the logic advanced here, schools should provide similar opportunities in the arts and humanities, too, because there are careers for which that background would be useful. Perhaps one could retort that the "best" careers (i.e., the highest-paying) require math and science, hence the point of emphasizing those areas. As common as that assertion is, though, it is not clearly true, and even if it were, it would make a huge — and astoundingly narrow — assumption about what people might find fulfilling.[17] The essence of Noddings's argument is that if happiness is our aim in education we should expand the range of educational experiences open to students and educators.

Appeal to needs is only one way to think about the objectivity of well-being.[18] However, the discussion at least indicates the point of exploring a subject-relative alternative. As I suggested before, I am not sure the subjective–objective distinction is very helpful. While we should be concerned if conceptions of well-being exclude all reference to individuals' particular attitudes and concerns, one rarely sees that sort of argument. We are further ahead if our question is *how* reference is made and not *whether* it is.

As we have noted already, one way to make reference to individuals is through their attitudes of favor and disfavor, through the psychological or emotional dimensions of their experiences. One candidate with a long history is happiness.

## HAPPINESS, SATISFACTION, AND WELL-BEING

"This is boring!" "Why can't we do more fun stuff in this class?" I imagine all teachers have had students say such things. Those comments might be merely amusing, or they might be disturbing, suggesting students' failure to perceive the value of activities, or even their belief that their own enjoyment should be their and their teachers' primary concern. But in America we have complicated attitudes about happiness. For example, on the one hand, the abundance of self-help books about achieving happiness suggests that happiness is, indeed, very important, if not supremely important.[19] And even if we do not go that far, most people would grant happiness some legitimate place in life and education. If a student enjoys writing a haiku it would seem he is doing better than if he hates doing it. Still, on the other hand, there is the attitude that other things — duty, accomplishment, discipline, suffering even — are more important than happiness.

Philosophers often use "happiness" and "well-being" interchangeably, although not without considerable qualification. I call my topic "well-being" rather than "happiness," though, for the sake of clearly distinguishing well-being from common understandings of happiness, which revolve around things such as joy, play, fun, pleasure, and amusement, because not everyone is careful regarding the difference between well-being and happiness. For example, Haidt cites a study that shows prostitutes in Calcutta rate their lives as more satisfying than dissatisfying, and so, "the lives of these prostitutes are much better from the inside than they seem from the outside."[20] There is nothing wrong with having happiness rather than well-being as your topic, and perhaps it is worth knowing that even prostitutes can find happiness in their lives. However, as with contended slaves, the fact that prostitutes are happy or satisfied does not show that they are doing well. Haidt acknowledges that the prostitutes "suffered privations that seem to us in the West unbearable,"[21] but if we are concerned for the well-being of these women we need to think beyond the fact that they are able to bear what seems unbearable to us. Maybe we should marvel at these women's resiliency, but at the same time we need to insist their well-being consists of more than their satisfaction with their lives.

As I will be using the words, "happiness" is not the same thing as "well-being." Even so, we should consider how happiness, in the run-of-the-mill sense of that word, has a legitimate and important place in a life well lived.

As mentioned earlier, there is a history of skepticism about happiness. To give one example, we have Nietzsche's crack that "Man does *not* strive after happiness; only the Englishman does that."[22] From this passage we can glean two issues: the meaning of happiness and the goal of people's striving. (A third issue is the use of "man" or "human being" as the standard. I return to that issue in Chapter 6.) Let's consider the meaning of "happiness" first.

What is "happiness"? The Englishman to whom Nietzsche refers is the utilitarian. Early utilitarians construed happiness as pleasure. Jeremy Bentham states the principle of utility this way:

> By utility is meant that property in any object, whereby it tends to produce benefit, advantage, pleasure, good, or happiness (all this in the present case comes to the same thing) or (what comes again to the same thing) to prevent the happening of mischief, pain, evil, or unhappiness to the party whose interest is considered.[23]

The problematic claim here is that benefit, advantage, pleasure, good, and happiness all come to the same thing, and it was that claim that rankled Nietzsche.

Equating happiness with pleasure does present problems. One is that pleasures are qualitatively different. Pleasures and pains always have meaning. The pleasure of hearing a good joke is not the same as the pleasure had when hearing a baby giggle or when a difficult task is completed or when an annoying colleague dumps his coffee in his lap. So, well-being and happiness cannot be judged in terms of some singular quantity, "pleasure." In addition, pleasure is absent from many things that people pursue and that clearly benefit them. Life-saving surgery is not pleasurable but clearly is beneficial (other things being equal). How many times have our students, and we, come to realize that we are thankful for experiencing things we hated at the time (and perhaps still are not exactly happy about) — piano lessons, family reunions, *Silas Marner*?

Equating happiness with pleasure also presents the normativity problem. Doing well cannot be reduced to having some mental state such as pleasure. We could imagine a situation such as in the movie *The Matrix*, where people are plugged into a machine that creates pleasurable mental experiences. But such a situation is abhorrent to most people. People enjoy *things*; they take pleasure in other people, activities, events, and so on. They want to really do things, to be and become particular sorts of persons. It is not merely the mental state that is sought.[24] This takes us to the second aspect of Nietzsche's complaint. People do not strive after happiness (pleasure); they strive after accomplishments. Happiness might accompany those accomplishments, but it is not the immediate or primary goal.

Still, Nietzsche clearly values joy and cheerfulness highly. For example, he attacks the "Spirit of Gravity" that makes life a "desert."[25] What is important are the accomplishments people strive for, in Nietzsche's case, things such as healthy self-love and continual critical thinking aimed at "self-overcoming," but happiness is the result:

> The ancient philosophers . . . never tired of preaching: "Your thoughtlessness and stupidity, the way you live according to the rule, your submission to your neighbor's opinion is the reason why you so rarely achieve happiness; we thinkers, as thinkers, are the happiest of all."[26]

Dewey makes the point by speaking in terms of "enjoyeds," which he prefers to "enjoyments" because the former term "emphasizes the fact that actual events are involved; we do not enjoy enjoyments, but persons, scenes, deeds, works of art, friends, conversations with them. And ball games and concertos."[27] I think Dewey overstates the case — I think we do enjoy enjoyments at times, enjoy the feeling of joy, wherever that joy comes from — but what I emphasize here is that while people enjoy things, they do *enjoy* them. Aristotle proposes that every activity is perfected by the pleasure appropriate to it.[28] Enjoyment is not the be-all and end-all, but happiness in the common sense of pleasure, play, joy, and so on still is a legitimate and important aspect of life and well-being.

As I noted before, we Americans have mixed attitudes about happiness in childhood and education. On one hand there is the "all-work-and-no-play" cliché. On the other hand, as, Dewey says, there is distrust of "amusement, play and recreation."[29] There was a time when recess was a standard part of an elementary student's school day. Many schools have gotten away from that. The argument or assumption likely is that recess is a distraction from more important "needs," "academics" usually. Recess still has its advocates, yet there too the assumption can be that recess is a distraction, the difference being the belief that occasional distractions are important to energize students for academic work.[30] Of course, there are teachers who try to combine entertainment and academics in classroom activities, maybe by teaching a lesson using a film or an internet simulation. But there too the attitude likely is that the play serves work.

These approaches can have value, but they all judge the value of play by how it serves work; play has little or no value in itself. Dewey takes the matter to a deeper level, positing the continuity of play and work:

> Both [play and work] involve ends consciously entertained and the selection and adaptations of materials and processes designed to effect the desired ends . . . Persons who play are not just doing something (pure physical movement); they are *trying* to do or effect something, an attitude that involves anticipatory forecasts which stimulate their present responses.[31]

In both play and work human beings exercise important powers such as forming purposes and plans to attain them. So, play can be good work.

A corollary of Dewey's point is that work is not the same as labor. Conscious selection and adaptation of ends, materials, and processes can be absent from work, turning it into labor, mere functioning. Even watching a movie or doing an internet simulation can be labor for students. For teachers at their start-of-school-year in-service training, the inspirational videos and get-to-know-you games can be laborious. In each case people might be entertained, but they need not be encouraged to entertain ends and possible materials and their adaptations; they need not engage in meaningful work or play.[32]

Dewey supposes that even under ideal conditions there will be a need for "special forms of action . . . forms that are significantly called re-creation."[33] Play and amusement can provide occasion for loosening boundaries and giving space for imagination, so that ideas, attitudes, and relationships can be reevaluated and re-created, if not anew, then with renewed commitment and understanding. These "special forms of action" have an important social and educational purpose: "Play and art add fresh and deeper meanings to the usual activities of life."[34] The point of giving imagination space through play and art is not simply to engage in self-indulgent flights of fantasy (although those might have their place, too). Playing with ideas can be beneficial to any sort of inquiry. And it can take us out of ourselves and put us in touch with something beyond ourselves, which is so important for our care for ourselves.

This leads to a final point. Dewey sees a moral purpose for play and recreation, which might seem strange in light of common understandings of morality that stress "serious" things such as industriousness, discipline, and responsibility. "Relief from continuous moral activity — in the conventional sense of moral — is itself a moral necessity"; the "careless rapture" of play and art is necessary for "softening rigidities, relaxing strains, allaying bitterness, dispelling moroseness, and breaking down the narrowness consequent upon specialized tasks."[35]

For Dewey, "casual and free intercourse" encourages "susceptibility and responsiveness," one of the three psychological aspects he deems essential for moral life.[36] The idea is that Dewey's other essential features — force of character and judgment — will not even be brought into play if the individual is not sensitive and responsive to situations that call for judgment and taking a stand. For this responsiveness, "[t]he informally social side of education, the aesthetic environment and influences, are all-important."[37] So, maybe showing a DVD can be a helpful component of the aesthetic environment, but, again, the question is how it is used. A DVD can be used to "teach," unaccompanied by formal or informal intercourse, responsiveness, or recreation.

We should take a playful attitude toward morality and other "serious" matters. It is a challenge to the sort of attitude Nietzsche identified as "The Spirit of Gravity." In a similar vein, Nussbaum points to the dangers of "serious" political movements and the need for art: "The revolution wishes to destroy the treasures of art in order to get everyone materially satisfied."[38] However,

> [g]reat art plays a central role in our political lives because, showing us the tangled nature of our loves and commitments, showing us ourselves as flawed crystals, it moderates the optimistic hatred of the actual that makes for a great deal of political violence, moderates the ferocious hopefulness that simply marches over the complicated delicacies of the human heart.[39]

We need not resort to extreme examples such as Stalin and Pol Pot to illustrate Nussbaum's point. In education it seems that there always is some "serious" political movement going on. Some people might like to see the *A Nation at Risk* report and the No Child Left Behind Act as revolutions attempting to get everyone materially satisfied. How many delicacies of the human heart have been trampled in the meantime, with the narrow focus on test scores and "what works"?

The foregoing discussion has identified several benefits of joy, enjoyment, play, recreation, and related things. Doubts still might persist, though. We might grant that happiness has value, but just how valuable is it when we compare it with other valuable things? One indicator of the value of happiness is how elemental and ubiquitous it is in human life.

Dewey argues that happiness is central to human experience:

> Human experience in the large, in its coarse and conspicuous features, has for one of
> its most striking features preoccupation with direct enjoyment, feasting and festivi-
> ties: ornamentation, dance, song, dramatic pantomime, telling yarns and enacting
> stories.[40]

Is Dewey right about that? Consider the Ifaluk people of the Caroline Islands in
the western Pacific Ocean, who lead a precarious existence.[41] Their small island
is densely populated. Typhoons regularly threaten their lives. Growing, harvest-
ing, and preparing food occupies much of their time; their lives depend on it. If
anyone should be concerned for survival primarily, it would be the Ifaluk.

In fact, the Ifaluk are suspicious of happiness. For them happiness/excite-
ment (what they call *ker*) is a pleasant but amoral emotion that yet can be
immoral because it suggests one is unafraid of other people.[42] Fear of other
community members is valued as an indicator of the seriousness individuals
attach to their relationships to other people. This fear is part of a complex social
structure that has preservation of the society as its central aim. Given the pre-
cariousness of their lives, all individuals know they could become needy. So, the
Ifaluk strive to maintain conditions for mutual aid and cooperation, conditions
threatened by *ker*.

Still, Ifaluk life is full of the sort of things Dewey mentions. They have
numerous rituals and ceremonies regarding naming children, caring for the
ill, taking leave from one another, grieving for the dead, and even just talking
with one another. These rituals and ceremonies might appear to have little to
do with "direct enjoyment"; it's hard to see what is enjoyable about grief or
saying good-bye to a loved one. But why should these people devote so much
energy and emotion to enacting and preserving these ceremonies, considering
survival is such a pressing "need"? As their suspicions about *ker* indicate, the
Ifaluk are not especially keen on happiness as excitement, but they enjoy one
another's company and have a sense of contentment and meaning with these
rituals.

The Ifaluk diversify and enrich their experiences in the way Dewey suggests. They are "more preoccupied with enhancing life than with bare living."[43]
Occasions for joy, sorrow, and wonder provide opportunities to enhance life,
to go beyond bare living. If some or a good deal of this seems not to involve
"direct enjoyment" that should not lead us to think people have no interest in
enjoyment — the Ifaluk clearly do — but, rather, to take an expansive view of
what enjoyment and happiness involve.

It is difficult to come up with one word that captures what is needed, but
something like satisfaction or fulfillment or contentment seems on the right

track.[44] As I noted before, "satisfaction" might seem an unsatisfactory aim. We might think that if people are doing well they are not just satisfied but are also happy; they are flourishing rather than just doing satisfactorily.[45] In education, people often construe doing well in terms of "excellence." Likely, they would dispute that education should be satisfying or satisfactory rather than excellent or the best it can be.

Kant, for example, proposes that people have a duty to perfect themselves, to raise themselves "out of the crudity of [their] nature, out of [their] animality . . . more and more to humanity."[46] Perhaps Kant has a point. Maybe people have a duty to themselves and others to live a life of dignity rather than one that is crude and animal-like.

However, why must we think that "perfection" is a desirable aim and that we get closer to humanity the further we are from the "crudities" of our nature? Our concern is *human* life, with all its frailties. Consider a person who reflects on his life and realizes he has not accomplished all he hoped he would. He sees shortcomings in his abilities and efforts. He has regrets; he has fallen short of "perfection." He could punish himself because of all that. But he could also reconcile himself to his life, come to be at peace with himself. He might not be "happy" in this reconciliation, but his satisfaction with it would seem to be a legitimate, major contributor to his well-being, certainly in contrast to the alternative of beating himself up. Yet satisfaction is not the same as resignation. Finding one's life satisfying, being at peace with oneself about it, can be a powerful, positive emotion.[47] It is not the same thing as happiness, but it can engender a similar sense of fulfillment.

Even if excellence were the ultimate aim, it is something most of us do not achieve, not completely, or in all, or even many, things. For example, it could be, as Haidt claims, that many human beings cannot be happy without friends.[48] That does not imply, though, that people who lack friends cannot live a life that is satisfying. Such a life might be difficult; the person might feel there is a "hole" in her life. Yet much else in her life can be meaningful and satisfying.[49]

Even if all this is true, one might argue that we still should keep happiness and excellence as aims in order to motivate us to improve ourselves and our situations. But if there is a point in aiming high, there are dangers in it as well. We need to ask how physically and psychologically healthy it is to strive for aims that consistently are out of our reach. Those aims can inspire and motivate, but they can also lead to frustration, guilt, or shame.

Perhaps one would reply that that is the way it should be. It seems that Kant thinks so.[50] Happiness should be hard to reach; one needs to earn it. I suppose we are inclined to think the happy criminal doesn't deserve his happiness.

However, to require that happiness be earned can be repressive. To students' complaints that they are not happy it would be too easy to retort, "Well, if you'd try harder to see the value of these activities, and put more effort into them, you'd be happier. You haven't done what needs to be done to earn your happiness."

Such an attitude also can be used to excuse the status quo. Consider, for example, the not uncommon idea that one should not expect life to be enjoyable. (Grandma Soprano comes to mind.) Perhaps it is thought that suffering is acceptable or even required for a reward that comes later. So, don't complain about your situation; accept it. However, it is difficult to see why people should be content with suffering.[51]

Of course, most human lives include some measure of pain and suffering. That prompts some thought about how we look at the world we live in. Luck can be a big factor in whether our lives are happy or sad, fulfilling or disappointing, yet we might think that, fortunately, suffering and bad luck are the exception rather than the rule. However, Dewey disputes the common belief that "[e]vils, rather than goods, are counted as evidence of chance."[52] Generally, theories of well-being construe well-being in terms of good things, realizing our wants, preferences, desires, and so on. But if the world is as Dewey describes it, where our desires and plans are as apt to be thwarted as to be fulfilled, we seem compelled to conclude that we should have no particular expectation that our lives will or should be happy. Maybe we should think so. Before accepting that conclusion, though, we should consider that well-being does not depend only on getting what we want. It is also helpful to have a reasonable expectation for the degree or sort of happiness that well-being requires and understand that the curveballs the world sends our way do not preclude a satisfying life. Things might not be completely rosy in our lives, but we can be doing well nonetheless.

Along with the nature of the world, we need to think about human beings, too, and what it means to be "human." Part of the story is told by psychology and physiology. For example, our ability to achieve happiness is partly determined by heredity. Our brains appear to be wired such that our responses to some stimuli are more or less automatic. For other things, some control is possible, but likely we have less control than we might like to think. Some patterns of conduct, regarding relationships, for example, seem to be largely set early on in life, although some change may be possible.[53]

There are numerous examples in fiction and history of people we hold up as models of strength, energy, and ingenuity because they do not allow themselves to be victims of fate and their own limitations. But we also have examples, notably in classical Greek tragedy, where disregard for chance is more a matter of hubris than fortitude.[54] We need to appreciate human frailty, that we are, as Nussbaum says in the passage earlier, "flawed crystals" who have limitations as human beings and weaknesses as individuals. In the film of *The African Queen*, Charlie tries to excuse his drunkenness by saying it's only human nature, to which Rose replies (in a Kantian fashion), "Nature is what we've been put on the earth to rise above." However, toward the end of the movie Rose prays that God will not judge her and Charlie on their weakness but rather on their love. Rose discovers something within herself; she has an epiphany regarding human frailty and "the complicated delicacies of the human heart." She could condemn herself and Charlie for not having the "best life"; instead she finds that their "weakness" has brought her to a new awareness of her life and its joys.

There are a few people — such as Leonardo da Vinci — who have seemingly boundless energy and talent that they put to fullest use. It is difficult to think how da Vinci's life as he lived it could have been better. Most of us are not in this kind of situation, though. We do not have boundless energy, talent, and commitment. We are not able to make maximum use of all our talents; we have to pick and choose what we accomplish. As Rose did, we should delight in human beings just because they are human beings with all their flaws, as "a parent who takes delight in having a child who is a child, and who reveals in interacting with the child that it is all right to be human."[55]

That does not imply that we should not guide children and adults by correcting their mistakes and having them make amends for their transgressions. But neither does it imply that our inevitable frailties condemn us to lives that always will be less than the best. Stocker distinguishes between "best" as a "relative superlative" and as an "absolute superlative."[56] One way to construe "best" is relatively, in comparison with other possibilities. Another way to think of it, though, is absolutely; that is, assessing it on its own terms without requiring comparison with other possibilities. So, why can we not think a teacher's life, committed to children and ideas, experienced as satisfying, is the best sort of life even if we can imagine other lives somehow "better" for her? Why not think that Rose's life with Charlie is the best sort of life, even if not "pure"? Perhaps what made her life with Charlie the best sort of life is just that it was so very human.

Maybe what this means is that we should learn to be happy with a "satisfactory" life. There is a point to that, but it still makes happiness the aim. At least in common understandings of the term, concern for "happiness" can engender considerable discontent, the "unhappiness of not being happy."[57] If we think the world is predisposed to serving our happiness, and particularly in America, with our ideas about a right to happiness, if happiness eludes us, it is tempting to blame others because they must have impeded what is naturally ours, or blame ourselves because we have failed to devote enough effort to its pursuit.[58] Of course justice and self-responsibility are relevant in the pursuit of well-being; however, I believe it would help if we had a reasonable conception of what we have a right to and what we should be pursuing.

There could be a point to thinking comparatively. There is the danger of settling for what really is not best. Weakness does not excuse everything. Even so, if "the best life" and "happiness" really are aims, they should be thought of as aims in Dewey's sense.[59] They should serve as guides to conduct without implying they are ends that must be reached. If we are concerned for *human* well-being we need to be sensitive to the nature and possibilities of human lives, imperfect and fragile as they are.

In light of all this, the facts of human frailty and the intrusions of a world that often is uncooperative, I propose "satisfying" as the sort of experience needed for well-being. I do not contend that this eliminates the problem happiness presents. "You/I should be satisfied" still can be an unreasonable and oppressive demand. The problem actually could be exacerbated just because satisfaction seems a more modest expectation. Even so, I think satisfaction is the more promising goal.

As with "pleasure," "satisfaction" does not name some singular quality. I will not devote much time to exploring the nature of satisfaction, *per se*. What I am concerned about are the sorts of experiences that can yield satisfaction. I will not provide an extensive typology of experiences. However, in the next section I discuss a fundamentally satisfying experience, the experience of meaning, which plays a central role in the conception of well-being I am developing.

## THE EXPERIENCE OF SATISFACTION AND MEANING

Dewey offers a starting point: "[E]very good, consists in a satisfaction of the forces of human nature, in welfare, happiness,"[60] and, "Good consists in the meaning that is experienced to belong to an activity when conflict and entanglement of various incompatible impulses and habits terminate in a unified orderly release in action."[61] Overlooking the details of Dewey's statements for the moment, he presents two broad ideas incorporated in the conception I offer. One idea is the connections among experience, good, well-being, and happiness. While we have just considered whether happiness is the mental state appropriate to well-being, Dewey believes some such favorable attitude toward one's life is central to experience and welfare. The second idea regards meaningful experience. In meaningful experiences we make sense of our lives, which at times might seem hopelessly confused and fragmented. Achieving meaning enables us to better pursue our well-being, and the experience of meaning itself can be satisfying.

For Dewey, satisfaction is not just a second best we might need to settle for. He construes happiness as a very basic human experience, the satisfaction of the forces of human nature. Satisfaction does not require extraordinary efforts or superhuman achievements. For example, in grasping sensory qualities — color, moist and dry, hard and soft — "the potentialities of the body are brought into functioning, while the activity of the body thus achieved brings in turn to completion potentialities in nature outside the body."[62] Thus, for Dewey, the good of "the satisfaction of the forces of human nature" consists largely of the realization of potentialities, potentialities for personal development and achievement, and potentialities the world embodies.

This satisfaction has two components. Dewey relates good and welfare to a meaning that is experienced, but it is not only a private mental achievement; it occurs in the world. There is the internal experience of satisfaction that accompanies an external unification of seemingly disparate or contending features in the person and the world.

Here, it is helpful to introduce two standards of worthwhile experience that Dewey offers: continuity and interaction.[63] The interaction Dewey is concerned with is between external factors and internal factors, between environing conditions and the emotions, attitudes, and other things internal to the person. Continuity occurs when "every experience both takes up something from those which have gone before and modifies in some way the quality of those which come after."[64]

Why should we think this sort of experience and satisfaction is so important for well-being? If you are moving out of your fifth-floor apartment and are unable to grasp the quality "heavy," fail to interact with the environment in that way, likely you will be frustrated or get a strained back if you pack boxes too full or neglect to get a dolly to take your refrigerator out to the rental truck. The potentialities of your body are not brought into functioning — not very wisely, at least — nor are the potentialities of nature, like gravity, and how that might frustrate you or aid you, appreciated. Dewey's emphasis is on progress and growth. Thus, really interacting with the world and making productive use of the potentials in one's body and in the world is a vital satisfaction, and one I imagine we all experience. In Chapter 6 I will talk about human capabilities, a notion similar to Dewey's "potentials."

Of course, it might be possible to just muscle a refrigerator out of an apartment, and that might bring certain potentialities into functioning. And maybe it is satisfying to some people to do things the hard way. However, for Dewey it is not enough that forces are satisfied as a matter of fact. The good that comes from it requires meaning, which for Dewey consists in sorting through various entanglements and arriving at an action that has order and unity. Continuity is part of that achievement. As an experience, as opposed to merely an episode or event, in moving out of your apartment you recall and use other things you have experienced about moving things, and through the present experience you learn new things that can be brought to bear in future experience. So, as a meaningful experience, your move isn't just an isolated event but demonstrates continuity with other aspects of your past and future life. Likely, muscling a refrigerator lacks continuity and unity.

We must do more to consider whether the sort of meaning Dewey advocates is necessary or important for well-being. Given the subject-relativity of well-being, we have reason to wonder whether it is; perhaps some people won't find "meaning" especially satisfying. However, we can see that meaning has a strong draw in human life. When tragedies occur, people ask, "Why did that have to happen?" Sometimes, for example in the aftermath of natural disasters, there may be "whys" in terms of weather dynamics, and that can be comforting if one is afraid of being singled out for God's wrath or fate's whimsy. Oftentimes, we can only say, "It just happened; there is no 'why.'" But in those cases people will often look for meaning in the sense of achieving some good out of the tragedy, say to prevent future tragedies, or to remind us to cherish our loved ones or fellow human beings and to appreciate the fragility of what is good.

To feel oneself at the mercy of what is arbitrary and capricious and so meaningless can be severely debilitating. In the film *Platoon* the young soldier Chris agonizes in a letter to his grandmother, "Hell is the impossibility of reason." In *Schindler's List*, the Jewish housemaid Helen tells Schindler how the concentration camp Kommandant shot a woman who was walking by him. Helen says the woman was no faster or slower, no taller or shorter than anyone else. She sobs that if only she could figure out the "rules" perhaps she would be able to survive. The common theme in these examples is the suffering people endure when they are unable to make sense out of situations.

Of course, to achieve meaning does not guarantee one will be happy. A student might be able to make sense out of being beaten up by a bully by saying, "It wasn't my fault; he's just a jerk," but it is difficult to see what is especially satisfying about arriving at that meaning. Still, it would seem a more satisfying meaning than, "I deserved it; I'm such a dork." Certain meanings might not be especially pleasant, but they can be satisfying in enabling individuals to better understand and give shape to their lives. Making sense of things and possibly coming to peace with oneself, while not fun, can be an important satisfaction. Achieving meaning is a key to achieving satisfaction and well-being in both the short term and the long term.

"Meaning" plays several roles in the conception of well-being that I propose. Meaning is a source of satisfaction. But meaning is not just one source of satisfaction among others such as the fulfillment of desires, needs, and other things. These latter things are sorts of meaningful things. This is another reason not to limit relevant meanings to specific things such as needs; there is much more that is meaningful in human lives. Finally, our ultimate concern is with the particular meaning "well-being."

What does it mean for something to have "meaning"? Again, Dewey offers a helpful (but problematic) suggestion. He contends, "When an activity is its own end in the sense that the action *of the moment* is complete in itself, it is purely physical; it has no meaning."[65] Hence Dewey's problem with "superficial compromises" and the victory of "impulse": "The unification which ends in act may be only a superficial compromise, not a real decision but a postponement of the issue . . . Or it may present . . . a victory of a temporarily intense impulse over its rivals, a unity by oppression and suppression, not by coordination."[66] In his view, these spurious unifications are complete in themselves; they are devoid of meaning because they lack adequate thought and do not look beyond the moment.

While Dewey has a point, I believe he overstates it. The meaning in "compromise" and "impulse" might be minimal, but it is not the case that they have no meaning. Imagine a student punches another student who made fun of him, or a teacher throws a student out of the classroom after the student insulted her. We might describe the retaliations as persons just lashing back, giving little if any thought to consequences and significance outside the moment. The retaliation is in that way its own end and lacks meaning in Dewey's sense. For him, meaning depends on relating events to things "outside" the moment, to ideas about proper relationships among students and between students and teachers, for example. Rather than see herself as a victim of seemingly arbitrary pushes and pulls — the student's anger, her own anger — the teacher who discerns meaning in her predicament is able to make sense of things in a way that enables her to act with more awareness and wisdom.

Even so, the events surely are meaningful to the people involved in the sense that they did not ignore the events; they perceived something significant at stake. And it could be said that lashing back released and unified contending elements in some sense — elements of anger and fear, perhaps. Dewey likely would reply that the proportion, order, and freedom introduced into the situation are still minimal. Perhaps.[67] Nonetheless, the meaning, even if minimal, can be significant. Even if the student and teacher do not think outside the moment, we can imagine that going through their minds are meanings such as "I am an object of attack" or "I am responding with anger." Even if the events are largely meaningless to them in that they would think, "I have no idea what's going on here; I can't make sense of it," they can also conclude, "I am in a situation where (apparently) meaningless things occur," which would make the situation very meaningful.

We are in dangerous territory if we think there are events or situations that have no meaning for people. It might lead people to try to separate meaningful experiences from other experiences. I heard a professor say that teachers need to focus on students' reading comprehension first and worry later about the meaning kids get from reading. I doubt many adults would put up with "meaningless" activities in that way. I don't see why young people should either. I also wonder whether students, having been inured to "meaningless" activities, will be receptive to a shift alien to their prior experience. We can imagine them complaining, "What's the point of trying to understand the significance of this novel? That's never been important before." Which brings me to a principal point. People are going to find meaning in things. Some sorts of meaning — such as the sort Dewey emphasizes — might not be achieved, but the meaning of events and situations is not singular. A number of legitimate meanings can be found in any particular event.[68]

We have to be careful not to carry the point too far, however. Haidt cites one of Dr. Phil's ten "laws of life": "There is no reality, only perception."[69] Apparently, this is a common claim in "pop psychology." I take the point to be that people should realize that they are not prisoners of reality but can alter their perceptions of things and give them different, and more healthy, meaning. But it is very different — and dangerous — to believe that there is no reality. Proponents of the "no reality" idea themselves cannot mean it literally if their claims are to be internally consistent, if for no other reason than they must make distinctions between ways of living that really are healthy and those that are not.

Educators need to be sensitive to the variety of meanings suffusing their lives and that of their students. The issue is not whether schooling will be meaningful but how it will be meaningful. Of course, I am not saying we can relax because education inevitably is meaningful for students and educators. The concern is about the sort of meanings that will be discerned: exhilarating, stupid, dull, intriguing, satisfying. If we are concerned about serving people's welfare, we need to work on the meanings that lead to satisfaction and understanding and those that hinder those things. Students might not see the meanings we educators wish they would, but just because their meaning is different from ours does not show it is mistaken. As discussed before, knowledge and perception inevitably are partial. Students may see or focus upon a different aspect of a situation compared with their teachers. Even if student meanings are partial, we should appreciate that they have achieved some meaning. At the very least, grasping some meaning is better than students allowing themselves to be like billiard balls knocked around by the elements of their environment with no thought or care regarding the purposes and consequences involved.

However, as much as I emphasize the plurality of meanings I do not propose all are equally valuable. For our purposes an exhaustive taxonomy of meaning is not necessary, but a few basic distinctions are helpful. The meanings we are particularly interested in are meanings relevant to an individual's well-being. In that sense, fine wine is not terribly meaningful to me whereas philosophy is very meaningful. Fine wine has no important place among my prudential values in contrast to philosophy. Other meanings have a more tenuous or distant connection to the individual. A good many school events are likely meaningful to students in this way. For example, *Romeo and Juliet* might be meaningful or increase in meaning for students if they can make comparisons between it and other plays by Shakespeare. Similarly, the x's and y's algebra students deal with might become more meaningful when they see how variables can be used to translate word problems into equations. This is a sort of meaning achieved when students are able to connect to other things, even if the connection to their well-being is not direct. The thing at issue no longer stands alone but has a place in a broader scheme of things. Finally, there is meaning that essentially is bare comprehension. *Romeo and Juliet* thus has a meaning it did not previously have, with students finally able to decipher Shakespeare's language and imagery even if they do not understand its meaning in the sense of its significance for Shakespeare's corpus of work, literature generally, or their well-being.

I think it is important to identify at least these basic distinctions. On the one hand, it reminds us that to achieve meaning in the latter two senses does not imply a connection is or can be made to the individual's well-being, which is the meaning we are aiming for ultimately. On the other hand, though, meanings not directly connected to well-being still can contribute to well-being. Simply being able to comprehend a difficult text can be satisfying to students even if literature is not at the top of the list of their prudential values. So, as important as it is to remember the differences between the types of meaning, all can have a proper place in the pursuit of well-being; we should look at their contribution to well-being as a matter of degree and context.

Again, though, we need to appreciate that people can discern a number of meanings in any one situation or event. A student might get satisfaction from completing a difficult task while also deeming the task itself as just another chore the teacher assigned. Or maybe a student refuses to put in the effort to decipher *Romeo and Juliet*. He might not get the satisfaction of understanding the play, but he is very satisfied by his refusal to do a task that strikes him as "meaningless." For him, what is meaningful and satisfying in the situation is his resistance.

## CONCLUSION

In this chapter I have begun to explore what it means to be in a world where one experiences well-being. Experiences of satisfaction and meaning are important factors.

We have also begun to see that experience can be complex. Events can have a number of meanings for people. People can find satisfaction in diverse ways. Because of that, I count the breadth of "experience" as a virtue of my conception of well-being. We have narrowed the experiences that serve well-being to those that involve satisfaction and some sort of meaning. However, much remains to be done to explore the nature of experience and whether experience provides what is needed for a conception of human well-being.

To continue to explore the nature and significance of the experience I advocate, in the next chapter I will compare and contrast my conception with a desire theory of well-being. Desire theory is only one alternative to the proposal I offer, but it serves well to present basic issues and challenges that need to be faced.

*Chapter 2*

# Experience, Desire, and Well-Being

Arguably the dominant approach to well-being currently,[1] desire theory makes the connection between values and well-being via people's desires. This approach has some promise. It is a subject-relative conception of well-being: something good benefits *my* life when *I* desire it. Also, people are doing well when their desires are realized and not just when they think they are realized. So, desire theory reflects the same concern for accomplishments expressed by Nietzsche and Dewey. And, as we will see, desire theory offers an account of motivation, of why people do and value the things they do: they desire them.

However, I will argue that desire theory does not provide the conception of well-being we need. As I will propose, desire theory assumes a separation between human beings and the world, and so precludes, or at least inhibits, the attunement and resonance with the world that is part of being in the world.

In the preceding chapter I began to argue for the necessity of experience in well-being. However, it is not clear what the role of experience should be, so I will start by responding to two criticisms of experience offered in Griffin's desire theory. One is the charge that experience provides too narrow a view on well-being because it excludes certain prudential values — namely, those that are not experienced. The second charge is that experience is too broad because of the place it gives to mental states. The problem Griffin anticipates is that favorable mental experiences will be taken to be sufficient for well-being. As a theme for the discussion I will use an idea Griffin introduces, that "a valuable life" means "a life I must lead."[2] What does it mean to lead a valuable life, and what place does experience have in that?

## WELL-BEING AND THE NECESSITY OF EXPERIENCE

Griffin denies that experience is required for well-being. One of his arguments regards what I call experience as awareness. He argues that for many valued things what matters most for people is that those things are realized, not that people experience the realization. Griffin argues,

> If I want to accomplish something, it is not necessary that I want my accomplishment to enter my experience — say that I know about it. That too is desirable, but it still is not the first desire. If either I could accomplish something with my life but not know it, or believe that I had but not really have, I should prefer the first.[3]

Consider an example, though. A teacher desires that her students be successful in life. For many teachers, their students' success in life is a major part of a fulfilling life and career. Often, however, a teacher will not know if former students are successful. Yet the teacher accepts this. She prefers that her students truly be successful without her knowledge to having a false sense that they are. As it turns out, her desire is fulfilled for some of her students and not for others, but she has no knowledge of how they fare. According to Griffin's view, her well-being is affected even though she is not aware of events.

In contrast, if experience is required for well-being we must say that the teacher's well-being is unaffected, at least in any direct sense. But from the teacher's perspective, that is exactly the situation. Without knowledge about her past students, she might assume success and feel good, or she might assume failure and feel bad, but neither of those assumptions is warranted. It is more reasonable for her to admit she does not know, and so be up in the air about that part of her welfare.

Griffin anticipates this sort of reply, using as an example the thorny problem of how to account for dead people's desires. If, as he claims, awareness is unnecessary for well-being, then it is sensible to contend that people's well-being can be affected after their death. It is difficult, however, to see how dead people can have a well-being. Griffin believes he has an answer. He asks us to imagine ourselves slandered by an enemy who is

> successfully persuading everyone that you stole all your ideas, and they, to avoid unpleasantness, pretend in your presence to believe you. If that could make your life less good, then why could it not be made less good by his slandering you with the extra distance behind your back that death brings?[4]

Griffin has a point. If we ponder what our whole life comes to, say how it benefits other people, but our accomplishments somehow are undercut by someone or some events, even if we do not know about it, our life will be diminished; it will not have the positive impact it would otherwise. So, Griffin describes exertions one might go through to prevent being slandered after death, claiming this shows the value attached to posthumous reputation, a reputation the dead person obviously cannot experience.

However, a major problem with Griffin's argument is that he talks about what could "make your life less good," but there is a difference between a good life and well-being. Let's suppose that a dead person's life can be made less good, say in the sense of what it contributes to other people: people claim her accomplishments for their own, or her contributions are misused, turned to evil purposes. So, when everything is added up, her life does not amount to much; it has contributed little if anything to making the world a better place, despite her great desire that it would. Even so, it doesn't follow that the dead person's well-being is affected. Again, there is a difference between living a good life (one that is beneficial to humankind, for example) and living a life experienced as worthwhile or satisfying.

Also, when Griffin describes efforts people go through to protect their reputations, his point is that people do not merely desire a sense that their reputations are secure; they want to secure their reputations. However, rather than show how people do not attach value to awareness or "sense" of accomplishment — here a good reputation that literally one cannot be aware of after death — these efforts show just how important experience as awareness can be. If posthumous reputation is important, one will want to experience that one has done what is needed to preserve that reputation, hence the exertions made prior to one's demise. One wants to lead one's life and not just be the victim of events and people. Experience as awareness is vital for that.

Let's get away from dead folk and think about living people. Consider another of Griffin's examples, parents desiring their child's success. The parents are not looking for any outward signs from the child. The child's appreciation might be nice, but at most it is only a secondary desire. If the child is successful, that is enough; the parents feel they do not need to know about it. So far as the parents leading their lives in light of their own priorities, Griffin's idea appears to be that this can be done without knowing whether the priority — the child's success — is achieved.

It might be that the parents prefer the child's success without their knowledge of it to the child's misleading them (not telling them about his drug addiction), but it would be an odd parent who would feel content or satisfied with the situation. Given the choices, probably most parents would rank their values the way Griffin suggests, but these are hardly the choices most parents would wish to have. I imagine that most parents' first desire would be that they didn't have to choose between not knowing their child's fate and being deceived about it. Under what circumstances might parents be forced into a preference for not knowing? Perhaps the parents and child are estranged and so the parents in fact have no knowledge of the child's welfare; maybe the child actively tries to keep the parents in the dark.

Likely, parents facing this situation would be loath to accept that they will never know whether their child is successful or not. Typically, parents do not merely wish for a child's success but do what they can to secure that success. Before being content with the estrangement, they likely would do what they can to maintain a relationship. The parents' aim need not be personal satisfaction or some return from their child. Their attempts to know about his fate are part of their desire for their child's success; awareness of his success is not just a separate and secondary desire. Their fuller experience of the situation, far from undercutting their highest prudential values, would appear vital if the parents really are to lead their lives in the way their prudential values suggest.

Yet Griffin is right that something important is at stake for well-being even in events beyond one's awareness. Returning to our teacher example, the mere fact of students' success or failure does not have a direct impact on the teacher's well-being, but it still is important, because of its potential impact. That is more plausible than saying the teacher's quality of life increased or declined even though she was unaware of it, which does not diminish the potential effects if she were to become aware.

However, insisting on the importance of awareness for well-being presents a problem. The necessity of awareness might appear to license wholesale ignorance and deception; what happens outside a person's awareness is irrelevant for his welfare so long as he remains ignorant or deceived.

A direct effect on well-being is not the only criterion for condemning or praising some action, though. Smearing a colleague behind his back is a bad thing to do, and it can be condemned for its potential to harm the victim. Relationships with colleagues might change for the worse, or the victim might be denied opportunities for advancement. Describing these as potential consequences for well-being does not lessen their importance. If we are concerned about well-being, we must be concerned for how people's lives are actually going *and* for how they might go, how they could go given the opportunities provided or denied those people.

The experience requirement does not justify decreases in opportunities so long as they do not decrease the well-being actually experienced by people. Also, an advantage of the experience requirement is that supposed benefits must actually enter into people's lives. Consider income-tax cuts that favor the wealthy. Typically, the claim is that the benefits of tax cuts will trickle down and benefit everyone. The experience requirement entails benefits that actually enter into people's lives — say, in the form of more and better paying jobs, more community recreation facilities, and so forth. For us educators, perhaps this implies that our promises to students that "someday" they will experience the value of what we teach them are not enough.

However, the experience requirement presents several other difficulties. For example, it implies that the well-being of brain-dead persons cannot be affected because they are incapable of awareness. That is a troubling implication, but I am willing to accept it. Certainly, the life and bodily health of persons in vegetative states are affected by whether they are cared for even if they are unaware of it; and they should be cared for.[5] The issue is the quality of life. Brain-dead persons do not have a quality life at least in part because they cannot be aware of their well-being.

The experience requirement also raises the issue of whether a person impacted by some good has to be aware of the impact *as* something beneficial if his welfare is to be served. For instance, I don't give much thought to my diet, and when I do I have the sense my diet probably isn't especially healthy. Unknown to me, though, I happen to take in the nutrients needed to keep me healthy. My diet benefits me, but I am not "aware" of that. However, although it might stretch the meaning of "awareness," at least in this case I am aware of my health because my body is functioning reasonably well (for now), and that is the relevant condition. I experience the benefit even though I am not self-conscious about it. What matters is that my diet has impacted my life in a way that promotes my satisfaction with my life. That isn't to say I wouldn't be better-off if I were more self-consciously aware. Greater awareness could help me lead my life rather than just bumble my way through it.

An important version of these latter problems arises in the case of young people who might not have the wherewithal to understand the benefits of things. Consider an infant with a serious infection who gets an injection of antibiotics. All the child is aware of is the pain of the injection. She might experience the benefit if her illness is cured, but if the inoculation benefits her, how is that a satisfying experience for her? In response, we could take the same tack we did in the previous example: it is enough that her health is benefited; she will experience more comfort and satisfaction than if her illness went untreated. That seems a reasonable interpretation. It implies that some satisfying experiences might come at the cost of unsatisfying experiences, but that seems inevitable.

That response can be too facile, though. What does a parent do when taking his child for an inoculation? Hopefully, he holds her, speaks soothingly to her, and sympathizes with her pain.[6] In other words, he tries to make the experience as satisfying for the child as possible. The pain does not disappear, but the parent tries to give the situation a meaning beyond "this hurts." The child is not self-consciously aware of the health benefits, but she can experience the satisfaction that comes from a parent's care.

So, for us educators, concern for students' welfare might necessitate we put them through painful experiences. But, like the parent, maybe we should admit the pain and not deny it, and offer solace and express regret so as to give the experiences a meaning beyond the painfulness. For example, if we educators must give students high-stakes tests — and I doubt that we must — let's sympathize with the anxiety and pain some students experience, and express regret for that.

Experience as awareness is essential for well-being. However, this does not imply that lack of awareness never contributes to, or is consistent with, well-being. Imagine a grandmother who sets aside money in her will that her granddaughter is to inherit after the grandmother's death. Obviously, when she is dead the grandmother will not know whether her desires for her granddaughter are fulfilled, and she has no desire to know. Still, she will do what she can to enhance the chances that her wishes will be carried out. She will try to find a trustworthy attorney to handle her estate, maybe tell other people of her intentions as a safeguard, likely try to get some sense of what would best benefit her granddaughter. She will want to be right in what she does and not merely have a sense that she is, but she cannot fulfill that unless she has some awareness that her intentions will be carried out.

Or maybe a teacher prefers not knowing how her former students fare in their lives, fearing that if she knows students do not do well she will become discouraged and her teaching will suffer. She will not know of the successes either, but she is willing to pay that price; she prefers not knowing students succeed to knowing that students fail. Yet here too, what counts for her well-being is what she is aware of, which is success at maintaining blissful ignorance.

Requiring experience as awareness does not deny Griffin's point that a person might prefer being unaware of a state of affairs to a false sense that the state of affairs exists. However, the discussion suggests a distinction in the notion of prudential value between the things people value as part of their well-being — what they value prudentially — and what actually contributes to their well-being — what *has* prudential value. Griffin states, "According to the enjoyment account [that requires experience], what affects well-being can only be what enters experience, and the trouble is that some of the things that persons value greatly do not,"[7] thus making a close connection between "what affects well-being" and what people "value greatly." However, those things need to be distinguished. When people consider what is important to them — what they value prudentially — they might rank achieving some desire above their experiencing that achievement. The experience requirement does not preclude that. It does require, though, that for something to actually *have* prudential value, it or its effects have to be experienced.

As I have said, one advantage of emphasizing experience is to remind us of the breadth of things that can impact our well-being. But is "experience" too broad? At this point I turn to another of Griffin's criticisms of experience. Griffin is suspicious of experience because it appears to open the door to "mental state" accounts of well-being. I will argue that making room for mental states is a strength of the experience requirement.

## EXPERIENCE AND THE INTELLIGENCE OF EMOTION

Griffin's fear is that with the experience requirement well-being will be taken to be only a state of mind; if you believe that you are doing well then you are doing well. But as we noted before, people can think they are doing well when in fact they are not. Hence Griffin's emphasis on desire satisfaction, which is a state of the world and not just a state of mind. It is not enough that you experience favorable attitudes or just believe your desires are fulfilled; the desires actually must be fulfilled.

Griffin's caution is well-founded. If, as Haidt and others appear to believe, there is no reality, only perception, then there is no meaningful state of the world; feelings or beliefs are the only relevant factors. Thus, Haidt proposes that "a sense of purpose and meaning" is the aim for a happy life.[8] But Griffin surely is correct that well-being requires more than a "sense" of purpose and meaning.

However, contrary to what Griffin seems to think, requiring experience does not lead back to a mental state account.[9] The experience of satisfaction is a necessary element of well-being; that does not mean the experience is sufficient.

Let's return once again to the parents who value their child's success but have no awareness of the child's welfare. It is easy to imagine that most parents would experience disappointment, regret, or even grief in those circumstances. Following Aristotle and Dewey, we could say that an emotional response is needed to complete or perfect the experience. At the very least, this shows that mental states should be factored into people's well-being. Realizing one's greatest desires can be accompanied by considerable heartache. Love is an obvious example. In some unfortunate instances, knowledge of a child's fate might be secondary to other values, but we should not conclude too much from that. Even if satisfaction or avoiding grief is not people's first or immediate aim, the emotions experienced surely can add to or detract from people's well-being. They can be important stimuli to action. They can offer insight into the nature and significance of events. We would know a lot about parents and the significance of events if parents did or did not grieve over estrangement from their child.

However, in America, and perhaps the West in general, emotions are looked upon with suspicion. There is a hands-off attitude, either because emotions are deemed irrational and so beyond the ken of rational understanding and modification, or because they are considered sacred and so not to be intruded upon.[10] Likely, such attitudes are behind skepticism about the connection between well-being and mental states.

However, Nussbaum argues that emotions are intelligent and related to persons' flourishing.[11] Regarding compassion, for instance, she identifies three cognitive elements:

> the judgment of *size* (a serious bad event has befallen someone); the judgment of *nondesert* (this person did not bring the suffering on himself or herself); and the *eudaimonistic judgment* (this person, or creature, is a significant element in my scheme of goals and projects, an end whose good is to be promoted).[12]

Similarly, regarding grief, "The notion of *loss* that is central to grief itself has [a] double aspect: it alludes to the value of the person who has left or dies, but it alludes as well to that person's relation to the perspective of the mourner."[13]

Nussbaum emphasizes the organic connection between the pains or joys in these emotions and the cognitive dimensions of the emotions. She proposes that we think of pain as "so closely linked to the thoughts that we might call it the affective dimension of the thought, a pain 'at the thought of'" the thing.[14] We might construe this as a causal connection; the thought of loss, for instance, causes pain. But Nussbaum also argues for a conceptual connection. That is, the pain of a loss is a particular sort of pain: "not any old throbbing or tugging will do, but only the sort that is 'about' or 'at' the misfortune."[15]

Does the causal relation work in the other direction, pain causing thoughts? Haidt suggests, "emotions can . . . cause thoughts."[16] The examples he uses are fear, anger, and sadness, and he says these operate by putting up "filters" that "bias" subsequent thought. It could be that emotions cause thoughts, but the way Haidt presents the idea, it loses the organic connection between thought and emotion Nussbaum seeks to establish. Part of the problem is the non-discriminating way Haidt uses "emotion." (Nussbaum's discriminations are presented shortly.) For example, sadness indeed can color our thoughts, making everything seem gloomier than it really is. But Nussbaum's point is that the sadness of grief is not just some generic, free-floating sadness but is a sort more or less particular to grief. It could be that we feel the pain of loss without fully comprehending why, and so to that extent the sadness precedes or prompts some amount of thought. However, if we do not just talk about sadness but about the emotion of grief, the causal connection becomes more complicated. If the pain of grief prompts thought, thought or perception also affects and effects the pain felt. The point is pertinent especially if the "emotion-causes-thought" claim is used, as Haidt uses it, to try to support the "reality-is-created" claim I criticized previously. From his discussion of causality Haidt concludes that negative emotions can "make everything bad."[17] Of course emotions can affect our thinking in ways largely beyond our control, but there is a difference between making everything bad and making everything *appear* to be bad.

Similar to Dewey's argument regarding meaning, Nussbaum's argument shows that it is misleading to think of emotions as mere mental states separate from cognitive connection to the world. This is another example of how something "in" a person resonates with the world outside. Emotions are not just private events that lack direct connection to events in the world; judgment about the world is involved. An emotion has an object; in the case of grief, loss of someone or something valued. But it also has a prudential connection to the subject. I grieve, not just because something valuable is lost, but something valuable to *me*. And the emotion is part of the judgment of loss. Emotional responses, then, are not merely secondary in the project of understanding and living a worthwhile life. They are central in forming, affirming, and experiencing one's prudential values.

This is true even for emotion-like states that are not so clearly object-centered and so might seem more purely "mental." Nussbaum distinguishes appetites — hunger, for example — from emotions because, although they have an object, appetites are value-indifferent. They are more a "push" in contrast to the "pull" of emotion.[18] Even here, though, there are connections to prudential value. Appetites are signals of neediness; we will have emotions about the things that satisfy those needs.[19] Generally, we do not just have "appetites" but appetites for particular things that are not substitutable. If I have an appetite for a good steak, I likely will be disappointed if offered a greasy hamburger. If students have an appetite for teachers recognizing their work, we should not think that appetite is satisfied with just anything. Gold stars might do little to satisfy the appetite for recognition.

Nussbaum also distinguishes emotions from moods — gloom, elation, irritation — because the latter lack an object.[20] One can be gloomy without really knowing why. It need not be prompted by a particular event; one might simply have a gloomy disposition. Yet surely mood affects one's ability to live a fulfilling life. Anyone who suffers from chronic depression knows how potent moods can be. For chronically depressed persons, it can be difficult to find satisfaction in accomplishing prudentially valued things. So, I do not dispute Haidt's claim that sadness as a mood affects people's outlook on life. However, even moods can have connection to particular events and need not be just free-floating psychological states. Gloom, for instance, can be triggered or deepened by events.[21]

Nussbaum also contends that some emotion-like feelings lack the self-referential element that other emotions, appetites, and moods have. Awe and wonder are two she considers. In experiences of awe and wonder one is "maximally aware of the value of the object, and only minimally aware, if at all, of its relationship to her own plans."[22] Yet, awe and wonder help "move distant objects within the circle of a person's scheme of ends."[23] The object does not stand as a distant fact or intellectual curiosity but exerts itself, overwhelms us.

Later I will do more to explore the plausibility and significance of Nussbaum's claims. At this point, I think the discussion of awareness and emotion at least gives us grounds to continue to pursue the idea that experience captures essential elements of well-being. Well-being is not just about having values satisfied but also about having the things one values prudentially actually impact one's life, both in the sense of enjoying the satisfaction (or suffering the pain) and in the sense that one is enabled to lead one's life when aware of and emotionally invested in one's success or failure at achieving the things most valued. Nussbaum argues, "The emotions are themselves modes of vision or recognition. Their responses are part of what knowing, that is truly recognizing or acknowledging, *consists in*."[24] Despite skepticism about mental states, we have reason to think the breadth of experience is an advantage because it brings in emotions and other mental states that are vital aspects of our being through which we understand and act in the world.

This brings us to what might be the central issue at stake in any subject-relative conception of well-being: What is the connection between valuable things and individuals' well-being? For example, I might be awed by a beautiful sunset, but the mosquitoes biting me severely decrease the enjoyment I experience. I can experience a valued thing, but what does that mean for my welfare? If desire satisfaction is the key for well-being then we have an answer: valuable things serve people's well-being if they are things people desire. Thus, I can explain why my sunset-watching experience was not terribly beneficial. I might have desired seeing the sunset, but I also had a strong desire to avoid mosquito bites. What does a conception of well-being based upon experience have to say about this issue? How can it link value to persons' lives? The essential claim will be that there is no link that has to be made.

## DESIRING AND EXPERIENCING WELL-BEING

Let's start with an example where it seems difficult to explain a person's welfare in terms of desires. Private Felix Branham, who landed at Omaha Beach on D-Day, 1944, says:

> I have gone through lots of tragedies since D-Day . . . But to me, D-Day will live with me till the day I die, and I'll take it to heaven with me. It was the longest, most miserable, horrible day that I or anyone else ever went through . . . I would not take a million dollars for my experiences, but I surely wouldn't want to go through that again for a million dollars.[25]

Private Branham's D-Day experience appears central to the quality of his life, a constant memory, perhaps a defining experience. He clearly values the experience — he would not trade it for a million dollars. Yet he also describes it as a tragedy, full of horror and misery; he would not want to go through it again. While Private Branham's D-Day experience is extreme, many of us go through situations where we are pulled in different directions, like in my buggy sunset experience. Teachers might have little desire to go through difficult episodes with students, colleagues, or parents — episodes filled with anger, frustration, sadness, and fear. They might hope never to have to endure such situations again. Yet they might also find that something worthwhile, satisfying, and even irreplaceable was achieved.

Supposing Private Branham's D-Day experience did contribute to his well-being somehow, how can that be explained in terms of desire? Because it was horrible, the experience might have little value in itself, but maybe it was vital for Private Branham's desires later in life, desire to be a strong person perhaps, or a person more (or less) sensitive to people's suffering and to the value of peace.

However, many war veterans do not look at their experiences only that way. They express pride and fulfillment about the experiences and not just what follows them. Maybe some are masochists who get a thrill out of their own suffering, but that seems not to describe Private Branham. So we look for some other desires. Soldiers often talk about their desire not to let their buddies down. Perhaps Private Branham had a desire to show courage in the face of the horror. Those things are possible, but it would also seem that a lot was going on that wouldn't be desired. And if Private Branham had certain desires in the situation, it is likely that he had a strong desire not to be in the situation at all.

One response to this complexity is to rank desires by their importance or intensity, to look for certain "higher-order" desires; that is, look for desires about one's desires. Perhaps what was most important for Private Branham was a desire not to let his desires to run or hide effect his conduct on the battlefield. His desire to be a certain sort of person was more important to him than other desires or impulses.

Again, that could be the case. Perhaps Private Branham confronted his fear and resolved to overcome it when the time came, forming a conception of himself that he hoped to fulfill. But it is probable that much of that went out the window on D-Day; at least, we get accounts from soldiers to the effect that they just acted, that they did amazing things just because they "had to." And even if it did not all go out the window, Private Branham really could not have known the good of duty, for example, until he had been drawn into the horrible and demeaning but courageous and noble events of that day. So, it is difficult to say just what his desires might have been or whether his strong desires can provide a helpful analysis of the benefits he experienced, if his desires were as tentative and complex as I have suggested. People can come to question the meaning of and their desire for things like duty when they experience all that's involved. It might be that in the heat of battle Private Branham had no idea what his desires were, and hence the plausibility of thinking "I just acted" or "I just had to do that."

Desire theory is charged with having an inadequate account of this "manna from heaven" — or, in Private Branham's case, "manna from hell" — phenomenon, when people experience unanticipated benefits. It would seem that people can get satisfaction from things they had little if any desire for.

Griffin acknowledges this possibility: "Good things can just happen; manna from heaven counts too"; one can discover values.[26] And he believes he has a desire-based explanation: "When you see what accomplishment [for example] is, you form a desire."[27] So, in Private Branham's case, it might be true that he had no particular desire to do his duty or had only a limited idea of what duty required, but when he saw it for what it was, he formed a desire for it. However, even if desires can be formed this way, it still requires that if Private Branham benefited from doing his duty he must have had a desire to do his duty, and I believe we still have reason to be skeptical of that, say, in contrast to compulsions he might have felt.

However, Griffin has another response: desires need not be conscious.[28] Therefore, even if Private Branham did not realize it or admit to it, if he benefited there must have been desires there. So, if Private Branham were to claim he was fulfilled by acting bravely, but had no desire to act bravely, he simply would be wrong. But it is unclear that for the sake of theoretical consistency we should ride roughshod over people's self-understanding. If we insist that people's self-understanding provides no evidence to challenge the role of desire, how can the desire theorist's claim ever be disproved? It would get to the point that desire would not explain anything at all.

Griffin need not take that tack, though. For Griffin, desires are an analytical tool. For example, Private Branham might not have desired to act bravely in the sense of having a motivation to act bravely. Nonetheless, insofar as Private Branham is able to understand the prudential value of his actions, he does it in terms of his informed desires. So, it might be true that Private Branham had no conscious or unconscious motivation to act bravely, but if we are to understand the prudential value of his brave actions, they have to be placed in a hierarchy of informed desires.

However, a hierarchy of informed desires is not necessary for making sense of unanticipated and complex situations of benefits and losses.[29] Say a teacher eagerly anticipates the beginning-of-the-school-year in-service training, because a nationally known speaker will give a presentation on using technology in classrooms, a topic the teacher is very interested in. Unfortunately, contrary to her expectation and desire, the presentation is disappointing. The speaker talks for too long, in a monotone, and offers nothing the teacher didn't know already. Supposing the teacher was made worse-off by this experience, how would we explain that? The teacher has a desire to use her time effectively, a desire to do things that will really help her teaching, a desire to listen to an engaging speaker rather than a boring one, and likely a number of other desires thwarted in the experience. Maybe the session even serves some of her desires, such as to see colleagues she hasn't seen for a while. It is not necessary to decide which of these desires are most important in order to see that the teacher has at least a good case for thinking her well-being has not been well served.

Should the teacher have been more informed about her desires? Perhaps, but if her unanticipated disappointment is stipulated to show inadequate information, that does not change the teacher's disappointment. What appears to count simply is her dissatisfaction.[30]

We might still believe that satisfaction or dissatisfaction has to reflect desires. Griffin proposes, "desiring something is, in the right circumstances, going for it, or not avoiding or being indifferent to getting it."[31] Thus, our teacher's disappointment regarding her in-service experience could be described as a manifestation of her desires; overall, she didn't "go for it." However, this relies on a very broad sense of desire. Sumner argues that if desire is stretched in this way, then it loses what is supposedly distinctive about it, its "prospectivity" feature.[32] That is, desire implies future-directedness. If I desire chewing gum, I do more than enjoy it: I seek it out. This prospectivity feature would distinguish desire from enjoyment, which does not imply there is some desire that is satisfied; I can enjoy experiences I have no wish to repeat. But hence Sumner's point: What does "desire" offer that distinguishes it from other favorable attitudes? If we deem everything we are not indifferent to a "desire" then why not just talk in terms of enjoyments?

In light of all this, it seems to me Griffin gives an inadequate account of the benefits and harms that accompany those times in our lives when we experience satisfactions and pains we had not anticipated. We need to expand the concept of well-being to include experiences in addition to the experience of desire fulfillment.

However, Griffin does leave us with a fundamental challenge. Immediately after the passage Sumner uses as the basis of his criticism given here, Griffin goes on to say "how little any of this shows."[33] Even if the criticisms here have merit, they show us little, because, Griffin argues, we still must account for how and why the things people find satisfying contribute to their well-being. Griffin does not deny that enjoyments have a role, but their role is in understanding values, which is just a step toward forming informed desires. The satisfactions and dissatisfactions our teacher experiences at her in-service training might help her gain insight into the value of the events she experienced and into herself, but we still face the question of how significant her experiences are: Is her dissatisfaction a major blow to her well-being or is it just a minor thing? Also, just how much do her satisfactions and dissatisfactions really show her? According to Griffin, we still need to explain how we get from recognizing value (of which enjoyment can be a part) to well-being, how those values do or do not contribute to an individual's welfare. And for that, Griffin argues, we need desire.

Before proceeding we should be clear about Griffin's challenge. As much as he emphasizes desire Griffin insists that its "push" is not more important than the "pull" of values. He posits a two-way or coordinated interaction of desire and understanding:

Once we see something as "accomplishment" [for example], as "giving weight and substance to our lives," as "avoiding wasting our lives," there is no space left for desire to follow along in a secondary, subordinate position. Desire is not blind. Understanding is not bloodless. Neither is the slave of the other. There is no priority.[34]

Nonetheless, even if the two movements, the pull of values and the push of desire, are equally important, Griffin says we still do need both. Griffin is right to argue that one cannot "explain our fixing on desirability features purely in terms of understanding,"[35] if we take understanding to be purely intellectual. As Griffin argues, understanding implies a sort of movement; understanding is not bloodless.

However, this brings me to a central claim of my proposal. Emphasizing that understanding is not bloodless is one way of stating the aim of my argument. Where I diverge from Griffin is in what accounts for the "movement" in understanding. Truly appreciating prudential values, or the prudential aspects or potential of certain values, entails appreciating their desirability features. However, desirability need not be in terms of desire. In language I will consider further shortly, the movement in understanding can be attributed to the normativity of reasons; prudential values provide reasons for action. As reasons they move us, whether or not we "desire" to be moved.

All of this will be further explained and defended in subsequent chapters, but the upshot is that there need be no divide, indistinct or otherwise, between understanding and the sort of movement Griffin attributes to desire. He wishes to make a close connection between reason and desire, but he maintains a distinction.[36] This is particularly clear when he talks about forming desires *after* appreciating something. Rather than the understanding of prudential value being a phase that must be complemented by desire that moves us, the movement resides in the thing, if you will. In that way, understanding *is* prior to desire; but we are talking about a particular sort of understanding here.[37] To understand the prudential value of some thing is to be moved by it; desire falls out of the picture. To introduce an idea to which I will return, to perceive or understand situations correctly is to have a correct conception of one's well-being. We do not need to take the further step of analyzing our perceptions in terms of desires we have or form.

## CONCLUSION

In this chapter I have argued that experience is essential to well-being. To be in the world, lead our lives, and live satisfying lives, we have to be in touch with ourselves and the world, physically, intellectually, emotionally, and spiritually. I have argued that desire does not provide the connection. To close this chapter I will consider what is at stake in the alternative I propose.

The essential issue is human beings' experience with the world and values. There was a time when people believed meaning and value were embodied in the order of the universe; they lived in what must be "the best of all possible worlds." Thus, to understand the world included understanding its inherent goodness. In modern times, though, the world has become disenchanted. It is neutral when it comes to its interest in our fate; if we human beings are to find meaning, purpose, and good in the world it is up to us to make that happen. This is a manifestation of the dominance of instrumental reason with its (mis)assumptions about our ability to control knowledge, value, and life in general.

I do not propose we return to an enchanted view of the world; that is impossible in any case. What we can avoid is a separation between persons and the world that a disenchanted view of the world has encouraged. We can see that the world can be understood and lived as a source of meanings and not only through laws yielded by science.

I see Griffin assuming or encouraging the separation in his scheme of desire and understanding. He wants to make an intimate connection between those things, but there still is a connection to be made. What is lacking from Griffin's account is what I have called attunement or resonance. Finding goodness and satisfaction in our lives is not like going to the supermarket and picking out what we like. It's more like getting vitamin D from sunshine. We may or may not like being in the sun, but it's going to impact us — for good or ill — whether we like it or not. I don't want to press the metaphor, because experiencing well-being is not automatic. Still, the world offers us good (and bad) things. Being in the world and living well is more a matter of opening ourselves to the world, being attuned to what the world offers, rather than a matter for our creation, choice, and control.

I understand how that could sound like a bizarre claim. In the next chapter I continue to develop this conception of life and value, beginning with further explanation of the notion of attunement.

*Chapter 3*

# Attunement, Motivation, and Reasons

T he attunement I am concerned about is attunement between human beings and the world and within and between human beings, "the grasping of an order which is inseparably indexed to a personal vision."[1] When I say attunement with the world I am not just saying we should respect the environment, although that certainly is part of it. I am not saying we should not use the world's resources for human benefit, although there is a difference between respectfully using what the world offers us and forcing things from it.[2] Nor am I saying we must be in perfect harmony with the world. We should expect conflicts and frustrations in our experiences with the world. Much of the world will and should be enigmatic toward us.

The urge to control is a source for the alienation that is the antithesis of attunement. Regarding alienation of aesthetic consciousness, for example, Gadamer says that aesthetic judgment has become focused on dominating artworks through analysis and evaluation. Instead, aesthetic consciousness should open us to be "seized" by a work of art, so that we no longer have freedom to "push it away from us once again and to accept or reject it on our own terms."[3]

I'll continue to explain what I mean by being "seized" or "seduced" by values and its significance for transforming the self.

## ATTUNEMENT AND ELEVATING THE SELF

Centrally, the attunement I seek involves recognition of the world as a source of prudential value we can access through languages that resonate within and among persons.[4] I want to be clear at the start that I am not reneging on my

53

claim that virtue need not be its own reward. The world offers us things that have prudential value, but those come packaged with a number of other factors. It is too simple to say that being disciplined, or honest, will benefit people, because other conditions can intrude so as to diminish or cancel their value.

To explain my point it is helpful to consider some contrasting views on value. The most obvious and egregious example is the attitude that the world is merely a source of data. Whatever value we get out of the world must be our own creation. The datum, "If you stick someone with a hot poker he will scream," is just a piece of information. If there is any value issue involved it is only because we decide to make a big deal out of causing pain. However, if there is an issue of forcing value here, it is force exerted to suppress sympathy, compassion, and sensibility to pain rather than to interject value where there is none.

That is only the most egregious example, though. Griffin, for instance, is not saying anything close to that. His two-way interaction between value and desire is a step toward attunement in that, on the one hand, our well-being is not a matter of simply reacting to value. If we hammer on a big bell our bodies will feel the vibrations whether we want to or not, but we might have control to the extent that we can restrain our inclination to cringe or cultivate awe at the power of the sound. On the other hand, as we resonate with value we respond to what is offered us; we do not just force or create prudential benefits. If our bell is made of tinfoil, we won't get an awe-inspiring sound, regardless how hard we hammer on it. Attunement implies there are two (or more) entities resonating with each other and not just one being moved by the other(s).

Still, intentionally or not, Griffin's conception reinforces a common inclination to separate humans from the world. In his view, we do not command the world of value; still, that world is in some sense separate from us. We understand values such as accomplishment, yet we still must form desires for them (if we do at all) if we are to experience their prudential value. The danger of that image is that it will be taken to be the model for prudential valuing, whereas it is only one sort of such valuing. To illustrate, let's go back to our datum that hot pokers cause people pain. Understanding what that means, we do what we can to prevent people from being burned. We're attuned to the world of value by understanding what it means to feel and to cause pain. But on Griffin's view, stopping torture in itself implies nothing regarding our own well-being. If stopping torture benefits us it must be because we desire to stop it. That seems odd, though. Stopping gratuitous pain adds quality to our lives whether we desire it or not.

There are obvious challenges to my claim. For one thing, some people seem incapable of empathy with human beings and other creatures; they even enjoy causing suffering. Even if someone sees benefit in stopping pain, it might only stem from desire to avoid being caught by investigators from Amnesty International. These people see and experience no prudential value from stopping pain, *per se*. What really is the problem there, though? On Griffin's view we might say it is lack of understanding, so we need to make more vivid to these people the pain and humiliation torture causes, and then convince them they really do not desire to cause pain and humiliation. But if that is the process we must rely on, we seem to have lost the game before it has started. If a person really understands torture he will see the effect of torture on the quality of his life. If he doesn't see that effect one has to wonder if he has the aptitudes and attitudes necessary for a productive examination of his desires.

Let's consider another challenge. Perhaps there are conscientious people who understand the horrors of torture yet doubt that it diminishes their well-being because their well-being depends on getting information from terrorists. Setting aside the issue of whether torture even is a reliable way to get useful information, let's admit that often we are faced with difficult trade-offs regarding our welfare. So, a person might say, "I have no desire to torture people, but I have a great desire to protect my loved ones, myself, and my country." I don't condemn such an attitude, but we need to be clear about the implications. If our well-being cannot depend on the state of the world but must be completed by the additional step of desire (or something else), it is easy to exclude inconvenient truths from our scheme of prudential values. I can say, "People are being tortured, but I have no desires for or against that; all that counts is my desire to be safe." To have no desire regarding torture is not the same as having a desire that people not be tortured but having a stronger desire to be safe. In the latter case, if people are being tortured a diminution of well-being is implied; there is a cost, a desire violated. My argument is that there is a diminution in the former case, too. Prudential benefits and harms can accrue from actions due to the nature of the actions and the world in which they are embedded. The benefits do not depend on their being desired; the harms cannot be escaped by eliminating them from our scheme of desires.

I must say how this claim relates to my proposal that well-being must be experienced. If persons really do not experience pain or guilt or regret about torture, how is their welfare diminished? Probably, we have to admit that their well-being is not diminished in a direct sense. However, I return to the idea of potential effects on well-being. A person indifferent to others' pain creates a particular sort of life for himself. He may never experience shame or guilt about that, but he lives in a diminished world nonetheless. Maybe he will come to an epiphany and reject his earlier attitudes. As praiseworthy as that might be, the potential for his well-being cannot rest on his reformed desires only. While the meanings of past events are malleable to some degree, there are limits. Past experience will intrude on a person who comes to understand others' pain, despite a desire to forget the past or a desire to be a different person in the future.

The experience requirement has a general difficulty with far-off events that are only indirectly experienced, if experienced at all. Perhaps pictures give us some vicarious experience of others' suffering (when the mass media deign to present them to us). Most of us have experienced pain and humiliation to one degree or another, which can give us some sense of empathy for torture victims, but it would be sheer arrogance to think we can fully understand their experience. But perhaps we can have the sort of experience Nussbaum refers to when she writes about "pain at the thought of." People who have not been tortured cannot understand what torture really means, but, even if we are conflicted about the need for torture, we can experience pain at the thought of people's suffering. We have to take into account other prudential values in order to understand the exact impact of that suffering on our well-being, but others' suffering is an evil that is a cost to our pursuit of well-being, whatever our desires regarding it.

Again, some people simply do not and will not see things that way, but to explain that we should not posit some inevitable gap between values and prudential value. Rather, we should consider how people perceive the world. As I said before, attunement implies some contribution from the individual. What the world offers so far as prudential value has to be perceived. People must be receptive to the world, but effort, aptitude, and education are required if people are to achieve that receptivity.

To explore further the nature of this receptivity, let's consider what attunement might mean within the individual and not just between the individual and the world.

For individual persons, attunement involves interaction of the various aspects of their being and humanity — physical, intellectual, emotional, and spiritual. There are glaring examples of what I would call lack of attunement — say, when intellect is valued and emotions devalued, and vice versa. Other examples are less glaring. Many people would value all the aspects of human beings and still separate them. For example, as noted earlier, people might value both intellect and emotion yet say they should not interfere with each other. Or, if there is legitimate interaction among the several dimensions there needs to be a hierarchy established. Thus Plato's notions about how reason should govern the other aspects of the soul.

In these examples, intellect, emotion, and spirit all have a place in the field and have some sort of interaction with one another. Yet, the interaction is largely competitive; supposedly each has its own more or less particular territory, and we must be careful because one or another is likely to intrude upon or overcome the others. Even for Griffin, who emphasizes that desire and understanding work together, there is suspicion of the emotional side of life. When I think of attunement I imagine a situation where the aspects of our lives do more to collaborate than compete.

Let's consider Private Branham again. We might imagine his emotions telling him to hide from flying bullets and his intellect telling him to do his duty. He's thinking and feeling a conflict. He might imagine his task as deciding which element will win out. He is seeing the conflict as a competition where thoughtfulness basically means not letting one or the other element exert too much influence. But what if we look at his conflict as a collaboration, where the elements are part of a unified movement?

Here I'm not talking about a compromise such that Private Branham would grant a bit to emotion and a bit to intellect — "My contribution to intellect and duty is that I'll fire my rifle, but my concession to emotion is that I won't expose myself in order to aim." That could happen, but what could also happen is that each element would contribute to something greater than the sum of the parts. For example, maybe it could lead to at least the first glimmerings of a more universal sense for how courage is at stake and what it would require. For Aristotle, courage is facing danger in the proper way and at the proper time. If fear tells us to be cautious and intellect tells us to remember duty, they both contribute to a perspective that transcends both. A person could experience a change in the level of the self, an elevation that opens the possibility for new ways of perceiving and being.[5]

Griffin's view of the two-way interaction of understanding and desire suggests a sort of collaboration; neither aspect is adequate alone. We might say they lead a person to a perspective that transcends both understanding and desire — namely, informed desire. Again, the difficulty I see here is that Griffin's view still stands on a separation between desire and understanding. Turning again to Private Branham, and imagining he acted bravely and benefited, the scenario sketched here is not well described as him understanding bravery and then forming a desire for it. Rather, his understanding his action would be part and parcel of experiencing courage and well-being. He has come to a new way of seeing his situation where his understandings of fear, duty, and bravery are not merely balanced but are transformed and find a new resonance within him.

I do not contend that Griffin's conception precludes the sort of transformation I'm suggesting, but I do think it makes it harder to recognize. Under

Griffin's scheme we can imagine Private Branham has some legitimate under-standing of courage — say, that courage is not the same thing as foolhardiness. With that in hand, he takes counsel of his fears and desires and determines what his informed desire is (which he might or might not then act upon). His determination is to fire his rifle while not exposing himself. In Dewey's terms, we could call this a meaningful action, a unification of contending elements that leads to at least some sort of sensible action. However, my issue is whether this is the best model for possible outcomes. The outcome I am emphasizing is a transformation or transcendence of Private Branham's understanding and self and not merely a negotiation between his current understanding and his desires. Under Griffin's scheme, Private Branham might come to better under-stand how, when, and if he might opt for courageous actions. However, his growth in his understanding of courage and of himself remains essentially a process of negotiation between desire and value. This does not imply advance in the sort of attunement with himself and the world that I am proposing.

If we imagine Private Branham in dialogue with himself and the world, the point is expressed in Gadamer's depiction of understanding: "To reach an understanding in a dialogue is not merely putting oneself forward and successfully asserting one's own point of view, but being transformed into a communion in which we do not remain what we were."[6] Imagining Private Branham's informed desires emerge from a dialogue between his understand-ing of value and his desires, the process Griffin describes would seem to be that each element competes to assert its claim on him. In contrast, the sort of understanding Gadamer writes about implies a communion where Private Branham does not remain what he was. He does not simply unify contending elements of his life but transcends the situation so as to see himself and the world from a different, more encompassing perspective. Through his experi-ence he will never look at and feel situations quite the same way again. We can imagine him having very different attitudes and understandings regarding fear, duty, courage, and so forth. For instance, rather than see these as contending elements that have to be unified, he might come to see that they do not contend at all. We can imagine him seeing that his welfare cannot be served through his choosing actions through the screen of his desires, but rather through a com-munion with events such that, in a sense, he allows actions to choose him. I am not saying these results are inevitable, or that if Private Branham had been more "in tune" he would or should do more than fire his rifle from his foxhole. The issue is how his emotions, intellect, and spirit are working together to do more than accommodate one another but to be transformed and so open up possibilities for his being that were closed to him before.

Likely, the sort of attunement I've been describing cannot always be fully attained. It will always be a matter of more or less for us human beings. And being fully attuned does not guarantee satisfaction. However, attunement is an essential element of experience and well-being that, at the very least, expands our view of how a good life can be lived beyond what alternative views offer. In particular, we are led to the possibility that attunement enables an optimal state for persons to see well, which is more than having an error-free understanding of values and desires. To see well is the essence of doing well.[7]

However, this claim about "seeing" needs more explanation and justification. In particular, why we should think someone attuned to the world will observe and understand it correctly?

## SEEING AND KNOWING

Dewey provides a first step for exploring the knowledge yielded by experience, returning us to the notion of "being":

> [B]eing and having things in ways other than knowing them, in ways never identical with knowing them, exist, and are preconditions of reflection and knowledge. Being angry, stupid, wise, inquiring; having sugar, the light of day, money, houses and lands, friends, laws, masters, subjects, pain and joy, occur in dimensions incommensurable to knowing these things which we are and have and use, and which have and use us . . . [T]hey can only be and be had, and then pointed to in reflection.[8]

Later I will dispute Dewey's distinction between "being and having" and "knowing," but here he does point to the important phenomena of being, having, and being "used" in ways that are not identical with the processes and outcomes of reflection. To be frightened, cowardly, or brave, to have a buddy's life in one's hands, a wound, or a bullet fly past one's head are not decisions to be made but experiences to be undergone. Private Branham could be "had" by courage or fear in ways that elude his attempts to "know" them.

Continuing with Dewey's argument, he says that experiences of goods (or evils) are needed before one can conceive of goods: "A hungry man [for example] could not conceive food as a good unless he had actually experienced, with the support of environing conditions, food as good. The objective satisfaction comes first."[9] Although Dewey's claim that experience precedes conceptualization is another one I take exception to, the basic idea seems correct. To face death and persevere, for example, can be fulfilling, regardless whether the experience ultimately is judged good or bad; the objective satisfaction comes first. Before such things are "conceptualized" — I think "specified" is a better word, which I will get into later — as good or bad, good or bad for oneself, they just are what they are.[10]

Dewey does not provide a full response to Griffin; however, he does provide an initial step for understanding how we might experience prudential value. If we are "had" by experiences in the way Dewey suggests, why not think that experience of prudential value can be part of the event? To be angry or stupid or to have friends or joy is not prudentially neutral.

Let us entertain a few examples that lend some plausibility to this idea. Consider the hungry person again. There is no mystery in a hungry person experiencing food as not just "good" but "good for me." Rather than think of the process as understanding something as good then figuring out whether or how it is good for me, it makes more sense to see the reverse movement: "I experience this as good for me. I wonder what makes it good?" This is an example of what I would call specifying a good rather than conceptualizing it. The task is less to conceptualize a good — one knows it is a good — than to specify its goodness. The distinction is important for my claims about attunement. The world offers us goods that we can experience as goods: food when we're hungry, companionship when we're lonely; there's nothing there that needs to be conceptualized. Yet if our understanding is to become more refined and intelligent, there is a point to analyzing and specifying the good or goods involved. For example, I experience companionship as good for me, satisfying for me. But does the satisfaction come from feeling safe, or from having someone to cuddle, or from being able to exert power over another person, or something else? In terms of satisfaction or enjoyment, the point is not that enjoyment is part of understanding some good; Griffin grants that. The point is that *in* the enjoyment prudential value is experienced and not just an understanding of the thing enjoyed distinct from its prudential value, even if the prudential value merits greater specification.

Obviously, not all food and companionship are particularly healthy, and people can control their food intake and relationships at least to some extent. Desires might have a role in explaining why people have the particular diets and companions they do. But those are special cases. Perhaps those cases need to be explained by desire, but not the prudential benefits that "have" hungry and lonely persons when they enjoy food and other people.

Maybe other examples are more difficult, though. Consider accomplishment again. A history teacher assigns her students an independent project. One student produces an elaborate DVD that required a lot of time and effort. When the teacher sees it she exclaims, "What an accomplishment!" However, to the teacher's surprise, the student replies, "Yeah, it's OK." Assuming the student is not just being modest or coy or ornery, it seems that the student does not see the project as an accomplishment. Maybe the student sees the project as a task completed adequately or even well, but that is not the same as seeing it as an accomplishment. It is significant whether a student sees a completed task as just a completed task or as an accomplishment.

As Griffin pictures it, for accomplishment to be prudentially valuable one sees what accomplishment is and then forms a desire for it. My claim is that to see accomplishment for what it is is to see its value for one's well-being. Similarly, if one does not see the prudential value of accomplishment, does not feel its satisfaction, one is not seeing accomplishment but something else.[11] Paralleling Nussbaum's point, accomplishment is something for which we experience joy at the thought of. There is nothing mysterious about the prudential value of accomplishment such that we need the added layer of desire to explain its contribution to an individual's well-being. In this student's case we need not think she fails to recognize the prudential value of accomplishment, but rather that she does not see how this particular activity is an instance of accomplishment. And if we doubt that typically people see the connection between accomplishment and their own well-being we need not conclude that the connection must be established but rather that people need to understand accomplishment better or have more opportunity to do things they can count as accomplishments.

Perhaps for some values, such as accomplishment, it is clearer that something is "in it" for persons. At least when I have accomplished something it is something *I* have done. But how about something like beauty, which might seem to be less clearly a candidate for prudential value? Imagine someone watching a beautiful sunset exclaims, "What pretty colors! Let's go get a taco." We might be tempted to think this person does not get it when it comes to the beauty of sunsets.[12] Where is the awe people feel in the presence of beauty? Awe is something that is fulfilling and that "has us" outside of our control over it. As Nussbaum proposes, perhaps awe and wonder are more distantly associated with our particular schemes of prudential values than things like grief or love. However, in some ways that makes the former phenomena particularly important. They can add to our lives just because they bring objects within our horizon of prudential concern that before might not have been present fully or clearly.

Of course, some people might not make sunset-watching a major part of their lives; one might be more interested in eating tacos or avoiding mosquitoes than watching sunsets. Again, desires might have a place in explaining such choices. Plus, there are people not turned on by beauty in the first place.

Here too, though, this need not be explained by saying such people understand beauty but have no desire for it; rather, they do not (fully) understand or receive beauty; the meaning beauty has for them is only partial or distorted. For some people anyway, when they are awed they tend not to feel hunger pangs or hear mosquitoes buzzing around their ears, despite what their desires might be.

The issue is the richness of the meaning beauty (and other values) has for people. I am not saying beauty is merely a "social construction," as if human beings could make beauty mean whatever they want. However, surely there is an educational aspect here. People need to learn what it means to experience beauty.

What does all this suggest about Private Branham's D-Day experience? Was it good for him? In the passages quoted earlier, Dewey suggests two senses of that question. In one sense, we do need to step back and reflect after having been "had." How does the D-Day experience fit into the whole course of Private Branham's life? What does it imply for how he understands and lives his entire life? Griffin's emphasis is on this sense of the question. However, in the other sense of the question we do not need to await that sort of reflection. Private Branham had experiences. Likely he experienced satisfaction, disgust, grief, horror, and exhilaration. People undergo fulfilling and unfulfilling experiences; they need not bridge to them. He might not have specified for himself the prudential value of his experiences, but the prudential value still could be experienced. And insofar as he did understand the meaning of what he did — understood his survival as an accomplishment, say — we need not appeal to some sort of desire to explain the prudential value he would have gotten from that.

As I mentioned earlier, one implication and purpose for the view I am expounding is to conceive human beings in a particular relationship with their world and their selves. Griffin sees this relationship as a sort of balance, an equitable contribution from person (desire) and world (value). My proposal shifts the center of gravity if you will, suggesting even less human control or initiative regarding well-being than Griffin's balance implies. As I have granted, this might strike modern ears as odd. If the world is disenchanted and value-neutral we would look for the center of valuing in human beings — say, in terms of motivation. If the world is value-neutral and exerts no "pull" on us, there must be something that "pushes" us to identify and pursue valuable things. After all, as we have noted several times, people are not always motivated to do good things. So, beyond my preliminary claims in the previous section, what does it really mean to say that the world "motivates" us to "have" the prudential goods it offers us, and can my claims really be sustained?

Griffin does not emphasize desire as motivation, but one purported advantage of some desire theories is that they account for motivation. White declares:

> It is hard indeed to see how anything could motivate a person to action unless it were at some point dependent on what he or she desired. In this, Hume's dictum that "reason is and ought to be the slave of the passions" appears to be on the right lines.[13]

Returning to Private Branham, it does seem natural to ask what possibly could have motivated him to risk his life. On White's analysis, he would only go through such horrendous episodes if he had some internal motivator — a desire — to push him. Contrary to White's claim, I will continue to argue that desire is not required to account for people's movement toward values; at least, the role of desire is more complicated than White suggests.

## MOTIVATION, REASONS, AND THE PRUDENTIAL POINT OF VIEW

One reason to question the need for desire as a motivator is that, for some objects and actions, there is no need to appeal to motives to explain why people enjoy or pursue them. Dewey contends:

> In every fundamental sense it is false that a man requires a motive to make him do something . . . It is absurd to ask what induces a man to activity generally speaking. He is an active being and that is all there is to be said on that score.[14]

What needs to be explained, then, is not what induces people to act but what prevents or discourages them from acting. This shifts the locus of interest from something internal to people to the environing conditions. Dewey does say that talk of motives has a place when we are concerned to influence action. For example, if a student does something harmful to herself or others we might ask what motivated her, hoping to understand what prompted her so that we can redirect her conduct. But White goes beyond that; he appears to believe that desires are needed to explain why anything can induce a person to activity.

Maybe we need to restrict the field, though. One might grant that motives are not needed to move someone to act "generally speaking," but reply that most prudential values present more difficult cases. But Dewey offers reasons to question that idea, too. Regarding hunger, for instance:

> If we like the form of words we may say a man eats only because he is "moved" by hunger. The statement is nevertheless mere tautology. For what does hunger mean

except that one of the things which man does naturally, instinctively, is to search for food — that his activity turns that way? Hunger primarily names an act or active process not a motive to act.[15]

Again, though, hunger might be a special case. Maybe hunger and other appetites represent natural processes, but valuing is different; it is not "natural." For example, how can we explain the prudential benefit gotten when a soldier charges a machine gun or a student chooses to devote her time to computer programming or a teacher undergoes angry arguments with a parent? At least on the surface, it is hard to see these as "natural" processes. It is no surprise people are drawn to food, but other examples of valuing might seem to require appeal to motives in order to explain them.

However, the real question here is not what people have a motive to do, but what they have reason to do. Even someone like White does not claim that anything one has a motive to do something necessarily constitutes a good reason to do it. I might have a motive to kick my friend in the shin — he made fun of me for buying an ABBA CD — but that is not a good reason for me to kick him. If educators are concerned with helping students toward a sound understanding of their well-being, we need to consider what form that help should take. If we are unable to provide reasons for what we do and recommend we must resort to some non-rational alternatives, say the brute exercise of power, through threats, bribes, or a teacher's overpowering personal charisma. Before concluding those are the only means we have, we should consider the possibility of more rational processes such as argument and persuasion. So, the issue is the nature of reasons, particularly the motivation reasons can or should provide.

The motivation issue can be located within what has been called the externalist and internalist debate on the nature of reasons. The externalist argues that one has reason to act simply because of the nature of objects and events. Thus, from that point of view, Private Branham would have reason to do brave acts simply because they are brave acts. The internalist, however, argues that there must be something internal to the person that "pushes" him toward such acts; the nature of the act alone does not provide reason to act.

To illustrate what is at stake, imagine a student who appears unable to see the value of some school activity. And let us suppose that the activity really does have value; again, the subject-relativity of well-being does not imply that the value of things is dependent solely on people's attitudes. Furthermore, let us suppose that the teacher gives a sympathetic, thorough, and sound argument for the activity's value. Nonetheless, the student remains skeptical. On an externalist view, we would be justified in saying that the student isn't listening to reason.

We need not blame him for his failure of reason, but it still is a failure.

On an internalist view, we have a different account of the situation. To provide reasons for the student to act, the teacher's argument needs to make contact with something internal to the student. The charge that the student was not listening to reason would be unwarranted if the teacher has not provided reasons that can be recognized by the student. Suppose a math teacher tells students they should study math because it is needed for a career in engineering. It might be true that math is needed for an engineering career, but that need not constitute a reason for studying math for students who have no interest in engineering.

Clearly, my proposal regarding attunement with the world has an externalist character. White, in contrast, places himself firmly on the internalist side, going so far as to say, "no convincing argument has been put forward, to my knowledge, to support the possibility of external reasons."[16]

Externalism in a "pure" form is indeed implausible; at least, I do not advocate a pure form. That does not show, though, there is no externalist aspect of reasons; it shows that reasons are not purely external. But, by the same token, neither are they purely internal. Audi shows the variety of forms internalist and externalist views can take.[17] Because of the complexity in the internal and external character of reasons, Audi argues that if there is a helpful distinction to be made it probably is between instrumentalism and objectivism, which are extreme varieties of internalism and externalism, respectively, and not between internalism and externalism. White can be described as an instrumentalist who reduces the rationality of values to their service as means to other things, in White's case, desires.

White seems to think we have only two alternatives, a purely cognitive relation to values (a form of what Audi calls objectivism) or a purely desire-dependent (instrumentalist) relation: "[I]f we are acquainted with values in a purely cognitive way, then it is hard to see how they can affect our lives; but if the perception of them does affect us, this must be because of some desire we already have."[18]

White does have a legitimate concern about values that are purely cognitive. Values should have working contact with life; they should affect life and not just be intellectual. In Dewey's words, we want people to develop "moral ideas" and not merely "ideas about morality."[19] However, an externalist view need not claim that our acquaintance with values is purely intellectual. As I will propose momentarily, such a view can give desires or other affective states a role. But White does not claim that desires are a part of the explanation for how values move people; he claims they are the sole explanation, that desire is the only plausible explanation for how values can move us.

One very basic problem White faces is that people do not just follow their desires; they question their desires. In general at least, they seek what is really good for themselves and not merely what satisfies a desire. If instrumentalism were true, a person would have no reason to be moral unless that person had certain desires. At the very least, that clashes with common beliefs about moral reasons; they have a claim on us regardless of what we happen to desire.

White believes he has answers to that problem, appealing to two ideas we already have encountered — higher-order desires and informed desires — that rely solely on desires. Again, the idea of higher-order desires is that we have desires about our desires. What is important for my well-being is not satisfying just any old desire — like kicking my friend in the shin — but the desires that are most important to me — not being the sort of person who loses self-control and kicks people. The other part of White's answer is that the relevant desires have to be informed. So, if I go ahead and kick my friend, even though I might think that that satisfies a higher-order desire, it might not, if my desire was not informed. If I had thought about it, I wouldn't have desired to kick my friend.

However, this approach has difficulties if, as White seems to think, reason is the slave to passions. For that implies higher-order desires are simply what one is most passionate about. If my strongest passion is to kick my friend, it isn't clear why I shouldn't. I might find my intellectualized higher-order desire to be thoroughly unmotivating.

Appeal to informed desires is problematic, too. For example, on White's view it would appear that the only information one would listen to or accept would be information one desires to hear. Yet people take in all sorts of unwanted information all the time. At least, if a person aims for the sort of experience Gadamer articulates (and that I explore extensively in Chapter 4), where he aims to "belong" to what he encounters, he "must hear whether he wants to or not."[20] This is another place where one could insist that a desire just has to be there; we just are not acknowledging it. As suggested before, though, this explains nothing. We might as well insist that there has to be a little gnome in our heads pulling levers, pushing buttons, and making us do things.

White believes he has a follow-up answer, though. He appeals to "certain innate desires" that human beings have and from which all other desires can be built up.[21] So, maybe there are desires deep within us that keep us in line without our being aware of them. Here, too, we see some surface similarity with Dewey. Dewey claims, "[A]ll conduct springs ultimately and radically out of native instincts and impulses."[22] So, if Dewey is correct, White may be on to something when he appeals to something innate in human beings. However, there are problems with basing morality on instincts. Conduct might "spring" from native instincts and impulses, but it does not follow that good conduct can be reduced to instincts. At the very least, to trace all reasons for conduct back to antecedent desires would be convoluted. Human beings have all sorts of "innate desires," for love and for destruction, for compassion and for hatred, for greed and for generosity. It is difficult to see how what we commonly believe morality to be can be built exclusively from interaction of these often conflicting desires. Plus, as Dewey remarks, a number of people's activities do not require "motivation" to explain them. And among "native instincts and impulses" Dewey includes much more than desires. For example, as suggested before, a propensity to distrust desires would seem to be a native impulse.

At least some decisions about value cannot easily be justified only in terms of desires. Imagine I have a terminally ill friend who does not know she is terminally ill. She has no other friends or family, so it is up to me to decide how and whether she should be told about her condition. Do I tell her the truth that she is dying? Do *I* tell her or do I leave that to the hospital staff? On White's view, I must consult my desires and decide which of my informed desires are "highest." So, I think hard and honestly about it and decide that I would be terribly uncomfortable talking with my friend about her impending death. I find my comfort is much more motivating than any desire I have to deal with my friend. So, I decide to let the hospital personnel handle it. Or, maybe I decide my desire to talk with her is stronger than my desire for my personal comfort. I then find that my desire to tell her the truth is stronger than my desire to avoid the pain the truth might cause her. So, I tell her.

Perhaps all these courses of action could be acceptable. The problem is not with the decisions but how they are reached. My desire for comfort, for instance, is a singularly poor reason for leaving the matter to the hospital, regardless of how strong my desire is. Rather than ask myself, "What do I most desire?" a better question would be, "What is best for my friend?" I should ask the latter question regardless of what other questions I would prefer to ask, and act upon the answer to the question whether or not the answer is one I desire to accept and act upon.

In response to my scenario, one might say my decision to duck out on my friend only shows I was not informed about my desires or was not getting at my real desires. That could be the case, but the objection still is too facile. Being genuinely wellinformed does not guarantee one will arrive at the right decision. Desire theorists such as White have to accept the possibility that, if they base ethical judgment solely on desires, that judgment might yield conclusions that are suspect ethically.

However, another response could be that it is all well and good to say what people should do, such as listen to reason, but we have to consider what people are able to do. So, maybe I should have hidden the truth from my friend, but I couldn't; I could only act on my desire. But as suggested before, that does not seem right. It might be difficult, but surely it is possible to resist one's desires.

However, let's say I seriously try to inform my desires with the thought of doing what is best for my friend. That too is difficult to explain only in terms of desires. At least part of knowing what is best for my friend would require I listen to her own wishes. But then my friend's sense of her well-being could be entirely incomprehensible to me. According to White, my sense of prudential value ultimately can only derive from my own desires. If my friend's desires are radically different from mine, she might appear crazy to me. I could desire simply to act according to whatever it is my friend desires or would desire, regardless how crazy it seems to me, but that too is a poor basis for action. People should try to do what is best for their friends and not simply do what the friends say they desire.

Now, if reasons have an external element that doesn't preclude the possibility that people won't understand the reasons other people act upon, but at least the prospects for reasonable argument and discussion are better if we suppose that the persuasive power of reasons does not rest solely on the lucky happenstance of people's desires coinciding.

The bottom line is that desires alone cannot explain the draw of value. Sher criticizes the sort of subjectivism White espouses, the position "that desires *confer* value on their objects, that things *acquire or inherit* value by being chosen, that value flows from desires or choices *to* their objects, and so on."[23]

However, maybe these criticisms are off target. It is unsurprising that some values might not satisfy a particular individual's desires, but we are interested in prudential value, and perhaps for something to have prudential value it does or would satisfy a person's desires.

However, as I began to show before, it is unclear that prudential value requires that sort of link between values and persons. Returning to the notion of meaning, values such as accomplishment, beauty, and friendship have a prudential meaning, or prudential benefits as part of their meaning. That does not imply that persons who accomplish things or witness beauty or have friends actually will benefit. If people are to benefit we might need to work on their understanding of accomplishment, beauty, and friendship and what objects and actions manifest them. White doubts that such understanding alone can move people. As noted before, though, reasons themselves can have prudential value; "[H]ell is the impossibility of reason." People seek and benefit from meaning in their lives; acting on reasons is a way of acting meaningfully. To act on reasons, even when they clash with one's desires, can have prudential value in itself.

The sort of desire theory White offers has severe problems. But his other line of argument is a call for an externalist view to do better. He challenges:

> In so far as one does hold that values are independent of desires, one has to show not only what their metaphysical status is, i.e. what kind of existence they can be credited with, but also how they can have any bearing on our lives.[24]

White doubts that these things can be shown.

I'll respond to the "bearing on our lives" challenge first, and to do that we need to develop our conception of reasons more fully. Audi offers what he deems the most plausible "reasons" internalism, calling it an epistemic form of "accessibility reasons internalism." This view holds that "a reason for action, normative or motivational, must be such that the agent can, in a suitable psychological sense, *have* it, for instance be appropriately aware of it."[25] Here I cannot do full justice to Audi's complex and subtle argument, but the main points can be identified. First, the significance of "reasons" internalism is that the position holds that reasons can be normative. That is, people are moved by reasons; they act according to norms of what is right, good, beneficial, and so on and not just on their desires. That is the epistemic aspect of Audi's favored position; the reasons "internal" to people are not only based on desires but also on knowledge and understanding.

This contrasts with "motivational" internalism, which holds that making a positive judgment about something implies having a motive to do the thing (even if one does not follow through on it for some reason); something cannot count as a reason for action unless it actually provides a motive to act on it. White adopts something akin to this latter view. If I identify something as an accomplishment, for instance, I have reason to pursue the thing only if I am motivated — have desire — to pursue it. So, "That is an accomplishment" cannot be a reason for action for a person who does not desire accomplishment.

In contrast, reasons internalism suggests being told "That is an accomplishment" can be a reason for a person to seek it independent of the person's desires. Yet there is an "accessibility" factor. For our skeptical student, the difficulty is not that "That is an accomplishment" provides her no reason to do or value her project; she could understand very well that accomplishment is a good thing, a beneficial thing. If she deemed something an accomplishment she would be moved toward doing it. However, in her situation, "That is an accomplishment" is inaccessible to her as a reason to do the project or take satisfaction in it; she doesn't count her work as an accomplishment. For example, imagine the student produced her DVD using some software program but without the technical knowledge of how the software works, and because of that she discredits what she did. Despite the teacher's attempt to convince her otherwise, for the student, "That is an accomplishment" is no reason to feel pride or satisfaction, because she does not see her work as an accomplishment.

Or taking a different scenario, imagine that the student has somehow gotten the attitude that school success means playing safe, not doing things that might go beyond the guidelines teachers set. In other words, she believes she is in an environment where accomplishment does not count much as a reason for action. The student understands "That is an accomplishment" can be a reason to do the thing, but what she can't access is the idea that accomplishment counts as a reason in *this* environment.

When it comes to my dying friend, I might have a normative reason to tell her the truth (or not) — say, based on my knowledge of her wishes. I have to battle my desires; I really dread telling her the truth. "She'd want to hear the truth" would be a reason to tell her the truth despite my desires, but I have difficulty accessing the reason. I might never desire to tell her the truth, but I still could work on my experience so that I can see reasons where I had not before. Maybe I would need to think very hard about who she is and what our relationship requires: Have I done enough to feel her pain? What does real friendship require of me?

Or for Private Branham, if he did benefit from his D-Day experience we need not suppose that at some level of analysis his actions must have stemmed from some desire or motive he had. "That is a courageous act" provides him a reason to do the act (which does not mean he should do it), and reason to get satisfaction if he did act, without appeal to a desire he must have had. True, the reasons would not be "moving" reasons for him unless he had certain sensibilities, attitudes, and understandings. But these would constitute receptiveness to reasons, even contrary to his desires to avoid danger.

This "accessibility reasons internalism" does not make reasons and value completely independent of people's internal states, which would be an objectivist view, in Audi's terms. One can have a normative reason to act, but having that reason does not imply having a motive to act on it. Hence, there is an external aspect to reasons. However, reasons must be accessible to people if the reasons are to be completed, if you will. There must be an appropriate internal state that might include desires, but could include awareness, understanding, emotions, and other aspects as well. These sorts of things would empower people to be receptive to reasons.

So, what is at stake for education in all of this? Audi concludes:

[I]f we expect people to be moral, we must educate their desires, emotions, and sensibilities, not just their intellects . . . [B]ut then desires, emotions, and experiences, like judgments, can provide normative reasons for action as well as motivation to perform them.[26]

Here Audi's particular concern is moral action, but his points pertain to reasons relevant to well-being as well. The first point is that, similar to how one must adopt the moral point of view in order to fully understand and feel the force of moral reasons, people need to adopt "the prudential point of view" in order to understand and feel the prudential value of objects and acts. We cannot expect that to just happen or come naturally; people's attunement or receptivity must be educated, and education includes more than intellect.

Advocating that people adopt the prudential point of view does not imply ethical or prudential egoism, that the ultimate reason for action must be one's own benefit. I watch a beautiful sunset because it is beautiful. I help a friend because it is my friend. However, just because I appreciate beauty or friendship, that does not imply I will experience the awe that can fill one's soul when witnessing beauty or experience the fulfillment that comes from true friendship. People need to be taught that it is acceptable to adopt the prudential point of view and how prudential benefits can be embodied in the world.

The second education-related point in Audi's passage is that, when educated, desires, emotions, experiences, and so on can themselves be reasons for action. That is a controversial claim we will continue to explore. However, Audi sets the stage for the idea that for experienced persons their emotions, for instance, can provide reasons for action and belief. Recalling the example of the teacher who angrily lashed out at a student, I proposed (Chapter 1, note 67) that our judgment about the wisdom of such a display might depend on who the teacher is (as well as other factors). It could be that an experienced teacher's anger is a reliable guide for her actions.

Our issue has been how values can have working contact with human lives. I've begun to present a conception of values and reasons that involves attunement with the world, where one is receptive to what the world offers. When it comes to White, he might be read as having a similar concern for attunement. His emphasis on desires, especially innate desires, could be read as an attempt to naturalize value and so make values appear less alien to the human condition. However, in actuality I believe White provides an example of the instrumentalism that is destructive of attunement because it results in alienation from the world. White emphasizes how human beings are shapers of value; our desires confer value on things. Human beings are not just shapers of value, though; we are shaped. That is the upshot of Audi's argument regarding normative reasons; we are moved and shaped despite what our preferences might be. People might choose some prudential values — say, to indulge in fine cigars — but values can "choose" people too, as I began to argue regarding Private Branham and other examples. If there is creative and productive power in human nature, there is sensitivity, receptivity, and reverence, also. We can access these abilities if we relinquish the urge for control and educate our being, with due regard for emotion, experience, and other elements of our being, as well as intellect.

Before I leave White I should respond to his other challenge. Recall that he said an externalist view of reasons had to address the contact-with-life problem and also the issue of the metaphysical status of external reasons. So, what is the metaphysical status of reasons that have the external quality Audi proposes? I have to admit that my first response is, "Who cares?" As Dewey argues, "moral principles are real in the same sense in which other forces are real . . . they are inherent in community life, and in the working structure of the individual."[27] Values, wherever they come from, are a part of human life. If I skid on an icy road and crash my car into a tree, it is largely beside the point whether I consider the tree as a living thing with a soul of its own or as a mere collection of molecules. The tree is going to have an impact on my life whatever the tree's metaphysical status.

That response is too glib, though. Surely there is a point to pondering the status of values. I have been offering my own metaethical notions about the nature of values. So, I do not deny the status or source of values can be a good question to consider. Nonetheless, we do not have to get that all sorted out in order to help people live fulfilling lives. What we can do is learn to live with complexity, plurality, and uncertainty, and use various views to explore, understand, and critique people's ideas about their well-being and the conditions and actions that conduce to it.

## CONCLUSION

We have been interested in how "being" is the basis for truth and knowledge. Not just any sort of being and experience will do. In this chapter I have proposed attunement as a fundamental way of being in the world. An implication of attunement is that things can be prudential values and reasons without being desired.

Even so, what provides reasons to some people might not to other people;

their sensibilities and dispositions could be such that reasons will not exert the same power for everyone. I've claimed that people's internal states can be critiqued and educated. But that's a tall order. How might it be accomplished? The central issue is how people experience their world. For some people, experience seems to do little to affect their being. When it comes to receptivity, perhaps experience even hardens their attitudes. (There's the possibility that "familiarity breeds contempt.") We need to take a closer look at the nature of experience, and we will do that in the next chapter.

*Chapter 4*

# Perceiving and Valuing in Hermeneutic Experience

The aim in this chapter is to continue to explore the nature of experience and, particularly, the question of how it yields knowledge of value. Again, Dewey provides some initial steps. Recall his point about "being and having" certain things. He also argues:

> Empirically, the existence of objects of direct grasp, possession, use and enjoyment cannot be denied. Empirically, things are poignant, tragic, beautiful, humorous, settled, disturbed, comfortable, annoying, barren, harsh, consoling, splendid, fearful; are such immediately and in their own right and behalf.[1]

These claims of Dewey's point us toward the sort of experience of prudential value I have expounded. I have claimed that in experiencing the good of food, for example, part of the good that is grasped is "good for me." I might then wonder why the food is good for me — say, in terms of its nutritional value, its effect on taste buds, and so forth. But such analysis might show that the food actually is not good for me. So, how can we say that in perception true value judgments or evaluations are achieved?

## THE PHENOMENON AND KNOWLEDGE OF PERCEPTION

If Dewey's notion of "direct grasp" takes us a step in the right direction, it is a small step. Griffin and Dewey have an essential orientation in common; both would dispute my claim that judgments of prudential value are made in the "direct grasp" of experience and perception. As we have seen, Griffin does not deny enjoyments a role in understanding. So, experiencing some thing as poignant, tragic, and so on could be an essential part of coming to understand the thing. And he likely would agree that such things have some inherent attractive or aversive qualities. Nonetheless, a further step is required if a person is to know if the things contribute to her well-being. The need for a further step is the significant point Dewey shares with Griffin. For Dewey, enjoyment, satisfaction, and so on are what judgment is *about*.[2] Objects of direct grasp are then "pointed to in reflection." "Enjoyeds do not provide evidence of value in their bare occurrence."[3] In Dewey's view, we might take in beauty, accomplishment, bravery, or annoyance and report the fact of that perception and the enjoyment or pain we experience, yet we do not take in or report the value of that experience.

Concern for the accuracy of perception is one reason we might doubt that value is grasped in perception. Griffin argues, "My truly having close and authentic personal relations [for example] is not the kind of thing that can enter my experience; all that can enter is what is common to both my truly having such relations and my merely believing that I do."[4] Griffin's claim is that experience cannot be relied upon because it cannot distinguish between correct perception and mere belief, between truth and appearance.

In contrast, John McDowell argues:

Traditional epistemology accords a deep significance to the fact that perception is fallible. It is supposed to show something like this: however favourable a perceiver's cognitive stance may be, we cannot make sense of subjective states of affairs constituted by a subject's letting the layout of the objective world reveal itself to her. As the objector insists, something that is not a glimpse of reality, since the subject would be misled if she took it at face value, can be subjectively indistinguishable (at least at the time) from experiences that are veridical. That is supposed to show that the genuinely subjective states of affairs involved in perception can never be more than what a perceiver has in a misleading case.[5]

Griffin and Dewey appear to adopt this "traditional" view about the fallibility of perception. McDowell's criticism is that the fallibility of perception does not imply that "the very idea of openness to facts is unintelligible."[6] Experience can be misleading, but that does not

deprive ourselves of 'taking in how things are' as a description of what happens when one is not misled . . . *That things are thus and so* is the content of the experience, and it can also be the content of the judgment: it becomes the content of the judgment if the subject decides to take the experience at face value.[7]

So, how might a person "take in" an authentic friendship, say? What would it mean for a person, call him Dense Dennis, to believe he has a true friend when in fact he does not? Assuming Dennis is merely dense and not delusional, his problem is not that he depends too much on experience but, rather, too little.

How would the false friend, Fred, create the deception? Likely, he would do things with and for Dennis — going out for an occasional beer, sending birthday cards, offering succor when Dennis was feeling blue. But did these things happen only when it was convenient for Fred? How much did he sacrifice himself? Are Fred's actions thought out and personalized or just superficial and generic? Sure, it can be difficult, but people are able to distinguish between true and false friends and between closer and more distant friends and acquaintances. Good advice to Dennis would be to take a closer look at his experiences with Fred and other friends to get a better sense of their relationship.

I am not suggesting that friendship is reducible to overt acts. Intent matters. Fred might show all the outer trappings of real friendship but only for the sake of getting something from Dennis in return. Still, that does not show experience is impotent. It is possible to develop an accurate sense of persons' intent from the history of their actions.

Let us consider a different example of an apparent clash between appearance and reality. There is a person who has genuine concern and affection for Dennis. However, the person, Reticent Rita, is shy and socially inept and so is unable to show her concern adequately enough for Dennis to perceive it, and so Dennis does not believe Rita is a genuine friend. Rita has the right intent, but her intent does not enter into Dennis's experience.

One might advise Dennis to look past what Rita does not do and focus on her attitude. Dennis might prefer a person who really wishes him well to a person who does not yet does all the "right" things. Nonetheless, merely wishing people well is not friendship in a full sense. If Dennis is magnanimous and discerning he might realize Rita wishes him well yet reasonably conclude Rita is not a real friend. Rita might be "real" in the sense of being authentic in her feelings, but she is not real in the sense of doing what friends do for each other. Like the false friend, Rita may be unable or unwilling to sacrifice herself for Dennis, to do things that are difficult or uncomfortable for her. Suppose Dennis had a tragedy — a loved one died — and looked to his friends for solace and support, but Rita did nothing overt. Maybe Rita grieved privately for Dennis, but, being socially inept, she was unsure about what to do for him. We need not blame her for that; many of us feel at a loss in such a situation. Even so, true friends stretch themselves for the sake of each other. Maybe Rita is a friend of some sort, but "being" a friend is not the same as doing what good friends do.

These examples suggest that it is possible for a person to "take in how things are" respecting friendship and other states of affairs. People will be better able to take in how things are and not be misled if they have had experience with friendship and other personal relationships and so are able to compare and contrast a variety of relationships they have had.

However, here we are moving from a broad sense of experience as awareness to a particular discerning sort of experience. While I argue that well-being must be experienced, it does not follow that all sorts of experience must contribute to well-being. I am not primarily referring to "bad" experiences. For example, while friendship must be experienced to be beneficial, some people might do well without their experience of friendship being particularly deep. It is possible for people to benefit from casual friendships or quasi-friendships without being especially discerning regarding those experiences.

However, if we are to carefully consider the role of experience in human well-being, and its epistemic role particularly, we need to explore beyond the vague sense of experience I have been exploiting to a more sophisticated account. I have claimed that people can perceive the world accurately in and through experience. What sort of experience is this?

## HERMENEUTIC EXPERIENCE

Following Gadamer, I will call the sort of experience we are interested in "hermeneutic" experience. Historically, hermeneutics was concerned with interpretation of ancient texts, the problem being how to understand a text distant in time and/or culture. However, Gadamer expands the relevance of hermeneutics to understand the whole "text" of personal and social life. Here we will consider a sort of hermeneutic experience that is particularly demanding and adventurous, a sort of experience that might not be central to some people's well-being and which can only be occasional in any case. However, Gadamer also sees hermeneutic experience as "the mode of the whole human experience of the world."[8]

As I noted, Gadamer's hermeneutics is the task or process of understanding, especially some text or person or event that is alien because of historical distance, cultural differences, or some other factor. We might think these "alien encounters" are occasional or rare, but Gadamer argues that they constitute our experience, at least insofar as we do experience our world and lives rather than drift through them blindly or semiconsciously: "There is always a world into which experience steps as something new, upsetting what has led our expectations and undergoing reorganization itself in the upheaval."[9] Our expectations might not be upset always, and Gadamer does not say they should be (although shortly we will consider how the potential is inherent in all our encounters with the world); however, while we can "live" our lives without upheaval, that is different from "experiencing" our lives.

But we need to do more to describe and understand this phenomenon of "hermeneutic experience." Extending upon Hegel, Gadamer argues,

> What Hegel . . . describes as experience is the experience that consciousness has of itself. "The principle of experience contains the infinitely important element that in order to accept a content as true, the man himself must be *present* or, more precisely, he must find such content in unity and combined with the *certainty of himself*," writes Hegel . . . The concept of experience means precisely this, that this kind of unity with oneself is first established. This is the reversal that consciousness undergoes when it recognizes itself in what is alien and different.[10]

My concern for attunement can be stated in terms Gadamer uses here. Can one be present or certain of oneself, if there is some inevitable, even if bridgeable, gap between the world and the person, desire and understanding, passion and reflection, emotion and intelligence, enjoying and valuing? Griffin and Dewey propose some sort of unity, some connections among elements, but theirs is not the sort of unity needed.

What does it mean to be present in the manner of being certain of oneself through "reversal of consciousness"? That sounds rather cryptic. And we can increase the mystery by bringing in Gadamer's claim that the requisite presence involves "self-forgetting,"[11] a "loss of self-possession."[12] On the face of it, it is difficult to see how forgetting oneself is consistent with certainty of oneself.

Gadamer uses the metaphor of play and games to illustrate the sort of experience he has in mind.[13] When one is "present" in a game, "the real experience of the game consists in the fact that something that obeys its own set of laws gains ascendancy in the game";[14] the play gains ascendancy over the consciousness of the player.[15] In that way, the person is not completely free to act as she wants. A softball player, for instance, has to take her cues for action from the flow of the game. Of course, a player will make her own unique contributions to the game, and a manager might use strategies so as to allow the player to best utilize her talents. Even so, the "subject matter" of the game is not simply adapted to the individual's particular interests or talents. A power hitter who swings for the fences when her team is behind by one run with bases loaded and two out in the final inning likely is thinking less about what the game requires of her and more about her own interest in being a star. She is not really present with the game. Hence the place for "self-forgetting," or "loss of self-possession." The point is not that a self is absent or unimportant but that reversal of consciousness occurs. The player's consciousness is focused on the game, not on herself.

Obviously, players' selves have to be present in some sense; there is no game without the players. Still, getting the players involved is not a matter of connecting them to some independent subject matter; the subject matter exists only as the players produce it. The player's actions are the individual's expressions, but what essentially is expressed is not a "true self" so much as the game through the medium of the individual. There is a self present *in* the situation, but even more, a self present *to* or *with* experience so that the person can undergo and extend the experience.

However, Gadamer argues that this loss of self-possession is not *experienced* as a loss of self-possession. Rather, he characterizes the experience as "the free buoyancy of an elevation of oneself."[16] This is the point made earlier when I described change in the self as a change in the level of the self, about Private Branham transcending himself and his situation. The softball player who is really into the game likely has a heightened sense of herself and her presence; she is sure she is there. Her eyes and ears are working intently; her muscles are tensed. She is observing and thinking; she is not merely being reactive in the sense of allowing events to knock her around. But neither is she in possession of herself — say, in having self-conscious control over her senses and muscles, or of the objects and events around her. More than her choosing what to attend to, the objects and events draw her attention to them. In these ways one is not in control of oneself; but in allowing oneself to be drawn into the movements of the game, one is drawn to a heightened sense of one's presence. One is certain of one's total presence rather than distracted by thoughts about whether one's uniform is dirty. This is certainty that "I'm all here."

This implies a particular conception of the "I" or self. For Gadamer, "[t]he self that we are does not possess itself; one could say that it 'happens.'"[17] Similarly, Merleau-Ponty proposes, "Vision is not a certain mode of thought or presence to self; it is the means given me for being absent from myself, for being present at the fission of Being from the inside — a fission at whose termination, and not before, I come back to myself."[18] So, we might say that the loss of self-possession, the vision that allows one to be absent from one's self, that one undergoes in experience is confirmation that one cannot possess one's self in the first place. Hence the problem if we think a "self" is the starting place for education and that then is connected to the subject matter, and vice versa. Self and subject matter happen and develop together.

In addition to certainty that "I'm all here" one needs to be certain that "I belong here." This is an implication of Gadamer's point about recognizing oneself in what is alien. Gadamer describes belonging as subject and object belonging together;[19] one is able to make one's own what the "text" says.[20] Belonging isn't always easy in the face of what is alien. One reaction is to feel like an outsider, distanced and at a loss about what to think, say, or do.

Consider our ball game example again. A rookie just brought up from the minor leagues, sent to bat in a clutch situation, might be uncertain of himself in the sense of feeling he doesn't belong; he's too nervous. He can't fully recognize himself in the alien game situation. He might have been in clutch situations before, but not in the big leagues. In contrast, veteran players often want to be in clutch situations. They can't be certain they'll get a hit, but they are certain they're ones to try. At least, the veteran player likely would be better able to be present to the situation than a rookie who is most aware of his sweaty palms.

How many students or teachers undergo what the rookie in our example does? We might go to great lengths to tell them they "belong" in the school regardless of sexuality, race, abilities and disabilities, and so forth, but do we provide environments in which they can belong in a more profound way?[21] I have to wonder.

So, what recognition of oneself is required in certainty of belonging to what is alien and different? Gadamer's notion of "fusion of horizons" is helpful here. To belong in a shared horizon is not to be part of the in-crowd whose membership requires like-mindedness, nor is it to consider oneself a native among people whose culture or perspective is fundamentally different from one's own. Rather, one finds a place with other people in a broader landscape of concerns and "first principles." Even a rookie belongs in the sense of recognizing the first principles of baseball. For example, she'll do what she can to help her team win rather than lose. At least she is able to see the point of what is going on around her. Sure, being unable to be "all there," her horizon will differ somewhat from her veteran teammates. But she still can belong; horizons can be fused.

Plato's *The Republic* provides an example more closely related to education. One of Socrates's achievements in the dialogue is to help his interlocutors belong to the discussion. This is not just a matter of making them feel comfortable; after all, Socrates potentially is an intimidating figure. He is unrelenting in dismantling speakers' views. It is easy to see how some people might feel "out of his/her league," that they do not belong in the discussion. However,

Socrates helps create a situation where people contribute, apparently willingly and sincerely, with a sense of belonging.

Socrates encourages this by having his partners initiate discussion. For example, early on in *The Republic* Socrates moves the conversation by encouraging Thrasymachus to look at his own words and their implications; Socrates says, perhaps rather disingenuously, he wants to understand what Thrasymachus is saying. So, there is belonging in the sense of some equality in who carries the discussion and who has worthwhile things to say. However, we might get the sense that Socrates is merely setting up the poor fellows (Adeimantus expresses that feeling). But Socrates's target is not the people but the content of their statements; hence, it is an example of working toward "unity of content." Admittance to the group isn't based on agreement on answers to the issues at stake but a common interest in exploring the issues. Socrates assumes his partners' ability to follow the logic of their subject matter. He proceeds to dismantle people's proposals, but, again, belonging is not a matter of associating with people whose opinions agree with yours. Belonging is consistent with the frustration, inadequacy, and anger people can feel.

A superficial reading might suggest, as I have heard people say, that Socrates is just "leading people around by the nose." However, when, at the start of Book VI, Glaucon asks what question they should pursue next, Socrates replies, "Surely . . . the one that follows next in order." Socrates is not in control of the game; he's the mouthpiece for what the game demands.[22] This supplies a way of understanding Socrates's several claims not to know. Obviously, Socrates knows a lot. Yet if he has particular insight into what questions follow next and how to explore the implications of various claims, his position is similar to his interlocutors' in that he does not have the final answers or a lesson plan to follow. The truth of the logic, or logos, of the subject matter can only emerge.

Of course, many of Adeimantus's and Glaucon's replies to Socrates are limited to things like, "Yes," "Clearly," and "Very true." That might seem to constitute minimal participation. However, Socrates gives his interlocutors the opportunity to confirm or disconfirm his statements, and Glaucon and Adeimantus are in a position to respond. They are present in a way they wouldn't be if they could only say (like poor Thrasymachus, perhaps), "Gee whiz, Socrates, I don't have the foggiest idea." They are able to state or affirm what the logos of the subject matter demands from point to point in the dialogue. And their engagement certainly goes beyond agreeing with Socrates. They challenge him with questions and counterexamples at several key points. They do not necessarily defend contrary views, but they recognize themselves in those alien views in the sense that they see the place for the challenges in the logos they are revealing; they see that the challenges deserve a careful response. And Socrates affirms those questions and counterexamples as important elements of the dialogue.

What about Thrasymachus, though? In Book VI Adeimantus speculates how people involved in the discussion would be so muddled by Socrates's wordplay that they would have nothing to say. That appears to be exactly what has happened to Thrasymachus. After his appearance in Book I we hear from him only one other time. Socrates has demolished Thrasymachus's claims; because of his silence we might wonder whether Thrasymachus has lost self-possession or rather has become terribly conscious that he doesn't have much to say. Likely, he still has "opinions," but perhaps he senses they do not transcend to the logos.

Even so, we get clues that Thrasymachus has been engaged even if he hasn't spoken. Early in Book V, he pipes up to agree with Glaucon and Adeimantus that they are going to keep Socrates until he gives a satisfactory account of the issues. Thrasymachus still belongs and is present to the extent that he is able to state a common first principle of the group's aim by joking with Socrates that they are not there to find gold but to hear discourse. The upshot is that presence might be a matter of form and degree; Adeimantus and Glaucon are more clearly in the game than Thrasymachus. Yet outward signs can be ambiguous. Even Thrasymachus shows he's attuned to the course and content of the dialogical experience, rather than stewing about how he can get back at Socrates. Students don't have to talk in order to be engaged and thinking.

However, while the preceding discussion does something to describe experience and presence, what initiated this discussion was the question of how experience can yield accurate perception and knowledge of prudential value. Following McDowell, I've argued that experience can yield those things, but let's return to the issue to explore it further.

## EXPERIENCING PRUDENTIAL VALUE

If a person's perceptions are to yield accurate insights into their selves and their situations, they must be receptive to what the world offers. One sort of receptivity might be a radical openness to the world such that the world somehow "hits us" without any sort of interference on our part. The putative epistemic problem is that the world as it really is must exert some sort of check on people's vision if we are to have a correct perception of the world. The image of the mind as a *tabula rasa* is an example of this. Supposedly, the mind is a blank slate that is written upon by the world without any intervening distortions. That view has been decisively criticized. Yet, the problem still occupies some people: How can human beings make undistorted contact with the world as it really is?

Similar to the tack we took before, McDowell's approach is not to solve the problem but, rather, deny that it is a problem. There is no problem because "the relevant conceptual capacities are drawn on *in* receptivity [and] not *on* an extra-conceptual deliverance of receptivity."[23] We need to give up looking for unmediated contact with the world, because that is impossible. Yet neither is it necessary.

To be present to experience of friendship or accomplishment, including its satisfactions and enjoyments, does not imply people somehow must be blank slates or neutral in their perceiving. Indeed, to attempt that would be self-defeating. Perception is in terms of meanings and not brute facts. Again, this does not mean reality merely is a "social construction." It does mean our grasp of reality will be partial and selective. So, much hinges on the conceptual capacities one brings with one's presence. People will perceive the things they do via meanings, such as accomplishment or drudgery.

It could seem that Dewey could agree with much of Gadamer's conception of presence. Earlier, Gadamer quotes Hegel as advocating presence "in order to accept a content as true."[24] If this means that presence is a precondition for knowledge then this would be consistent with Dewey's claim that "grasping" things is important to know *with*, but not the same thing as having knowledge. However, that is not what Gadamer is saying. Before going further with Gadamer, though, let's consider some of what is at stake in the dispute.

Dewey has several aims in making his claims. Reflection is important, but it should not dominate. Dewey resists a role for judgment that would encourage automatic skepticism about the epistemological, ethical, and psychological value of immediate experiences. One of Dewey's criticisms of modern science is that it treats objects' "secondary qualities" as "irrelevant and obstructive" in the search for the "reality" of objects.[25] Even if they are not value judgments, "enjoyeds" are vital components of life and valuing and serve perfectly well much of the time. "Enjoyeds are judged only when there is doubt about their value."[26]

Another aim is to defend the rationality of valuing. Some people might note the emotional aspects of valuing and conclude therefore that values are no more than "feelings." Dewey is right to challenge that view. The problem is how he challenges it. He replies by granting some part of the claim — enjoying is, indeed, "unregulated by intelligent operations" — but then proposes that's no problem for the rationality of valuation, because enjoying isn't valuing anyway. Enjoying only provides the starting place for valuing, the latter being the rational or intelligent process. Unfortunately, by taking that approach Dewey buys the rationality of values at the cost of separating intelligent valuing from experiences of direct grasp and enjoyment.

For Dewey, "intelligent operations," at least in their paradigmatic form, are self-conscious, systematic (though not "systematized") operations. In contrast, enjoyments are "unregulated by intelligent operations." According to Dewey, we must not make the mistake of taking "enjoyments which are casual because unregulated by intelligent operations to be values in and of themselves."[27]

However, I propose that rational, intelligent, correct evaluation does, or can, occur in perception; it does not require a step subsequent to perception. This is part of the picture of the human condition I am developing, an example of the sort of attunement to the realm of value I believe is possible and desirable.

## EXPERIENCE AND INTELLIGENT VALUING

Consider an alternative to Dewey's conception of judgment. Klein observes the thought processes of people such as firefighters, military commanders, and others immersed in real-life situations. He concludes, "the sources of power that are needed in natural settings are usually not analytical at all — the power of intuition, mental simulation, metaphor, and storytelling."[28] Surely, thought is involved in intuition, metaphor, and the other things, yet they are ways of knowing that do not require some additional reflection to complete them. This is knowledge reached within experience itself. In relevant cases people just know what to do; they do not "decide" what must be done. One firefighter commander went so far as to say, "I don't make decisions . . . I don't remember when I've ever made a decision."[29] Klein argues that generating a single course of action is a sign of expertise. It is not the novices who act on the first course that occurs to them; it is the novices who need to reflect and consider different options.[30] Experienced people are able to act well just because they have extensive experience to draw upon, and have vivid images or stories of those experiences to guide them.

Dewey grants that good people can trust their "direct responses of value," but this is only appropriate "in simpler situations, in those which are already upon the whole familiar."[31] In the case of emergency workers, for example, the salient aspects of situations might be similar enough that reflective thought is unnecessary and even dangerous because it is time-consuming. However, describing these situations as "simple" and these actions as "casual" would not do justice to the intelligence required. The way Klein portrays the thinking he studies, there is a lot of intellectual activity going on that is not just casual but is not reflection in the sense Dewey emphasizes, either.

We can expand the point to life in general. As Dewey shows in his attention to habit, Gadamer also has a keen sense of the limits of our ability to make things problematic for ourselves. For example, he argues that questions arise more than that we raise them. However, Gadamer argues:

> It is clear that the structure of the question is implicit in all experience. We cannot have experiences without asking questions. Recognizing that an object is different, and not as we first thought, obviously presupposes the question whether it was this or that. From a logical point of view, the openness essential to experience is precisely the openness of being either this or that. It has the structure of a question.[32]

If there is a question of "this or that" implicit in all experience, intelligence can be at work more pervasively than Dewey grants, if active intelligence, in contrast to habit, implies sensitivity to the thwarting of our expectations, to seeing things as different. Dewey suggests we do not confront questions until they confront us; Gadamer agrees, but also proposes that experiencing always presents questions. We might express the difference in terms of the default position one takes. One might treat experiences the same until shown they are not. Or, one might treat experiences as different until shown they are the same. Dewey appears to adopt the first position, Gadamer the second. Such a view is consistent with Gadamer's insistence on our limited powers to see things differently. Bringing to an experience the question "Is this the same as the other experience?" does not imply one will necessarily catch all the relevant differences. Experienced persons are particularly sensitive to the newness of experience, but they still might need help perceiving what is new or problematic. Also, as Klein shows, openness is consistent with actions that, from the outside, might appear merely routine or habitual. Likely, emergency workers are very attuned to how different situations are different, but determine that the differences do not call for different actions.

Perhaps what we should conclude is that there are two sorts of valuing going on here. Unifying and directing one's life, placing a situation in a broader context of meanings, is important. There is an issue of priority here, though. Even if Dewey would acknowledge the processes Klein describes to be valuing or judgment, he also contends that ethical life has its "center" in reflection during "periods of suspended and postponed action" when we seriously consider alternative aims.[33] Dewey does not propose that every experience should be a reflective experience; however, he does propose that "the crucial educational problem" is to procure postponement of action until reflection has been brought to bear.[34] But if Klein is correct, judgment "in the heat of the moment" can be no less important and legitimate than reflection in a "cool hour" and might reflect greater insight into value than is manifested when alternative aims or options have to be pondered. Ability to make immediate judgments can be an indicator of experience and knowledge; it need not be a sign of naiveté or ignorance or rashness.

However, our concern is not just valuing but prudential valuing in particular. Turning more directly to the realm of well-being, Klein's account has affinities with Aristotle's conception of the person of practical wisdom. For instance, Aristotle says that a person's reactions in the heat of the moment are surer signs of courage than when the person has had a chance to prepare.[35] According to McDowell, Aristotle implies "there is nothing for a correct conception of doing well to be apart from [the] capacity to read situations correctly."[36]

That might seem woefully insufficient, though. For example, just because a person can read a situation correctly — "I am being beaten viscously by a big guy with a bat, and it really hurts" — that hardly seems equivalent to doing well. Clearly, McDowell is talking about a particular Aristotelian conception of doing well that locates the core of well-being in people's character and perception, without denying that what happens to people matters, too. It is not too difficult to see the sense in this idea. What if the person saw his beating as an unconventional and overenthusiastic massage rather than a beating? We'd have doubts about his welfare in the very basic sense that he lacks a proper understanding of his world and what is good for him.

Still, McDowell's claim is controversial and complicated. Let's explore it further by returning to Evelyn Couch from *Fried Green Tomatoes*. Evelyn provides an interesting example, because in contrast to the calm professionalism we'd expect from emergency service people, it might seem that she was being impulsive, letting her emotions get the best of her when she trashed the girls' VW. What she did wasn't very nice, either. In Dewey's terms, we might think Evelyn's action lacked meaning. (Even Evelyn's friend Ninny worried that Evelyn had been taking too many hormones.)

However, it could be that Evelyn acted correctly and with understanding. That would seem to be the conclusion the movie urges upon us. I grant that we might have doubts about the correctness of Evelyn's actions, and I will do more to consider that issue later. For now, though, if we can imagine Evelyn did well for herself in the situation, her case is an example of how her reading of the situation shows she has a proper conception of her well-being. Had she read it differently — say, as a situation calling for restraint and caution rather than "Towanda,"[37] — likely we would feel she was making a mistake, reading her life in the same counterproductive way she had done previously.

Instead, Evelyn at last is present to experience. Before the parking lot adventure, Evelyn is doing more to resist her self and her circumstances than be attuned to them. Eventually, though, she finds belonging in the text of her life with the help of Ninny's stories. She fuses with the horizon that narrative offers. She has a reversal of consciousness where she can see herself in those stories. Suddenly, Evelyn is "all there." Rather than deny her emotions, she grips her car's steering wheel and gets angry. Here we see the way presence is necessary for knowing the truth. It is not as if Evelyn was present and then she gained insight. Rather, she could not truly be present until she had gained the insight she did.

Still, we might doubt that Evelyn did the right thing. I will not attempt a thorough defense of Evelyn's actions, but I will note a couple of things that should be considered. First, consider the "first principles" that appear operative in the horizon Evelyn shares with Ninny's stories. Surely, things such as dignity, freedom, self-reliance, and friendship, especially for women, are at work in Evelyn's experience and are worth fighting for. Prior to her epiphany Evelyn might have been able to give lip service to those ideas, but in grasping them she has finally understood them. And she has made the connection to her own life. As she has begun to develop a grasp of universals from Ninny's stories, she has begun to see particulars in her own life in light of them. Her understanding of first principles and particulars grow together.[38]

Consider the cost, though, we might say. What Evelyn did wasn't very nice, for instance. But hence the movie's message that the valuable things in our lives confront us with complex and often conflicting demands. Even if we were to conclude that Evelyn's conduct was bad, we have Griffin's point mentioned earlier: it might be better to be bad and preserve one's life than to be good and lose it. What life did Evelyn have to preserve? Her physical survival wasn't threatened by the girls; but the episode represents a crossroads where we likely have the sense that if Evelyn hadn't acted as she did she would have lost all chance to truly live.

Our doubts still might persist. As long as I've mentioned survival, maybe a big reason we might think Evelyn did the right thing was that she was simply lucky. What if the girls had pulled out a gun and shot her? But to read a situation correctly does not imply omniscience. Consider again the guy being beaten with a baseball bat. When I mentioned that before, I left out attention to the circumstances. What if the guy was beaten because he tried to intervene when another person was being attacked? Let's imagine that he had an even clearer view of dangers than Evelyn; he saw that the other guy was swinging a big wooden bat and outweighed him by 150 pounds. Does our victim do well by reading the situation as one that calls for his intervention? That's a tough call, but I think at least we would see some potential in showing courage as opposed to ignoring the situation. Similarly with Evelyn. Without for a moment denying that luck and consequences of actions play a role in well-being, to read situations in particular ways is the core of our well-being.

However, this brings me to another way Evelyn might have just been lucky. Even if Evelyn's perceptions were correct, she could merely have stumbled upon them. That is, what about the intelligence of her perceptions?

I've already made some case for the intelligence of perception, but Evelyn's example presents some challenges to consider. Let's deal with an obvious factor first: Evelyn's anger. Typically, we'd hope emergency workers aren't angry when they're working. Anger is an emotion or passion commonly thought to be an exemplar of impaired reason or judgment. We should question that attitude. For example, returning to the Ifaluk people, among them justifiable anger or righteous indignation (what they call *song*) is considered prosocial.[39] Not all anger is valued, but *song* has an important place in Ifaluk life. It is not just a "personal" reaction; it is a way of calling attention to salient aspects of social relationships, especially when those relationships are endangered or unclear.[40] Similarly, we might view Evelyn's anger as justified and even welcome as a way of calling attention (to put it mildly) to a breakdown of social relationships in the girls' rudeness.

However, even if we grant Evelyn's anger is understandable or even socially valuable, we still might deem it a surrender to mere impulse or passion. But the girls treated Evelyn shabbily. Perhaps shabby treatment is something we should feel anger at the thought of. Of course, anger can be blind or excessive, but that does not describe Evelyn's anger. She did not ram just any old car. She did not run over the girls. Evelyn was controlled, saying simply, "Face it, girls; I'm older and I have more insurance."

Here it is helpful to bring in Gadamer's take on the sight metaphor. Gadamer argues, "The opposite of seeing what is right is not error or deception but blindness"; it is losing "the right orientation" within oneself.[41] In Evelyn's case, the problem is more her being slow to achieve the right orientation than losing it, but the point still holds. Her problem was not that she misread things or was deceived by people, as if had she only looked harder she would have seen what she needed to. Her problem was that she was not in a position to see in the first place; she was blind to what needed to be seen. Returning to the game metaphor, Evelyn did not need to immerse herself more in the game; she needed to see what game she was involved in. As Taylor argues, there comes a point when a response to "I don't understand" has to be "Change yourself."[42] That is what happened to Evelyn. She underwent a fundamental transformative elevation in her self-understanding.

Is this a matter of Evelyn creating herself, as Foucault argues, or did she discover and elevate her self?[43] Evelyn's change was pretty radical, so it might appear to be a good example of self-creation. Her change did not happen all at once, however. She did not create her discontent. She revealed her discontent with her earlier persona through expressions of frustration — as when she was pushed aside by a teenage boy at the supermarket — and through humor — as when she begged off looking at her vagina, supposedly because she needed help getting her girdle off. Slowly, she uncovered and released the "Towanda" within herself.

Does it somehow invalidate or cheapen her achievements if we interpret them as discovering something about her self as opposed to creating something? If anything, I think the former does more to help us understand and appreciate the slow, painful struggle she went through to peel away the obstructions to her understanding of her self. And if we would see ways she should continue to grow, I think we would be reluctant to say, "create a new self for yourself," because she has largely "arrived"; she finally has come upon something fundamental in her self that should not be altered.

Along with Foucault, we might say that there is artistry in achieving a self; but art need not be a making or adding-on. For example, the ancients considered sculpture a matter of revealing what already was present in the marble.[44] Perhaps we cannot buy completely into that idea today, but contemporary sculptors and carvers express a similar attitude when they talk about having respect for what their material offers them; the material puts limits on what they can do with it.[45] That hardly diminishes their art. If we do want to care for the self, perhaps we should take a lesson from these artists and respect the material we have to work with. Evelyn's self-discovery was long and painful. We might wish it had not been that way, but the "material" that was Evelyn did not allow for a different process.

Evelyn's shift might appear impulsive. However, if Evelyn's change was rapid, that does not make it impulsive. We can see parallels with Kuhn's notion of a gestalt shift in science.[46] This shift constitutes a fundamental change in how the world is perceived. Such a shift cannot be forced or created: it happens. Yet it doesn't just happen. It is preceded by considerable effort; people need to reach a standpoint where a shift can occur. So, a good deal of effort could be needed for perception to occur, but the perception itself might seem spontaneous or effortless.

I suppose one thing that endears Evelyn to us is that she did try so hard. All that effort, which from our outsider's perspective might seem ill-advised, put Evelyn in a position where she could finally attain the right orientation to her life. In terms I used earlier, Evelyn finally came to feel the power of reasons or to finally see that she had reasons to think and act as she did. Maybe we could understand this as new reasons entering her horizon, a reason such as "Towanda." Perhaps other reasons exited. "That would be dangerous" or "that wouldn't be nice" might have been reasons that counted against action before but not now or not in the same way. Or perhaps it was a matter of shifting priorities. Evelyn's dignity might have become a much stronger reason for action than it was previously. Or perhaps we could think of it not as her dignity being relatively unimportant before but that she finally really understood what it implied.

If Evelyn elevated her self so as to finally see, we need not interpret that as cutting loose from reason — a charge leveled against Kuhn — but as establishing contact with reason.[47] If she was alienated from reason, that occurred more before her road rage than during it. Reasons finally became accessible to her.

Does this analysis speak against Dewey's idea that the perceptions Evelyn had were things to know with rather than knowledge? We might have sympathy with Evelyn and maybe even think she was doing something good for herself when she trashed that car yet still be nagged by the thought that it was only a start; Evelyn still has a lot to figure out. Of course she still has a lot to think about, and shortly I will say more about the value and nature of deliberation of that sort. But, to introduce a distinction I will pursue now, to understand why something is true, or to understand the implications of a truth, as Evelyn did, is a different task than establishing something as true.

There is a major danger in the view I espouse, however; we could fall back into the epistemic skepticism regarding perception that Dewey was trying to avoid. Again, his aim was to establish perception's legitimate place in the process of knowing. If perceptions are claims to knowledge then we appear to reintroduce the problem. However, accepting that perceptions can be mistaken does not require us to be skeptical of perception *per se*. And if we do have reason to question perceptions, we need not eschew claims to knowledge but, rather, ask the right sort of questions regarding our perceptions. As McDowell describes the transition from "that" which is perceived, to its justification, the "because":

[I]n acquiring the *because* one would not be adding new material to what one acquired when one took possession of the *that*, but coming to comprehend the *that*, by appreciating how one's hitherto separate perceptions of what situations call for hang together, so that acting on them can be seen as putting into practice a coherent scheme for a life.[48]

We can justify Evelyn's perceptions and actions in the parking lot by under-standing their "becauses." They make sense because they hang together in a coherent scheme of life that Evelyn finally achieved. Reason-finding can involve "moving from unreflective satisfaction with piecemeal applications of the out-look to a concern for how they hang together, so the intelligibility accrues to the parts from their linkage into a whole."[49]

That might seem to be a very inadequate sort of justification. A hardened criminal might "justify" his crimes by how they hang together in his life. However, what is the point of justification?

Cavell proposes:

> The point of the assessment [of a knowledge claim] is not to determine *whether* it is adequate . . . the point is to determine *what* position you are taking, that is to say, *what position you are taking responsibility for* — and whether it is one I can respect. What is at stake is not, or not exactly, whether you know our world, but whether, or to what extent, we are to live in the same moral universe.[50]

So, regarding Evelyn, the relevant question need not be "Is her perception cor-rect?" but rather "How do her actions make sense?" "What is their place in 'a coherent scheme of life'?" "Can we live in 'the same moral universe' with her?" Our discussion has given us grounds to think that Evelyn was acting within a coherent scheme of life, and although we might not like what she did, perhaps we can live in the same moral universe with her.

This doesn't mean we must stop looking for reasons why people's actions are or are not justified; perceptions can be mistaken. But rather than believe these reasons have to be something external — say "external" in the sense of being subject-independent or external to any particular moment, like one's stable value priorities — reason-finding can involve "moving from unreflective sat-isfaction with piecemeal applications of the outlook to a concern for how they hang together, so the intelligibility accrues to the parts from their linkage into a whole." So, if we are concerned that Evelyn is making a mistake when smashing the girls' car, we need not doubt the correctness of her reading of the situation, yet we might ask how her action fits into the whole of her life.[51] Saying, "You know, you'll probably get into trouble for this" could be significant for some people, but it might not fit the same way into Evelyn's changed life.

This sort of internal or immanent critique of one's life still might seem an unsatisfactory answer to the normativity issue. We might wonder, for example, whether a couch potato pressed to ponder the fit of the elements of his life would be moved to see anything wrong with his life. But if so, we also should wonder whether confronting him with some different "objective" image of a good life would have much effect, either. As I suggested earlier, if we want to help people conceive and live lives that genuinely are good for them we need to do more than speak the truth to them: we need to persuade them.

Persuasion likely will be more effective if it appeals to reasons, in the sense of internal reasons presented before. Deliberation about "fit" takes this approach. Even a couch potato might acknowledge he has reasons to get off his tail and do something. He might believe he has found a satisfactory fit among elements in his life, but I would guess all of us have experienced doubts when prodded to consider whether our actions and prudential values really do fit together very well. This does not imply people shouldn't be confronted with new possibilities for themselves, but it does imply these should be possibilities to which people can be present, to which they can belong.

Consider again the exchange between Socrates and the unfortunate Thrasymachus. Socrates starts from what Thrasymachus "knows" about justice. Clearly, the point is that Thrasymachus really does not know. To get to that point, though, Socrates does not say something like, "Well, let's see what Anaxagoras had to say about that." Rather, he moves to what else Thrasymachus knows. Proceeding through several points to which Thrasymachus can accede, even if reluctantly, Socrates brings Thrasymachus to a point where he sees his earlier claims do not fit with other beliefs of his.

This talk of fit prompts us to consider further what fit involves. One sort of fit is among elements of a whole life. I will consider that sort of fit further when we discuss "structure in a life" in the next chapter. But consider another way Evelyn manifested fit. What if the parking spot had been taken by a guy with a shotgun in the gun rack in his pickup truck or by a harried mother with six screaming kids in the car? Or what if the teenage girls had apologized about taking the spot? We don't know how Evelyn would have reacted in such circumstances, but I think we get the sense that Evelyn would have read those situations differently. Experiencing persons are present to their experience by being attuned to context, the particulars of the experience, the way a ballplayer is attuned to the action of a game.

However, this sort of attunement to time and place presents a difficult issue for thinking about value and leading a life. For there could be a number of ways to find fit among the particulars of an experience. Griffin argues that we want to avoid an "eclectic" approach that throws us upon "haphazard intuitions" when making decisions.[52] The problem is this: Let's grant that Evelyn thought hard and intelligently during what led up to her trashing the girls' car. But what about the choice of action itself? She had a number of options to choose from. And this presents a question if, as Ruth Chang argues, "[a] comparison of the alternatives is necessary to the justification of choice."[53] Gadamer says something similar when he claims knowledge implies treating possibilities as possibilities.[54] However, given the way I have described Evelyn's action, it would appear that there was little, if any, comparison of alternatives; she simply saw what had to be done. I've even suggested that if Evelyn had paused to compare alternatives, that would be a mistake. I will argue that there is comparison of alternatives in "seeing" and that experience is essential to that.

## COMPARISON AND THE INTELLIGENCE OF CHOICE

As I just mentioned, Griffin decries an eclectic approach to choice. He looks for some sort of single principle — informed desire in his case — that yields a systematic way to make or analyze choices: consulting a hierarchy of informed desires. One does well when satisfying one's greatest desires. Hence his emphasis on primary desires compared with those — such as experience — that are "merely" secondary. A choice is rational if one chooses the desire higher in the hierarchy than the alternative. Here my concern is not desires *per se* — I think we have sufficient reason to question that framework — but to challenge the general idea that the reasonableness of some choice is judged by how it conforms to some set of priorities.

Taylor agrees that pondering the importance of goods in one's life, as Griffin does, is a vital activity, and one discouraged by a good deal of modern moral philosophy. However, he also argues that the choices we must make as we live and give shape to our lives cannot be made only with attention to what is most important but also with attention to the "complementarity" question, how the diverse things we value fit together in a whole life.[55] Among these diverse things is the concern "to be and become a certain kind of human being," which cannot be reduced to being faithful to the ranking one gives to one's values.[56]

Turning to what this means for Evelyn, I hinted at this point before when I suggested she was at a crossroads for her life. Let's say preserving her life is one of her priorities. In light of that, we might say she acted unwisely, even if teenage girls were her targets — they can be pretty nasty, after all. But Taylor's point is that leading a life is not only a matter of following our priorities. There are times in our lives when our priorities should not take priority. The question one must ask is not only, "What do my priorities demand that I do here?" but also, "What do this time and place in my life demand for me as the person I am and aim to be?"

Perhaps the actions Taylor emphasizes are just impulses — he describes them that way — but if they are they still have an important function to prevent one among a plurality of values to overwhelm the others. We do want to treasure the important things in the world and in our lives,

> but this is not all. We also want to cherish and develop a certain way of understanding and responding to the world — in short, a certain reverence . . . [S]ingle-minded pursuit of the results, without any concern whatever for what kind of people we are becoming, would be more than questionable.[57]

To illustrate further, let's return to our example of the parents estranged from their child. Their child's success in life is their priority, and from what friends say, the child is doing well. Yet the parents are grieved by the estrangement. One day, they can restrain themselves no longer and go unannounced to the child's apartment. When their son comes to the door, they plead to be let in, but he slams the door in their faces. What are we to think about the parents' actions? For several reasons, we might think them unwise. They rank their son's welfare over their own feelings and their desire to have a relationship with him, so they appear to be acting against their own priorities, and maybe even in a way that puts things they value at risk. We might even wonder whether they are being selfish — say, by burdening their son with a guilt trip. Or we might sympathize with the parents but then say there were better ways to make overtures to their son. Or we might sympathize because of the inherent unpredictability of consequences. Who knows how the son might react? But let's suppose that the parents thought a good result unlikely, even expecting that the door would be slammed in their faces. In all these ways, it would seem the parents are making mistakes because they're not acting according to what is most important among their own priorities for their well-being.

However, on Taylor's view, concern for what is most important is only part of what is at stake. A parent should also think about the life he is leading, the sort of human being he aims to be and become. This does not imply doubt about the rank given the child's success or about risks to what is valued; it does imply judgment about how that value fits into the parent's life at this place and time. The parent might aim to be and become the sort of parent who loves deeply and makes that love clear to his child. After all, it would seem to take a loving parent to wish the best for his child even as the child rejects him. The parent might still value his child's success above his own expressions of love, all things considered, but the concern is what the present circumstances portend for his ability to be and become the loving person he aims to be. To advise him to "stay cool" is to ask him to defer or maybe even deny the imperative that is pressing upon him.

Perhaps we'd advise that there will be other opportunities to express love, but that assumes a lot about the similarity of experiences and of people from one time in their lives to another. To repress the urge to express love rather than be receptive to it might make it even more difficult for the parent's becoming the sort of parent he aims to be. Perhaps without action now, the gulf between child and parent would only continue to grow. Sometimes, opportunities are irretrievably lost. (We will return to this issue in the next chapter.)

A parent in our example "may agree that the cause [of her child's success] in a sense comes first — that is, one ought to be ready to sacrifice a great deal [for it] . . . at various crucial moments. But the path of becoming a person of reverence is something one should never abandon."[58] The parent could admit that she might feel and act differently at some later time, "but she cannot now, given where she is."[59] If that sounds selfish, we should remember that the ultimate point, as Taylor frames it, is to cherish and develop reverence, a humility or receptivity that stops us from narrow-minded pursuit of what is "most important." That would seem to hold a good deal of value for all people and not just the person acting. Whether or not the parent's choice is correct or "thoughtful," the point is that one's welfare involves not only what one values most but how the things one values fit together, especially at particular times of our lives that present particular conditions for decision and action.

Taylor's point about reverence is similar to Nussbaum's point about awe and wonder. Even if reverence does not intrude in the way awe and wonder do,[60] it is an attitude with an object — the world and our ability to be responsive to it — that brings within a person's scheme of ends factors that a ranking of values cannot fully capture or deal with in the face of the choices that confront us at crucial places and times in our lives.

Similarly, Evelyn's parking lot episode was a time and place where she had a choice about becoming a certain sort of human being. While it might seem paradoxical in light of her aggressive action, we can describe Evelyn as exhibiting a sort of reverence or humility in the face of what her life and Ninny's stories were trying to tell her. Evelyn had been trying so hard to take control of her life, but what she really needed to do was let go.

The argument is that a hierarchy of values does not provide all that is needed for comparing choices, but we still seek some way to compare possible actions or possible lives and make some nonarbitrary judgment about which might be better. But, again, I think it is easy to imagine Evelyn saying about the alternatives to ram or not ram the car, "There is no comparison."

Literally, of course there is a comparison. What Evelyn's imagined comment likely would mean is that the value of one action far, far exceeds others, such that there is no real question about their relative merit. There's the rub, though. We can imagine someone, such as Evelyn's husband, complaining that it seems that way to her only because she has adopted the particular (weird) perspective she has. A "real" comparison requires some perspective that is neutral between the two contending alternatives.

This leads us to another aspect to account for in the intelligence of experience and choice. In our lives we can be confronted by choices that are incommensurable. It is the "you-can't-compare-apples-and-oranges" situation. Comparability sometimes is taken to be a particular problem when we are confronted with incommensurability, and my pluralism presents just that issue.

However, as common as the "apples-and-oranges" idea is, it is false. One certainly can compare apples and oranges even if we lack a single scale for comparison. That is, incommensurability does not imply incomparability. The fact of incommensurability does not tell us incompatible entities cannot be compared; it does tell us what we need to do in order to compare them.[61] We have to compare them in multiple ways rather than in a single way.

If we were to judge apples and oranges on the basis of which is tastier, we would not get far, because apples and oranges are tasty in different ways. So, we look for multiple ways to compare. The orange is sweet and the apple is tart. Is the orange therefore better tasting? Perhaps the fruit's consistency matters for taste, too. The apple is firm and crisp; the orange is soft and juicy. And maybe there are other things to consider before we decide which is the "better" fruit. Each has seeds, but it's easier to eat around them in an apple. Plus, you don't have to peel an apple if you don't want to. On the other hand, the orange's peel can be an advantage; the apple bruises more easily. All this makes it tough to decide which fruit is better.

But maybe we could just tot up the pros and cons of the one and the other. One often hears that kind of advice. If you aren't sure what to do, put all the plusses of doing something in one column and all the minuses of doing it in another, then see which list is longer. One problem with that, though, is that it assumes what counts as a plus and a minus. Does the tartness of the apple count against it or for it? Also, we need to account for intensity. For example, as I survey my list about apples and oranges, I note that an orange is juicier than an apple, and in addition, I really want something juicy. So I give the orange two plusses. Or should it be three? One and a half?

Systematizing our judgment in any helpful way seems to elude us. Yet we can and do make decisions in these situations. We can make a judgment about whether an apple or an orange is a better fruit, at least for certain purposes. Griffin's example of the trees along Paris streets is another example. Planting trees comes at the cost of some drivers' lives. Are the trees somehow worth more than people? Of course not. We tend to believe that the worth of people's lives cannot be compared in terms of the monetary or other value of other things. Yet, as Griffin argues, we do make such decisions, and they are perfectly legitimate.

In the context of my discussion, what we face is the "you-can't-compare-value-priorities-and-reverence" problem. As I described it, these concerns can be incompatible, implying incompatible actions, such as going to a child's apartment and not going. My proposal is that there is no further value or principle that provides a single scale for choosing value priorities or reverence at a time and place in a life. So, when we wonder whether value priorities or reverence better serves a person's well-being, we are facing a decision like whether an apple is better than an orange. Saying we have to look at Evelyn's action only in terms of her value priorities would be like saying we have to judge an orange by how much it's like an apple.

However, this only takes us so far. The argument suggests that deliberation might not yield a clear answer always. We have to accept that. Because of the plurality of values and the complexity of their interactions, we should expect indeterminate rankings that represent a range of acceptable answers rather than one correct one.[62] Perhaps this just shows the limits of rationality. Maybe that is not a problem. If two incompatible actions are equally justified it might be acceptable just to pick one. But people tend to balk at that when important choices are involved.

What might all this mean for the intelligence of Evelyn's choice? Let's imagine that Evelyn deemed "Towanda" to be the reason that justified her action. In the movie she says "Towanda" right before she plows into the girls' car, and we can imagine "Towanda" as Evelyn's way of capturing what she had been thinking and experiencing regarding her life, her values, and Ninny's stories. We have described her as doing little, if any, deliberation about her action; she simply saw what she needed to do. Plus, whatever deliberation she might have done, we are supposing that Evelyn is considering two options, such as being/becoming "this person" or being/becoming "that person," that cannot be straightforwardly compared with each other, and, in fact, the comparison seems skewed because the criteria Evelyn is using for the comparison favor "Towanda." Evelyn appears to have a problem; she seems not to have compared alternatives, at least not fairly or seriously.

However, Chang argues, "[a] reason can justify in virtue of something that is no part of the justification but is what gives the reason its justifying force."[63] In other words, justification and comparison involve more than the head-to-head comparison of alternatives for action at some particular point in time. "Towanda" might justify Evelyn's action in virtue of something that is no part of the justification. What might this "something" be? I propose that it is experience, essentially. "Towanda" justifies Evelyn's action because she can say, "I've tried the other way, and it is a dead end." As the movie portrays it, Evelyn's life implicitly, if not explicitly, has been a comparison of lives. She takes classes to add "spark" to her marriage and get in touch with her genitalia. She tries to be "nice" and play by the rules. None of those things remedies the emptiness and frustration she feels. Ninny's stories offer her an alternative for being, albeit being experienced vicariously prior to Evelyn's action. "Towanda" is a reason that gets its justifying force from the experiences Evelyn has had.

Similarly, we can credit "to be a loving parent" as a justifying reason for action in our other example if our parents were experienced. Contrast them with parents who had not pondered their lives and values, who had not struggled to accept the distance between themselves and their child, who had not undergone the emotional turmoil of their love and grief, but rather one day just decided, "Let's go show up at Johnny's door and show him how much we love him." "To be a loving parent" does not have the same justificatory power if the parents had not experienced serious comparison of alternatives.

But maybe I have skewed the question of rationality by appealing to what are more likely to look like reasons. "To be a loving parent" seems a good candidate for a reason. Maybe even "Towanda," although unusual, looks like a reason. But I have been advocating the role of emotions, so what if Evelyn's reason for action was, as she suggests at one point while relating the incident to Ninny, "I got mad," or if, in our other example, the parents' reason was "We simply were overcome by grief"?

Already I have defended the rationality of emotions, and the discussion here suggests that emotions can have an experiential basis that speaks to their rational justification. Perhaps that is not terribly controversial. But I want to be clear about the nature of emotions as reasons. First we should think about the reasons appropriate to persuasion and argument. There is a common image that "nonrational" emotions can be rational but only if governed by the intellect. Persuasion is directed at the intellect that then will exert its effects on the emotions, keep them in check. However, Gadamer has "a deep skepticism about the fantastic overestimation of reason by comparison to the affections that motivate the human mind."[64]

I have misgivings about the contrast Gadamer makes between the power of reason and of affections, yet he makes a good point that appeal to emotions is a reasonable way to persuade. We might need to offer "rhetoric" rather than "argument," but rhetoric still can be reasonable: "If rhetoric appeals to the feelings, as has long been clear, that in no way means it falls outside the realm of the reasonable."[65] If appeals to feelings serve people's welfare, we have reason to make such appeals.

Emotions themselves can be educated. It might be that we should be suspicious of our emotions at a stage when they are not well developed, but with experience they can become more reliable in the directives they offer. McDowell argues, "a directive-issuing state can be constituted (by 'persuasion') out of psychic materials that, before the formation of character, are not a source of rational prescriptions."[66] Recall that Audi made a similar point when arguing that desires, emotions, and experiences can provide normative reasons for action. If anger, for example, is a psychic state that cannot issue rational prescriptions prior to its proper constitution, that does not imply it cannot issue correct directives subsequent to the formation of character. With Evelyn we get the sense that her character (finally) has been properly formed, and because of that she needs to heed her anger. Her anger is telling her something; it's a reason to act.

The upshot of all this is that we have grounds to think that the appearance of "impulse" and passion, rather than cool reason, does not imply that the comparison and justification Chang requires for rational action is absent.

## CONCLUSION

In this chapter I have described hermeneutic experience that entails an individual's presence and belonging in the world so that the self is "forgotten" but can be discovered and elevated. A principal concern has been to show how an experienced person can perceive and value and act in justifiable ways. These persons' way of being in the world, with all its feeling and emotion, does not merely provide things to know with but also can yield knowledge itself.

This does not mean that cool, overt deliberation is unimportant. In particular, as I mentioned before, our concern for "fit" that gives meaning and sense to life extends beyond the fit that can be achieved regarding particular choices. We are also concerned with what happens after and around particular choices, the sort of fit experiences do or do not have in one's life as a whole. The issue is not just that lives should make some sense rather than be haphazard but also that we need ways to judge if lives are being lived well or not, if they are progressing in beneficial ways rather than detrimental ways. The next chapter explores those issues.

*Chapter 5*

# Structuring and Evaluating a Life

Human beings are confronted by a plurality of things that do or might contribute to or detract from their welfare. There are things that people need and things that people desire. There are things we seek to have and things that have us. We have priorities for our lives but also times and places when reverence for our being puts priorities on hold.

However, it is difficult to live a good life if one's life is just a haphazard collection of values and actions. Educators have a responsibility to help people find some sort of structure in their lives, so they can find meaning in what they believe, do, and become. In this chapter the issue is how some sort of structure can be achieved in a life that is sensitive to and responsive to value plurality. As we have seen, one approach is to organize our prudential values in a hierarchy. I have questioned whether any single principle, such as informed desire, can provide the structure needed and so advocate a stronger sort of pluralism holding that values are not subject to a complete rational ordering.[1] But let's explore that further.

## VALUE PLURALITY AND SINGLE-PRINCIPLE LIFE STRUCTURES

My criticism of informed desire and other single-principle structures gets especially tricky when we consider a life over the long term. For example, Private Branham might have benefited from his D-Day experience without desiring those benefits, but the benefits of those experiences cannot be fully understood except within the whole course of his life. The meaning of his D-Day experience would seem quite different if he made the military a career or if he became a pacifist. I do not dispute that desire (and other things) gives us insight into the meaning of experiences. The issue is the sufficiency of any one structuring principle.

Let's examine another example — this time a movie adaptation of a musical. Consider Tevye from *Fiddler on the Roof* and the episode when he spurns his third daughter, Chava, who secretly married a Christian. Tevye is an interesting example for several reasons. For one thing, he provides an example of someone facing complexity in his life and trying to make sense out of it. Also, he gives us an opportunity to revisit other issues we have considered regarding the intelligence of perception. For instance, I imagine his action sits less well with us than Evelyn's. We might wonder if Tevye's "sight" is especially good. For another thing, Tevye appears to deliberate when facing difficult decisions regarding his three daughters; he regularly ponders "the other hand." Yet, with his third daughter he concludes, "There is no other hand." So, he gives us a chance to think more about comparison of alternatives in perception and judgment.

To begin, I propose that Tevye is present to his experience. He is a thoughtful, passionate, and very spiritual man. When he thinks about his daughters he does not just think about them; he pictures them in his mind. He endorses tradition, but he is playful about it, at one point shouting "Tradition!" but then shrugging his shoulders as if to say, "Eh." Tevye comes across as a man who is thoroughly involved in the "game" of his life and not just conforming to what tradition seems to dictate about how the game should be played.

I'll also say Tevye "belongs," but complexity intrudes here. Surely he belongs to his Jewish community, although there too he's not above poking fun at certain aspects of the faith. But the movie also prompts us to wonder about how he belongs to the other life texts with which he is confronted — through his daughters' challenges and those of the Christian townsfolk, for instance — situations where he feels confused, marginalized, or persecuted.

Tevye is an example of the many "belongings" people face and negotiate. Tevye makes attempts to cross borders, albeit cautiously, as when he accepts the invitation to dance with the Gentiles in the tavern and, contrary to tradition, dance with his wife at his first daughter's wedding. Probably, he does not fully understand the narrative his first two daughters are developing for their lives, yet he manages to fuse with their horizons. He is similar to Glaucon and Adeimantus; he might not fully understand what is going on and might even feel somewhat muddled, but he exhibits a sense of belonging even if it is partial and tentative.

So, we get the sense that Tevye is present and able to see. But what does he see regarding his third daughter, Chava? We encounter something similar to

Evelyn when Tevye says, "There is no other hand!" Did Tevye go through a comparison of alternatives? He appeared to begin that, but if there is no "other hand," did he make a serious comparison?

What reasons might justify Tevye's choice? Perhaps his faith ranked higher in his priorities than his daughter's happiness. If so, we can see the sense of his choice. However, I'm not sure the priority would be well described as a desire so much as a matter of duty or compulsion. We can also imagine Tevye resisting the idea that his choice was a matter of priorities. Recalling Taylor's point about reverence, we might imagine Tevye saying it was not a matter of priorities but of what was crucial to his being and becoming. As he contemplates accepting Chava's marriage he says, "If I bend that far I'll break." But if, like Evelyn, one option was not really an option, where was the comparison of alternatives?

Like we did for Evelyn, for an answer to that question we look to the course of Tevye's life. In the movie he is confronted by several choices, most prominently regarding his two eldest daughters but also regarding his fellow Jews and the anti-Semites in his village. His life and his values are tested and pushed. Is his love for his daughters stronger than faith or tradition? How, if at all, might he do justice to both? He compares alternatives for his being and becoming. His concern for his being and becoming might not have entered explicitly into his thought about Chava, but we can see it as a justifying reason. Tevye might have appealed to his faith in his choice, but that reason justifies his action only because of the experiences he had. "My faith" would be less a reason and more a mere excuse if it was only a dogma and not a faith he lived and struggled with.

We might have misgivings about Tevye's choice. It might be difficult to see rejecting Chava as an "elevation" of his self, just because we wonder if Tevye expanded his vision or narrowed and hardened it. Yet he progressed in the sense that he found in his self a clear vision of how his turmoil had to be resolved. Sure, the results were not perfect, just like getting beaten up when trying to help someone being attacked. We get the sense that Tevye was not "happy" about his decision, but that it was meaningful and "satisfying" nonetheless. The challenges Tevye experienced could have broken his life into pieces, but he made the pieces hang together in his response to Chava. And we get the sense that Tevye still belongs with Chava's horizon. Later in the movie he does not respond to Chava when she says good-bye before leaving the village with her new husband, but neither does he rebuke his eldest daughter or his wife when they speak with her. His only complaint is that his wife is broadcasting family business. And he himself blesses the couple under his breath.

Tevye found a fit among his beliefs and actions, but it is a fit that is not captured in a single principle like desire or some other priority. As with Private Branham, we might wait to see the fuller significance of Tevye's experiences. If he comes to desire reconciliation with Chava we likely will see his experiences in a different light than if he does not form that desire. However, even if we can analyze Private Branham's and Tevye's lives in terms of desires, that captures only part of the meaning and significance of their experiences. Gadamer argues:

> [E]xperience is [not] just something that flows past quickly in the stream of conscious life; it is meant as a unity and thus attains a new mode of being *one* . . . Everything that is experienced is experienced by oneself, and part of its meaning is that it belongs to the unity of this self and thus contains an unmistakable and irreplaceable relation to the whole of this one life. Thus, essential to an experience is that it cannot be exhausted in what can be said of it or grasped as its meaning.[2]

To illustrate what's at stake, let's continue Tevye's story. We continue to worry about him. Maybe he is right to do what he did with Chava, but he gives signs that he might be confused or inadequately thoughtful about his priorities. So, we take him to an infallible psychic who can tell him what his stable priorities will be across the rest of his life. She guarantees that he will continue to resist reconciliation with Chava and be at peace with himself about that. She tells Tevye that it's a close call, but his priority is for his faith and community, with the welfare of his family a close second. She also tells him that his family will accept his decision even though reluctantly. So, she advises Tevye to continue with his attitudes and actions. With our doubts now put to rest, we turn with a smile toward Tevye and say, "I guess you were right, you can put this out of your mind." To our surprise, he replies, "No, I cannot accept that conclusion." Of course, we are incredulous. After all, the psychic has infallible insight into what Tevye himself most values.

How does Tevye's imagined response make sense? Outside of fantasy examples, most of us would hesitate because we're skeptical of fortune-tellers. But we're imagining that Tevye's doubts don't stem from that. He accepts that the psychic's predictions are true. We might say that, like many of us, Tevye doesn't like being told what to do or think. But the psychic isn't telling him what she wants him to do and think; she's telling him what he himself will want to do and think. Perhaps Tevye could accept that; yet, say, he wants to figure that out himself, another inclination I suppose most of us would have. However, if doing well means satisfying value priorities, such resistance would be mere stubbornness. Unless one has a greater desire to figure out how to do well than to actually do well, the sensible thing to do would appear to be to take the shortcut and get right to satisfying one's greatest priorities.

However, there is a problem with shortcuts that goes beyond wanting to figure things out for one's self. Tevye cannot follow the psychic's advice because he cannot understand the advice. Tevye's resistance is sensible because he does not structure his life only around his value priorities. The psychic and we are asking Tevye to violate the principle that "experience is [not] just something that flows past quickly in the stream of conscious life; it is meant as a unity and thus attains a new mode of being *one*." Similarly, Taylor argues that "making sense of my present action . . . requires a narrative understanding of my life, a sense of *what I have become* which can only be given in a story."[3]

Even if we can assure Tevye he will become or continue to be a particular person, to ask him to be that person now is to treat a segment of his life as merely "flowing past quickly," as a dispensable component of his story that essentially is meaningless in itself, because it is only an element in a process that supposedly can be short-circuited thanks to the psychic's omniscience. Even if he can accept the psychic's prediction as true, Tevye cannot make sense of it abstracted from the experiences that would lead up to it. If priorities do have meaning for Tevye's life, they do so only so far as they have *a place in his life*. Appealing to desires, even desires Tevye himself will have, is asking Tevye to isolate one aspect of himself from the unity of himself.

If we want an education example, let's think about what we often tell students in order to justify the education we offer them: "You will need this later in life." Oftentimes, students are skeptical about such claims (bless their hearts), but the problem is not getting them to believe the claim. The claim might in fact be true. The students might believe it is true. The problem comes when they and we treat their school experience as detached from the unity of their lives and see the meaning of their education experience only or principally in its relation to some future self. Dewey sees the problem, which he describes as failing to get out of experience all the potential that it holds, with the further self-defeating consequence that students are inadequately prepared for the future, which was the supposed goal.[4] However, the point I'm stressing is not just about the quality of experience and what preparation for the future really requires. The point regards the reverence and humility experience demands of us educators: reverence because experiences are irreplaceable parts of a whole life that belong to the person living that life; humility because the full significance of experience inevitably is enigmatic.

The educational aim is not simply to multiply the potential meanings students' school experiences might have in an attempt not to short-circuit students' being. What is essential to experience cannot be grasped in what can be said about it regardless how rich and complex our language might be. The uncertainty of what a whole life will bring, the complexity in individuals and situations, and the multitude of possible meanings implies that the significance of experience will always be elusive. Desires (or some other priority or principle) might help us *explain* lives, but that does not imply we *understand* lives.

This does not mean we should abandon the search for meaning, explanation, and understanding. In Part Two, I will argue that an essential task for educators is to engage with students in that search. And a vital aspect of the search is to find a way to give some structure or meaning to the multiple elements of persons' well-being as they are living it and seeking it.

## STRUCTURE AS A CONSTELLATION

"Constellation" is the metaphor I employ to describe the structure needed. Quoting Martin Jay, Richard Bernstein describes a constellation as a "juxtaposed rather than integrated cluster of changing elements that resist reduction to a common denominator, essential core, or generative first principle."[5] The metaphor is apt because the fit we are after is fit among a cluster of elements in a life that can be in tension, elbowing us in different directions.[6] These elements are not static; with time and context they change in form and significance. Connections important at one time need not be at another. So, we do not look for fit in relation to an essential core — say, the core provided by a life plan or an unchanging self — nor in terms of a generative first principle, such as informed desire, authenticity, or some other priority.

Probably, rather than talk of structure and fit in a life, we should talk about structures and fits. As we work to achieve meaning in our lives we likely will have to settle for a piecemeal approach, making sense out of some aspects of our lives as others have to wait. We have to start somewhere; we cannot make everything fit at once. As we live we might achieve greater, more encompassing meaning in our lives, yet the eventual outcome is unlikely to be some point where finally everything all hangs together. Instead, we probably will have to settle for a variety of structures, some expansive, incorporating a good deal, while others are more restricted. Perhaps we can achieve some integration among structures, but we should also expect some juxtaposition. Schizophrenia is juxtaposition taken to the pathological extreme, but I imagine many of us recognize parts of ourselves that don't hang together all that well — like my interest in my health and my enjoyment of cigars — while still living lives that are satisfying, and deserve to be so.

Tevye is a good example to return to. Likely, we have the feeling that Tevye hasn't integrated all the elements of his life. He's decisive and persistent in rejecting his daughter Chava, yet we sense the elements involved there and in other aspects of his life are undergoing change through his experience with his other daughters, his family's forced move to the United States, and the persecution that brought that about. Whatever plan Tevye might have had for his life, it's been radically disrupted. Family, faith, and community are not going to be what they were. Probably, there are some structures he really hasn't faced up to, such as family.

Tevye's life is full of tensions and uncertainties. Some of these he seems to have a good handle on, others not so much. Yet, despite the lack of a solid structure, he is making sense of his life. We see that Tevye is not adrift in a mishmash of disparate elements. Granted, we might say that he hasn't given enough thought to giving his life a real structure. But why must we think that is a problem? All things considered, Tevye seems to be doing pretty well. We might even be glad he hasn't sought a tighter or more extensive structure just because his constellation holds the possibility for him remaining sensitive and responsive to the difficult and important questions he faces.

In a constellation we do not have an overarching principle to hold things together, but we do have a center of gravity — the person who is living this constellation as her life.[7] Even so, we still look for some criteria by which we can judge the quality of a person's life, the prudential value of their constellation. Here I will begin to suggest some criteria and continue in Part Two, when we talk about the judgments educators have to make.

## EVALUATING THE CONSTELLATION OF WELL-BEING

There are two basic approaches for judging the quality of some state of affairs. One is in comparison with some goal. For instance, depending what the relevant end point is, I am doing well if I have arrived at a place where my happiness is authentic or my desires are informed and satisfied or my rational life plan is realized. No one of those goals captures the essence of well-being. However, that is not the deficiency I focus on now, for we could see each of those goals (and others) having a proper place in the constellation of a person's life. The problem in a goal approach is that it relies on goals. There is no guarantee that having reached a goal the person will be well-off. That can be attributed to having a poor conception of the goal, but that leads to the problem of the inherent difficulty in knowing when a goal is adequately informed or rational or authentic.

Different theorists do offer criteria for the adequacy of some end point.[8] However, there is a different approach to try. We can judge the quality of a state of affairs, not in terms of arrival at some point but in the *arriving*, in the progress *from* some state of affairs and the potential to lead to further progress. If we give up the goal-oriented approach, we still can compare positions by focusing on the transition between them.[9]

I should say right off that this approach has a fundamental problem of its own, presented by the subject-relativity of well-being. Progress itself will have different prudential value for different people. A person can recognize some life as better for himself while deeming it not worth the effort and other sacrifices it would require to attain it. Recalling the distinction between absolute and relative superlatives, it cannot be assumed that one's aim must be a life that is better than all possible others.[10] With that proviso in mind, however, we still can look for ways to judge well-being, for even if progress is not an unqualified good, we should be in a position to judge whether progress is warranted or not, as in the case of the "contented slave."

We should not look for a single criterion but, rather, think in terms of a cluster of criteria that each can contribute something valuable to the complex task of comparing alternative ways of life. We have considered a number of possibilities. For example, we could look to see if a person's constellation allows for Deweyan interaction or the presence and belonging vital for hermeneutic experience. For Tevye, for instance, the "externals" in his life — events, faith, family, tradition, poverty, prejudice — are not inert. He lives those things and their implications. His interactions with them do not always have happy results. In his constellation there are repulsive forces at work as well as attractive ones. Yet they hold together because Tevye thoroughly experiences them as parts of his life. Tevye is present with and to his life, and, as we have seen, presence implies "I'm all here" and "I belong here," which in turn imply a deep and thorough interaction of the external and internal.

However, heavenly bodies influence one another. There is only so much a human being can do to make things hang together. If the constellation of a life is to hang together there has to be some appropriate balance among the various meanings and experiences and not just between them and the person.

Dewey's idea of continuity applies to continuities among experiences as well as continuity within some experience. Consider Tevye once again. The parts of his life are not isolated from one another; there is continuity. I have mentioned several times how in Tevye's struggles — with his daughters, for example — he brings into the struggle his prior beliefs and experiences, and those undergo modification. He makes connections between his experiences with his daughters, in which tradition is challenged, and other experiences where he is faced with challenges to tradition, as when he dances with his wife at Tzeitel's wedding. He ponders what his daughters teach him about paternal love, and he connects that to his relationship with his wife, asking/singing, "Do you love me?" Aspects of his life interact and coalesce when he sings/daydreams, "If I were a rich man." His poverty, faith, and thoughts of prestige in the community come together there. Granted, the modifications he undergoes might be more or less in different situations, but the point is that there is continuity among his experiences; they are not isolated from one another nor inert so far as their affect on his life.

I want to explore a bit more what sort of continuity this is. Particularly, continuity has some connotation of linearity, and we should be careful not to expect continuities in a constellation to be clear and direct. We educators need to appreciate the complexities of continuities not only to understand students but also to think about how to guide their education. For example, continuity is relevant to the question of when students get "off task."

I'll use an example from Dewey to illustrate. Dewey imagines a person confronted by a ditch standing in the way of her getting to some destination.[11] Dewey uses this example to illustrate features of a good experience. For instance, he notes the importance of "surrender." There are two basic "surrenders" the person must undergo. One is to the facts of the situation; the other is to ideas about what to do. If one is fixated on jumping the ditch, despite the fact that it is 40 feet wide, one is not being receptive to reality and alternative possibilities for action. In other words, interaction is needed. One has to be receptive to what reality presents — the ditch is wide, deep, and full of water; it has sheer, slippery sides. To cope well, one has to be open to possibilities for action: Maybe I could build a bridge; maybe the ditch is easier to cross somewhere else. In turn, the possibilities are tested via return to the facts: Are bridge-building materials available? Can I find a narrower or shallower spot? Do I have time to look for another spot to cross? For Dewey, this sort of receptivity, acknowledging that one cannot be master of planning but must be sensitive to the limitations of knowledge and circumstances, is essential for reflective thinking.

We can discern continuity in Dewey's example. The person brings past knowledge and experience to bear — about bridges, for instance. There is continuity in that the investigating and reflecting leads to something; one solves the problem or at least learns something about the problem, perhaps even that the problem isn't what one thought it was. I imagine that for many people attracted to Dewey and problem-solving approaches to education, this represents a paradigmatic case of learning through experience.

But consider a modification to Dewey's example. While examining the bank of the ditch to see if it offers a foothold, I notice a whitish, pointy thing sticking out of the bank. My curiosity aroused, I look around for a stick I can use to dig around the object and expose more of it. After digging at it for a few minutes, I am able to grab it and pull it out. It appears to be part of an antler.

How are we to describe this experience? There appears to be some amount of Deweyan reflective thinking happening. I am sensitive to what the environment provides — "There's an odd object there." I formulate a "problem" — "I want to get that object." I come up with a suggestion — "Maybe I can dig it out with a stick." And I return to the situation to test my suggestion — "Are there sticks around that would be suitable for digging?" In other words, there appears to be a good deal of interaction and continuity present here.

However, what might prompt criticism is that by playing around in the muck I have forgotten my "real" problem — getting across the ditch. To put it in educationese, I have let myself get off task. I suspect Dewey would not share that criticism but would see a number of good things in my antler hunt. It has the characteristics of what Dewey deems real experience, an aesthetic experience that includes elements of curiosity, appreciation, perception, and enjoyment.[12]

Nonetheless, I think Dewey might also question the extent of reflective thought involved. At least, I would appear to have done rather little to postpone "immediate action upon desire until observation and judgment have intervened."[13] True, I thought enough not to just start kicking at the curious object and risk breaking it, but neither did I stop to wonder about whether I should take time with the object rather than get back to my ditch-crossing problem. In other words, we might wonder if there is real continuity in my constellation of actions, thoughts, and values here or if I am just being impulsive or addle-headed.

Maybe I am just being addle-headed, but that is not the inevitable conclusion. Continuity could be present, but to see it we would have to expand our view beyond the putative task at hand and the factors most directly related to it. For example, why not see continuity through the fact that I am simply a curious person? Maybe I'm not especially intrigued by paleontology, but ditch-crossing problems don't float my boat, either. Or maybe the continuity is not in terms of specific interests but, rather, in my inclination and ability to be present to circumstances beyond what is required for a particular interest or task. What might appear from the outside to be a thoughtless person, always flitting from thing to thing without taking any one thing really seriously, could reflect some more basic, though less obvious, continuities.

Continuity can exist even if there are many side trips and detours. Gadamer argues:

[E]very experience has something of an adventure about it ... An adventure [as opposed to an episode] interrupts the customary course of events, but is positively and significantly related to the context which it interrupts. Thus an adventure lets life be felt as a whole, in its breadth and in its strength . . . It ventures out into the uncertain . . . But at the same time it knows that, as an adventure, it is exceptional and thus remains related to the return of the everyday, into which the adventure cannot be taken. Thus the adventure is "undergone," like a test or trial from which one emerges enriched and more mature.[14]

So, maybe my antler digging is just an adventure. Perhaps I even know that it is exceptional and that I must return to the everyday and find a way over the ditch. But that does not constitute a discontinuity in life and experience. The adventure interrupts *something*; it isn't as if it appears arbitrarily out of nowhere. If I were sitting outside just staring out into space when the antler fairy drops an antler into my lap, I probably would not have the sort of adventurous experience I'd have digging in the bank. True, if I'm modestly conscious I might take the magical appearance of an antler in my lap as an interruption of my beliefs about the existence of things. But that's the point; something would be interrupted. If I were really just sitting like a bump on a meadow, there would be nothing for the magical antler to interrupt. There would be no adventure, no real experience.

Experiences that have the quality of adventure interrupt the flow of things, but therein lies their value. In their novelty they prompt consciousness of what is "normal." They let life be felt as a whole. As noted before, experiences are irreplaceable parts of a whole life. We can see how that might happen in my example. Getting across a ditch might be an interesting and practical task, but we don't want such things to be taken to be all that life is about. My antler adventure might remind me of parts of my constellation that have been out of my sight while I focus on the immediate world around me. Engendering awe or wonder or reverence, getting "off task" might bring things within the boundaries of my constellation of prudential values and so enrich my life. But these results are unlikely unless I experience what the interruption offers, unless I treat it as something to be present with rather than as a distraction to resist.

The upshot is that educators need to be careful about what continuity amounts to. As we see with Tevye, even daydreams can be important for continuity and interaction in experience and life. There needs to be time for adventure and interruptions. At the same time, thinking of these as adventures reminds us that life cannot always be an "experience."

Interaction and continuity give us ways to think about how elements of a constellation hold together. They also give us two criteria for judging the quality of experiences and life. They are far from sufficient, though. We also need to consider whether the interactions and continuities are headed in a good direction.

"Satisfaction" is an obvious criterion to try, given my conception of well-being. We might not be able to know when the ideal satisfaction has been reached, but perhaps we can judge when one state of affairs is more satisfying than another. It's clear Evelyn was more satisfied with her life after trashing the girls' car than before. Satisfaction is tricky, though. For one thing, satisfaction isn't open-ended. When people's situations change for the better (or worse), there tends to be a short-term increase (or decrease) in satisfaction, but with time the tendency is to return to a baseline level of satisfaction that is more or less stable.[15]

Also, as I have said many times, while satisfaction is necessary for well-being, it is not sufficient. Just because a contented prostitute becomes even more contented, that alone does not show that her well-being is improving. In addition, satisfaction is not a single thing; different satisfactions have different qualities. For example, the satisfaction Evelyn got from crunching the car is different from the satisfaction Tevye got in resolving his situation with Chava. His satisfaction probably involved much less joy than Evelyn's, but that reflects a difference in the quality of the satisfaction and not only in the quantity.

The other principal component of my conception of well-being — experience — has limitations, also. I have argued that experience as awareness is necessary for well-being. So, we might count a person's increasing awareness of herself, her surroundings, and what happens to her as valuable progress. However, awareness can be an unpleasant thing, and a person can reasonably choose against it. This becomes even clearer as we move beyond a broad notion of experience as awareness to hermeneutic experience and the efforts, attitudes, and aptitudes hermeneutic experience requires. I have argued that hermeneutic experience has benefits for people in terms of attunement, accurate perception and valuing, and elevation of self, but here too people can attach different legitimate prudential value to hermeneutic experience.

Another thing to consider as a desirable ability is practical wisdom. A person who is practically wise is able to see what is good and also why it is good. He will know how and when satisfactions are appropriate, what sorts of experiences are worthwhile. This suggests a standard. Wisdom does not guarantee happiness; bad things can happen to wise people, too; but at least wise people can see clearly.

Was Evelyn practically wise? We could dispute whether she did the right thing when she crunched the girls' car. We also could dispute whether she really understood what she was doing. We could entertain the same doubts about

Tevye. I have argued that for both people we have reasons to think they did see clearly and acted correctly and with understanding, but I don't propose that my claims are clearly true. Yet, a standard does not have to yield unequivocal judgments in order to be helpful. Practical wisdom is helpful for judging people's status in their pursuit of their well-being.

However, practical wisdom presents the same problems we considered with our other proposed standards. People can be quite happy or satisfied in their lives without being especially wise, at least not wise in Aristotle's sense. It seems that practical wisdom is a relevant concern but is just one more element in the constellation of relevant concerns we have been developing.

With all this complexity (of which I have just scratched the surface), how can one begin to judge whether a life is improving in quality? Science provides an example. A common conception of progress in scientific theory is that a theory is superior to a competitor if it can explain what the competitor theory can, solve some significant range of the problems the competitor cannot, and also suggest new problems and courses for inquiry. There are no neutral criteria that somehow can adjudicate incompatible conceptions of the world or of value. Also, as a constellation of elements, any one theory will not be perfect. It will solve some problems but not others. It might create new questions and tensions. Still, one conception can emerge as better than its rival.

The superiority of one theory over another might not be clear always, but superiority can be shown, and in terms both rivals can accept. One problem that we have seen can be overcome is incommensurability. Taylor says more about the process:

> The task is not to convince someone who is undividedly and unconfusedly attached to one first principle that he ought to shift to an entirely different one. So described, it is impossible; rather, we are always trying to show that, granted what our interlocutor already accepts, he cannot but attribute to the acts or policies in dispute the significance we are urging on him.[16]

Let's imagine the task is to persuade someone that movement of her life in one way is better than another way. Taylor does not use the words in the passage given here, but when he talks about appealing "to what our interlocutor already accepts" he is talking about the sort of immanent critique, critique from within a life, that I have endorsed before. The idea is not to convince the person to progress by accepting a new "first principle." Say she believes career advancement and a better life come from being docile, while you argue that she would be better-off if she were more assertive. The dialogical move is to something both of you already accept, say that her career is important. The importance might not be construed quite the same way; so, it's incumbent on both of you to be conversant in the other's language, in the manner of a "second first language," to use MacIntyre's term.[17] The dispute ends when one of you can no longer deny that career is or isn't improved by the change contemplated, or some other factor in the constellation emerges as decisive. Maybe your interlocutor continues to believe that docility is essential for career advancement but realizes it comes at the cost of what her career was meant to serve, perhaps respect from other people or self-respect. Or maybe it becomes clear that docility will only take one so far in the corporate world.

Of course, the point is not that this provides a foolproof recipe for rational debate and change. The point is that moving from one position to another can be a rational process, even if we lack some single or neutral criterion.

We can see this sort of progress in Evelyn's and Tevye's welfare. When we discussed Evelyn we proposed that when she came to her new "Towanda theory" she was able to make sense of and solve the problems she had been suffering with. In terms we have been using, Evelyn experienced progress in fit or meaning. This was not because she created a whole new set of first principles for herself; her internal dispute was over what she already granted, such as the importance of her dignity. She got to the point where her old conception of her self simply could not solve the problems arising around her dignity. And the change was not an end point but opened up a whole new set of possibilities for her life, compared with if she had run over the girls rather than just mash their car, for example. That would do more to preclude possibilities than create them. Similarly with Tevye. His theory of how to deal with Chava may or may not have been the best one, but it could represent progress in that he was able to make sense of his problems. And perhaps we have a sense that for him, too, this is not an end but will lead him to recognize and pursue new questions about family, faith, community, and himself.

However, there are some important disanalogies between scientific progress and progress in individual well-being. Perhaps Tevye's theory makes sense for him, and perhaps he will be open to further inquiry. Because of the subject-relativity of well-being, Tevye is the authority regarding those things (defeasibly). Science is not like that. Obviously, individuals conduct scientific inquiry, but ultimately it is a social endeavor. The scientific community determines if theoretical progress is being made. Maintaining openness to and pursuit of inquiry is a communal concern. Plus, science has a particular interest in progress that individuals need not have.

I draw two conclusions here. One is that while this idea of progress is an important addition to the criteria for judging well-being, once again we cannot escape the subject-relativity of well-being and the individual as authority regarding his well-being, including whether progress is a prudential value for him. After the episode with Chava, Tevye might continue to think and progress, but then maybe not. His wife, Golde, and his daughter Tzeitel might pester him incessantly to be more accepting of Chava, but if well-being is subject-relative Tevye would be within his rights as authority of his life to resist or reject their pleas. Of course, scientists disagree with one another, and some claim they know more and better than colleagues, but neither can they claim their views are authoritative just because they are theirs. They have a responsibility for openness that Tevye need not have.

The second, related conclusion, and one we have alluded to throughout this chapter, concerns the importance of the individual's attitudes and aptitudes. Scientists need certain attitudes and aptitudes of course, but the intelligence of science is largely a community matter rather than an individual one. For well-being, though, rather more hinges on the individual's perceptions and valuations because of the individual's authority regarding her welfare. So, if Tevye is to be open to possibilities and progress, much depends on his own willingness and ability to be open and progress. Of course, people and conditions can help or hinder one's attitudes, but, again, ultimate authority and responsibility lies with the individual.

Before we leave this issue, though, let's try one other tack. Perhaps as outsiders to other persons' lives, we have limited authority to persuade them to take their lives in a particular direction. But maybe it's enough that they are progressing, or at least keeping open the possibility of progress.

What I have in mind is something like Dewey's notion of growth as the aim of education.[18] For Dewey, the essential criterion for desirable growth is that it leads to further growth. This is a helpful addition to our criteria for judging people's constellations. However, it presents the same problem as our other criteria: because of the subject-relativity of well-being it can be reasonable for people to decline to grow.[19]

Gadamer offers a helpful revision, arguing, "The truth of experience always implies an orientation toward new experience. That is why a person who is called experienced has become so not only *through* experiences but is also open *to* new experiences."[20]

The helpful revision here is that Gadamer emphasizes an "orientation" to new experience, even if growth in experience is not actively pursued. Gadamer is suggesting that the point of experience is not knowledge but openness to further experience. It is not as if Gadamer is praising ignorance, but the point of experience is not to arrive at and be content with knowledge of the world and oneself but to keep people oriented toward new experience, among the benefits of which is the possibility of knowledge, rather than mere dogma. Gadamer argues that experienced persons are "radically undogmatic."[21] We can imagine that this is the attitude of the veteran ballplayer who is present in the game. Having "seen it all" she understands she cannot be dogmatic about her preferred actions. She knows she has to be responsive to the particulars of the particular game.

So, for Evelyn and Tevye, perhaps the correctness of their actions and their understanding of them are not the only important concerns. We should look to see what their experiences open them to. Maybe their experiences are questionable and risky adventures, but even so both persons appear to emerge enriched and more insightful. If, as I have proposed, judging people's welfare is an ongoing matter, a person's openness is a vital ability and virtue. The individual needs to be open to the possibility that there might be other and better ways to live their lives.

The openness of experience is related to practical wisdom. A practically wise person knows and feels that value issues are complicated. More often than not, being dogmatic about an issue is not a good idea. Experiencing the complexities of life and value can prompt one to be open in the manner required by practical wisdom.

However, here too, there are degrees of openness, and reasonable individuals can give it differential prudential value. For example, traditional communities such as the Amish in the United States do not give high value to openness to different possibilities for living their lives, yet their lives are fulfilling for many of them. So, like the other criteria we have considered, experience and openness have limited applicability to judgments of persons' well-being.

The upshot of all this, if it isn't obvious already, is that judging people's well-being is complicated, to say the least. We look to see if they are satisfied with their lives. We look to the quality of their experiences — say, the extent to which they are present in those experiences and find them meaningful. We see whether, as people live their lives, they are able to resolve problems they face and be open to new possibilities for themselves. We see whether they are wise and open people who can perceive their world well and take advantage of opportunities presented to them.

So, normative judgment requires a plurality of relevant criteria. They form a constellation rather than a system or hierarchy. They have to work together. For example, persons might be satisfied while merely avoiding the conflicts and entanglements in their lives, or closing themselves off from new experiences, or having choices forced upon them by other people, so their satisfaction cannot be the sole criterion for judging their well-being. Yet, new meanings can be painful, and new experiences need not be worthwhile for the individual, so satisfaction still must be considered.

Griffin expresses misgivings about an eclectic approach to judgment. If the scheme I offer is eclectic, it is not haphazard, nor does it throw us back on mere intuition. A constellation is a collection of elements connected via meanings and to persons. The meanings themselves and their connections to one another are complex. For a person judging his own or others' well-being, this likely will mean judgment must consider some number of possible lives. He'll have to compare apples and oranges, for possible lives can all be fulfilling while being fundamentally different. The course of a life will be affected by chance and changes in one's self. For these reasons, the task of judging the quality of a life is an ongoing process as that life is lived.

## CONCLUSION

My argument in Part One has been that we look to "satisfying experience" as a way to capture what is central to well-being. What does this conception of well-being as satisfying experience tell us? We should note how much it doesn't tell us. Because of the subject-relativity of well-being we cannot specify what experiences people will or should find satisfying. Throughout my discussion I have used language about what people "usually" or "typically" find satisfying, but what is typical for people does not provide decisive guidance. Similarly, if we consider what experienced people find satisfying that does not imply everyone will get satisfaction from being that sort of experienced person.

However, I do not count these limitations as failures. Experience is a broad notion, but its breadth is necessary if we are to appreciate all that is involved in well-being. We still have ways to make sense of and evaluate people's conceptions of their well-being and the choices they make. This structure is not provided by a single overarching value or principle. The structure is in interaction and continuity in a complex of meanings in people's lives. These meanings are plural, but there are ways to make good judgments about value and action while crediting the plurality. Not all meanings and experiences contribute to well-being. Not all meanings fit together very well. But the solution to the normativity problem is not in arriving at some particular state of being or conception of well-being but in maintaining conditions for openness, for ongoing personal and collective inquiry into well-being.

However, the plausibility of all this hinges on the capacity of our experiences and our perceptions to provide accurate insights into ourselves and our world. Without that capacity, my conception of well-being falls back into being a purely mental state account where meanings and satisfactions are no more than "beliefs."

Central to achieving that capacity is what I have called attunement between people and the world and within individuals. I have argued that a person is unlikely to be attuned and present in the relevant sense while being divided in ways I take Griffin and Dewey to suggest — divided between understanding and desire and between perception and evaluation.

I have argued that a person present to experience is enabled to see well, and following McDowell, "there is nothing for a correct conception of doing well to be apart from [the] capacity to read situations correctly."[22] I will not recount the arguments for that claim, but the implications need our attention. To read a situation correctly does not imply infallibility or omniscience; to have a correct conception does not imply having a perfect conception. Having a conception of a dictionary as a book, which is a correct conception, does not mean there is not much more that could be said about dictionaries. But perceptions can be legitimate and responsible judgments of prudential value.

Of course, as I have noted, to see well does not mean that one always will fare well. You don't have to be nearsighted to run into obstacles and problems. But in his statement McDowell does not claim good readings guarantee good results. He says that to be able to see well is to have a correct conception of doing well.

This is only a first step in the pursuit of well-being, but it is a vital step. Nussbaum argues:

> We live amid bewildering complexities. Obtuseness and refusal of vision are our besetting vices. Responsible lucidity can be wrested from that darkness only by painful, vigilant effort, the intense scrutiny of particulars. Our highest and hardest task is to make ourselves people "on whom nothing is lost."[23]

Many things can stand in the way of people achieving well-being, but Nussbaum challenges us to think what the root cause and solution might be. The important problems will not be recognized and addressed unless we have the vision required. Given the complexities we have explored, it will take persons of keen vision, who can scrutinize particulars of head, heart, and spirit, and of the world and the goods it offers, if we as individuals and a society are to progress toward a situation where all people can have at least an adequate experience of well-being.

Well-being as satisfying experience gives us a sense of the conditions needed if this is to happen. If perception and the experiences that sharpen and manifest it are central for pursuing well-being, those ideas give us a sense for the attitudes and aptitudes people need and how they can be educated.

I look at Part One, not only as offering a conception of well-being but also proposing some of the conditions that need to be present if well-being is to be pursued productively. Part Two explores how education might provide the requisite conditions and serve well-being. In line with the way we have concluded this chapter, emphasizing capability for experience, Chapter 6 argues that education aimed at cultivating "human capabilities" is among those conditions.

PART TWO

# Implications for Education Policy and Practice

*Chapter 6*

# Perfectionism and Human Capabilities

To begin Part Two and our further discussion of education for human well-being, I reiterate my central claim: Schools should be places where people experience, or at least are given a realistic chance to experience, well-being. Schooling should not be only a preparation for well-being. The relevant people are not restricted to students, although they are of special concern, of course. Teachers and other people associated with schools should have their welfare served as well.

So stated, the claim is extremely vague. We have to consider just what it might mean to serve well-being in the context of schools. Several aims are suggested by the discussion in Part One. People need opportunities for satisfying experiences. Ideally, they will achieve attunement, presence, belonging, and the sort of perception that yields accurate insight into their world and their well-being. They will form the values, beliefs, meanings, and activities in their lives into a constellation that allows for the adventure of experience while manifesting interaction and continuity.

In Part Two, we will consider some of what might be required if those aims are to be achieved. However, because of the complexity of well-being and the importance of the particulars of different people's lives, the pursuit of well-being in education has to be an ongoing project for individual and public awareness, deliberation, wisdom, and action. Thus, a principal aim in Part Two is to understand political, social, and educational conditions where people are empowered to conceive and live fulfilling lives for themselves and to engage meaningfully in public deliberations about individual and collective welfare.

What are some the complexities we have to face? Fundamental complexities arise from the possibility that schools are limited in what they are permitted to do, ethically and politically, to serve individuals' well-being. These limitations have several sources that I introduce only briefly here but that we will explore more fully as we proceed.

One obvious source of complexity is the subject-relativity of well-being. Well-being will constitute different things for different people. This leads to practical limits on what schools can do to serve individuals' welfare. Because resources such as time and money are limited — perhaps more limited than they should be or need be — there is only so much that can be done to serve the elements of well-being unique to particular individuals.

Also, there might be aspects of a person's well-being that we have no obligation to serve even if we could. Blowing up people might be central for a terrorist's well-being, but clearly that is no reason to aid the terrorist. Less dramatic, a person's well-being might require the amount or sort of resources that go beyond what is justly hers. It might be very important to an art student that she craft metalwork that requires expensive equipment and materials, but there are ethical limits on what a school and society in general are obligated to do to serve people's expensive tastes or activities.[1]

Finally, there are liberal arguments that it is not the state's business to establish or encourage particular conceptions of well-being. For example, that is the basic idea behind the separation of church and state in the United States. Public policy should not be based on particular religious conceptions of the good, conceptions that we cannot expect all citizens to share. This does not mean the state cannot or should not help citizens live good lives, but the help provided cannot be premised on any particular conception of a good life. So, teaching children to read, for instance, does not violate liberal principles because it does not presume a particular conception of well-being. Regardless of what people's particular conceptions of value and well-being might be, they can accept the value of literacy. The ability to read can help people to develop their own conceptions of their welfare, whatever those conceptions might be.

My task in Part Two is to sort through these issues and offer some suggestions for teaching and education policy that might enable schools to better serve people's welfare. In Part One, I presented a conception of individual well-being; here we need a political conception of well-being, one that can guide public policy and action. In the face of the complexities noted here, the inclination is to look for elements that are common and basic in different individuals' well-being. Here we turn again to "objective" conceptions of well-being. Recalling Sumner's argument, objective conceptions cannot provide adequate accounts of an individual's welfare because of the subject-relativity of well-being. However, at this stage of our discussion we are not dealing with what well-being means for an individual but with the political task of coming up with a conception of well-being, or fundamentals of well-being, that can serve as a basis for public education policy.

## A HUMAN CAPABILITIES APPROACH

The principal problem we are facing is coming up with a political conception of well-being that is relevant and beneficial for all or nearly all people and that does not confine itself to an unduly limited portion of human life. "Human life" would appear to be a natural alternative to try. All persons, whatever their subjective conceptions of their well-being, live human lives,[2] and so such a conception would be relevant for all people. And such an approach would provide a comprehensive view of human life and avoid being too restricted.[3]

"Human life" is the basis for the political conception of well-being I offer. This poses a number of problems we will confront. One, mentioned earlier, is liberal concern that "human life" takes us into territory where public agents do not belong. For example, maybe there are aspects of human life, such as religion, that educators should be neutral about, should avoid both promoting and discouraging.

This and other objections will get a fuller treatment later, but for now this liberal concern offers a chance to present the second main component of my political conception, which is that "capabilities" are the focus of education for well-being. The basic idea is that people should receive an education that will make them capable of experiencing a satisfying life. This provides some response to liberal concerns because capabilities are abstract and incomplete.[4] Keeping aims vague or abstract enables us to identify important goods while refraining from taking stands on particular forms of that good. So, for example, we can say spirituality is an important prudential good people should be capable of experiencing without also dictating that people experience spirituality through religion or some other particular way, or even that all individuals must be spiritual in order to have a satisfying life. Also, we need not claim that any particular set of capabilities or other goods is complete. It is enough that the set captures some adequate core that is essential to anyone's life.

So, with a capabilities approach educators need not dictate what sort of life people should lead. The idea is that people will be capable of a good choice for whatever sort of life they wish to have. Also, the capabilities approach offers a response to the problem of limited resources. Schools do not have to be all things to all people; they can confine their purposes to a limited number of fundamental capabilities.

I will use Martha Nussbaum's capabilities approach as a starting point for our inquiry. Nussbaum offers a list of ten "central human functional capabilities": life; bodily health; bodily integrity; senses, imagination, and thought; emotions; practical reason; affiliation; relations with other species; play; and control over one's political and material environment.[5] I will not defend the particulars of Nussbaum's list. She herself does not claim it is final. Yet her list at least moves in the right direction. We have discussed already the importance of play and emotions. It is not difficult to see that being able to take care of one's health and to protect one's body from violation are fundamentally important abilities. Practical reason is vital if people are to conceptualize and experience well-being, as is the practical freedom to control one's environment.

However, there are a couple of basic matters we should explore: the value of a capabilities approach in general, and the value of capabilities based upon the nature of human beings in particular. Let's consider the latter issue first.

## PERFECTIONISM AND HUMAN CAPABILITIES

Following Arneson, I will call a theory of well-being, such as mine, based in the nature of human beings, a "perfectionist" theory. Such a theory holds that "what is good for its own sake for a person is fixed independently of her attitudes and opinions toward it,"[6] and that this prudential good is "fixed" by human nature or activities and meanings characteristic of human life. I need to take some time to explore the significance of this approach, not only to show its merits but also to show how it is consistent with previous claims I have made.

For one thing, as the word "perfectionism" appears to imply, the aim is some perfect form of life, but I have contended that the "imperfections" of people's lives can be some of the greatest contributors to well-being. Some perfectionists argue that perfection should be the aim. For example, Hurka argues that perfectionism implies maximization: "We would not say of someone who was content with a reasonable development of his talents that he aimed at 'excellence' or was dedicating to 'perfecting' himself . . . [A] concern for human development goes naturally with a maximizing approach."[7] Here, although Hurka does not claim that there is one form of perfection, he does propose that perfection is the aim, such that a person who found satisfaction in "reasonable development" of his talents is making a mistake. Educators say such a thing to students all the time: "Always try to do your best"; "Don't just be good; be excellent." But that is bad advice. To live a good life, most of us cannot do our best in everything; we have to be selective. In addition, if maximization is the aim, that could justify differential distribution of resources to those people who have the best chance of maximizing excellence in their lives. That also is dubious.

If I reject maximization, perhaps the conception I am advancing is not really perfectionist. I have no special attachment to "perfectionist" as a label; if I need a different label, so be it. However, perfectionism is a complex position, and it is possible to tease apart at least a couple of elements of it. For instance, the principal reason I adopt "perfectionist" as a descriptor of my position is my "concern for human development." And I believe we can coherently speak in terms of the perfection of a life (if it's important to do so) without having to endorse maximization.

We already have considered one part of my argument with the distinction between "best" as an absolute superlative and as a relative superlative. In the present context, the point is that a person can live a best life (absolutely) without living the best of all possible lives (relatively), so in that sense maximization need not be the aim. Even if seeking a best life in the absolute sense is not the same as seeking perfection, the distinction at least allows us to agree with Hurka that there can be a problem when people are content with less than the best.

At the same time, there could be a relevant sense of maximization even if we think of "best" in absolute terms, but then we have to consider exactly what is to be maximized. If we think of an excellent life not as a "perfect" human life but as one well suited to the individual with all of his or her particular abilities, aspirations, and frailties, then a "maximized" life is one best suited to that individual and perhaps even an exemplar to others. That is what characters such as Tevye, Evelyn Couch, and Charlie Allnutt show us. These characters are not "perfect," but in spite of that — or because of that — they illustrate human life lived well. The aim of educating people in human capabilities is not some perfect specimen of a human being but to enable people to conceive and live a satisfying life.

However, there is another problem. I need to explain how my subject-relative conception of well-being is consistent with the objectivity implied in a theory of prudential value based on human nature or human functioning. My subject-relative conception of well-being holds that a person's welfare is not independent of her attitudes of favor and disfavor, so I might appear to make contradictory claims.

The apparent contradiction can be resolved if we note the ambiguity in "good for a person" and that the independence from and dependence on attitudes apply at different levels. (The ambiguity in "good for its own sake" also needs attention, and we will get into that later.) Recalling the discussion of reasons in Chapter 3, I argued that reasons have an external quality. So, for instance, "that would be an accomplishment" provides a normative reason for someone to do the thing independent of the person's attitudes; "accomplishment" is a beneficial thing, a human sort of thing. However, an individual's attitudes and understandings are relevant in a couple of ways. As I argued before, one's attitudes are important if the force of the reason is to be perceived and felt. Also, one's attitudes are relevant to what one considers an accomplishment. People do not pursue "accomplishment"; they pursue particular things that might or might not count as accomplishments. Or, to give another example, in terms of one of Nussbaum's capabilities, the argument is that play has prudential value independent of individuals' attitudes, yet that does not guarantee individuals will experience the prudential value of play or agree on what counts as play or make play central in their well-being.

There are other possible objections to a perfectionist view. One might dispute the claim that there is a human nature, given the variety of ways human beings live their lives. Of course human life manifests a great deal of diversity, and any reasonable judgment of the quality of people's lives must include attention to values more or less particular to their culture.[8] However, at least many of these differences can be attributed to different manifestations of common capabilities. Nussbaum constructs her list of capabilities in part from her work in India. Hindus, for example, might have particular relations with other species that carnivorous Christians do not, yet many of the latter get joy from pets, wildlife, gardening, and searching for extraterrestrials. So, while the particular relations with other species might differ, there is a shared aim and capability.[9]

Or consider the Ifaluk again. The Ifaluk highly value affiliation and control of their political and material environment and devote a good deal of time and energy to those things, although that control and affiliation might be much more a matter of ritual and custom than in our Western mobile, technological society. That sort of difference is fully consistent with Nussbaum's approach.

There might be cases that are particularly challenging. Take the Aztecs' practice of human sacrifice, for example. That practice might be considered inhuman. Perhaps we could propose that the Aztecs were simply showing a common human need for protein, but that would be "wildly reductivistic."[10] Yet we can search for other more fruitful aspects of a common humanness, such as religiosity and spirituality.

However, there might be the fear that the ways some people exercise common capabilities will be considered inferior to other ways. It surely is possible to use "human nature" to categorize people as superior and inferior. Even if we can understand the Aztecs, they could be, and perhaps should be, considered barbarous. As part of their specious justification for persecuting Jews, the Nazis denied Jews were human. Less extreme, Plato and Aristotle proposed that well-being consisted in exercising what is supposedly the highest part of our humanity — namely, our contemplative intellect or theoretical rationality. In light of that, the Ifaluk might be deemed "backward" and "primitive" in how they control their environment and in other ways.

This "higher/lower" issue is a basic one that will get fuller attention in Chapter 8. Perfectionists do hold that discriminations can and should be made about the quality of different activities and human lives. Some sorts of life are good; others are not. In light of that, people might fear from perfectionists an imperialistic impulse to impose capabilities on poor benighted people "for their own good." However, as will be argued more fully later, a perfectionist approach does not dictate what actions need to be taken when people have mistaken notions of well-being. The approach does tell us we should be concerned, but it is difficult to see how that is inappropriate.

If there are dangers in using humanity as a standard, there is also a powerful positive appeal in it. Many oppressed persons state their demands for justice in terms of being recognized as human beings. And even if people do not state their demands that way, or do not even ask for humane treatment, Nussbaum's capabilities give us grounds for aiding them. Recall the "happy" prostitutes mentioned in Chapter 1. At the very least, Nussbaum's capabilities provide grounds to question the idea that these women's lives are "better from the inside" just because they are able to find some satisfactions in their lives. The capabilities of bodily health and integrity clearly are jeopardized there. Those capabilities give us grounds for understanding and responding to the dehumanizing conditions in which those women are trapped.

There are dangers in appealing to our shared humanity, but the response is not to dispense with that appeal but to be careful how we construe our humanity and how we try to improve people's lives. I set that matter aside for now. I need to do more to present and explain the capabilities approach I propose.

## CAPABILITIES FOR THE EXPERIENCE OF WELL-BEING

In light of the conception of well-being I offer in Part One, Nussbaum's list needs two additions: capability for satisfaction and capability for experience. It may be that the things Nussbaum lists are the sort of things that tend to engender satisfaction, but, if I am correct in my claim about the necessity of "the prudential point of view," we cannot assume people will experience the satisfactions of those activities and states of affairs. Of course, as I noted in

Chapter 1, Nussbaum denies that satisfaction is the central aim for our and others' well-being. Again, while I agree that it is not sufficient, I do contend satisfaction is necessary and is a capability that can and should be educated. So, I count "satisfaction" as a capability that merits explicit attention.

It could be protested that satisfaction is different in kind from capabilities subject to political guarantees, which are the sort of capabilities Nussbaum advocates. For example, while it is reasonable to expect the state to guarantee its citizens adequate opportunities for health — by subsidizing health care, providing health education, inspecting and regulating food and drugs — and for leisure time and play — by regulating the length of the work week and the minimum wage — guaranteeing opportunities for satisfaction might appear more problematic. People find their satisfaction in all sorts of ways; it might seem impossible to identify a capability for satisfaction relevant for all people. There could be positive reasons against seeking such a capability because it might risk favoring some people's satisfactions over others.

However, these problems are not as severe as they might first appear. The political guarantee is not that people will be satisfied but that they will be provided adequate opportunities for being capable of satisfaction. The same thing is true of Nussbaum's capabilities. We might guarantee access to health care, for instance, but that does not guarantee people will be healthy or use health care services. In Chapter 1, we considered the dangers in claiming a right to the pursuit of happiness, but the problem is not in the idea of such a right but in what people take the right to imply. When we consider the basic requirements for finding satisfaction — the prudential point of view, the ability to find meanings and continuities in one's life — it is reasonable to expect the state, through its schools and other agencies, to promote the knowledge, skills, and attitudes needed.

However, we might grant that point but suppose that a capability for satisfaction is redundant with or subsumed by one or more other capabilities, such as practical reason and emotion. But while a capability for satisfaction depends on other capabilities, being able to exercise those capabilities does not imply one will get satisfaction from them. Capability for satisfaction is not redundant with Nussbaum's capabilities.

In addition to the capability for satisfaction, another capability should be added: hermeneutic experience merits explicit acknowledgment as a basic human capability. For example, while I have emphasized that emotions, senses, imagination, and thought — things included in Nussbaum's list — are important components of experience, to have emotions and so on does not imply one will experience emotion and other things in the sense of being present with and to them. One can affiliate while not experiencing affiliation in the hermeneutic sense. Here, too, there are particular capabilities for experience — such as presence — and they are not redundant with Nussbaum's capabilities. As I have acknowledged, hermeneutic experience might not be necessary for well-being, but it is something people should be capable of.

However, if such experience is unnecessary for well-being, that presents another possible problem. Nussbaum sees all her capabilities as necessary. If we emphasize unnecessary capabilities we raise again issues of what public schools reasonably can be expected to do. There are all sorts of nice things we might like schools to do, but they cannot do everything. Also, we again raise liberal concerns about promoting a particular conception of welfare, one based on hermeneutic experience.

I do not see these objections as especially strong. On the one hand, there is any number of things schools rightly provide that are not clearly necessities. On the other hand, if capability for hermeneutic experience is an aim it surely would take education in a particular direction, yet it does not dictate a particular conception of well-being. People can choose all sorts of things to experience — baseball, art, internal-combustion engines, even algebra. The point is that they should be able to experience these things in the full way implied in hermeneutic experience. That is not an unreasonable aim. I take it that it already is an aim many teachers have, to provide students the chance to experience their subject matter deeply.

Capabilities for satisfaction and experience merit inclusion in a list of basic capabilities, but we might try taking the issue even further. Given the importance I have attributed to satisfaction and experience, we might suppose they are not just additions to Nussbaum's list but should have a privileged place among capabilities. I resist that move, though, because the relationships among the capabilities are too complex. For example, life without satisfaction is bleak, but satisfaction is impossible without life. Experience and satisfaction are not free-floating capabilities but occur in and with play, affiliation, emotion, and so forth. In that sense, experience and satisfaction are dependent on those latter capabilities; yet the prudential value of the capability for play and other things is realized fully only if one experiences them and their satisfactions.

While I believe Nussbaum's human capabilities approach needs revision, it provides a promising starting point. However, as we have noted and Nussbaum acknowledges, it is vague. That is not all bad. However, a list of such vague items does leave us with several questions beyond those regarding the content of the list. So, let us push the question of just how much guidance a capabilities approach provides.

## CULTIVATING CAPABILITIES: BASIC QUESTIONS

One question concerns the point at which a capability is adequately developed, where adequacy is a matter not only of what individuals need and are capable of but also of what justice permits or requires. Perfect health is not necessary for well-being, but what is adequate health and adequate capability for health? For example, does a person's unhealthy lifestyle show she is capable of health but chooses something else? Or does it show that her capability for health was not adequately developed, because if it were she would not choose an unhealthy lifestyle? Even if we were to decide that the capability was inadequately developed in that sense, it might be adequate in the sense that it is the most that can be done within the constraints of justice.

Another basic issue is whether all the capabilities must be provided for all people. As I just mentioned, Nussbaum argues that they should. She bases this on a principle of respect for persons as equal citizens; all citizens are owed certain capabilities, even if we know that some capabilities will not be used.[11] For example, some people might forgo adequate nutrition because they believe physical beauty requires they be excessively thin. But, Nussbaum argues, we would disrespect these people if we "withheld from them the conditions of adequate nutrition and health care."[12]

However, there is a difference between withholding conditions for developing and exercising capabilities compared with giving people the chance to opt out of opportunities provided for them. The issue is especially pertinent for schools and other education agencies, for even if we were to agree with Nussbaum that people should develop all relevant capabilities, there remains the question of where those capabilities are to be developed. Must schools take responsibility for all the capabilities?

In addition, our concern for experience, presence, and belonging provides a reason to limit the range of capabilities addressed. Presence with some subject matter or capability could require focused, long-term commitment to some more or less particular subject matter or capability. If that is the case, experiencing presence might necessitate students forgo or minimize capabilities in other areas. In doing so, however, might they miss something important?

Thinking about what students actually do in school in terms of studies and choices brings us to a final issue regarding capabilities: Is it really sufficient that people develop capabilities for functioning, or must people actually function?[13] I have claimed that school should not only be about preparing students for well-being but also be a place where students actually experience well-being. So, it would appear that it is not enough that students be capable of well-being but that in school they actually experience well-being and function in ways that are worthwhile and satisfying to them.

Also, before, we breezed quickly over the idea that people should have the right to be unhealthy; our responsibility extends only to making them capable of health. But that is a troublesome idea. For example, given the precarious state of the health care system in the United States, perhaps citizens have some obligation to try to be healthy, for the sake of other citizens if not for themselves, so as not to be an unnecessary drain on scarce resources. So, here too, we might wonder if actual functioning is the aim and not just capability for functioning.

The issue is particularly urgent when we come to the education of young people. Perhaps for adults it is sufficient that they are capable of health and other things, but for youth perhaps we have the obligation to see to it that they really are healthy, at least to some adequate degree and for some period of time. Kids might eat junk food at home, but schools are not required to make it available.

Finally, and perhaps most basic, how can one learn to be capable of some thing without functioning with the thing? How can a child become capable of affiliation, for instance, unless he has practice actually affiliating with people?

Nussbaum emphasizes capabilities rather than functioning in order to meet liberal concerns about promoting particular ways of life, but educators have to help or even compel students to function. And that raises liberal questions all over again. For the sake of children's health, what do we teach them about sexual health, for example? With what sort of material do we ask them to function? Should they practice how to put on a condom? For the sake of developing students' practical reason, how far do we go to have them function with important but controversial issues? What about the lessons students might learn from the example of Evelyn Couch? Of course, I do not advocate that students function by actually ramming people's cars (although perhaps they could take field trips to bumper car rides), but maybe for the sake of healthy emotional life and controlling their environment students should function with an example such as Evelyn and ponder whether her car-ramming was a proper manifestation of emotion and influencing her environment. For the sake of affiliation, how far do we go to have children of different race, sex and sexuality, religion, interests, and abilities actually function with people different from themselves? For example, what, if anything, do we do about parents who homeschool their children in order to keep them away from people who are different? Or, what, if anything, should be done about same-sex schools, where affiliation is restricted in some sense but where the aim also is to improve affiliations, for young women for instance, whose affiliations in a mixed-gender school might not benefit them?

## CONCLUSION

In this chapter we sought a political conception of well-being to guide education. "Human capabilities" are at the center of the conception proposed. However, even if we accept this approach, we have seen that numerous difficult and persistent questions face us. If we as educators and citizens are serious about serving people's welfare, we cannot be content with the sort of simplistic prescriptions for education policy and conduct that are so prevalent nowadays. The issues we face are too important, complicated, and controversial for that. We need to establish conditions where meaningful and productive public deliberation can occur and where meaningful progress can be made in helping students and others experience well-being.

My principal task in the next two chapters is to show how these political, deliberative aims are consistent with and attainable within the perfectionist framework I have begun to describe. Already I have suggested, very roughly and tentatively, that a perfectionist approach to well-being in education can meet liberal objections. In the next chapters I will do more to develop the argument. I will argue that perfectionist deliberation has the potential to lead to a vibrant political climate where educators (and other state agents) are enabled to serve their ultimate responsibility — promoting the well-being of the human beings with whom they live and work.[14] This does not require the sacrifice of personal freedom and political stability; indeed, it can enhance freedom and stability.

*Chapter 7*

# Perfectionism, Liberalism, and Political Deliberation

My aim in this chapter is to begin to explain and explore what political perfectionism implies for public deliberation. The main theme is how political perfectionism can respond to the challenges that come from liberal political theory.[1] Rawls's basic question is, "How is it possible that there may exist over time a stable and just society of free and equal citizens profoundly divided by reasonable though incompatible religious, philosophical, and moral doctrines?"[2] His answer is that such a society is possible only if politics is appropriately neutral regarding the doctrines that divide people. He argues that perfectionist politics would lead to loss of freedom and stability.

I will challenge Rawls's claims. However, I want to begin my response by being clear that in the conception of politics I offer here, I see liberalism as an ally of perfectionism in a pluralistic, dialectical approach to public deliberation about education. So, perhaps I can label my view "liberal perfectionism" or "perfectionist liberalism."[3]

## LIBERAL PERFECTIONISM, PERFECTIONIST LIBERALISM

The perfectionist politics I propose shares the same basic goal with liberal politics: To establish a political environment that provides for all people their best chance to live well, within the constraints of justice. The approaches diverge in what they believe the proper political environment to be. Liberals will tend toward an environment that is more or less neutral regarding conceptions of

a good life. Perfectionists will tend toward an environment where some conceptions of a good life, or particular goods, are encouraged by the state, even
at the expense of others. The burden of my argument is to show how that sort
of environment is desirable and workable. Perhaps the biggest challenge is the
qualifier "within the constraints of justice."

Perfectionists themselves see dangers in perfectionism as a single-principle
approach to ethics and politics. Hurka, himself a perfectionist, concludes that
pure perfectionism "does not guarantee individual rights . . . or place other constraints on the pursuit of good consequences."[4] So, he entertains the possibility
that perfectionism at most can be only a part of a more complex ethical-political
theory. Similarly, my aim here is not to dispense with liberal concerns but to
see how they can be met or incorporated in a theory of public deliberation that
gives perfectionism a prominent role.

Even so, I believe Taylor is correct when he faults liberals, such as Rawls, for
encouraging "extraordinary inarticulacy" about the good because they tend
to "banish discussions about the good life to the margins of political debate."[5]
Even if many liberal concerns are legitimate, as I believe they are, educators still
cannot afford to take a neutral stance that would put issues of well-being out
of bounds. People's welfare is at stake, and if a neutral stance is taken, beyond
stunting public debate of education, in effect it surrenders the field to a few
articulate — or at least vocal — people who are more than happy to pronounce
on issues of the good. And people listen to them. We might bemoan that fact
and criticize the illiberal tendencies of education policies enacted and proposed,
but if liberal-minded people are unwilling or unable to meet proponents of
these policies on the perfectionist field of play I have to wonder whether effective replies or resistance can be marshaled.

Questions of the good are inescapable. Perhaps things like reading and writing can be considered neutral or objective values in the sense that they can be
widely endorsed. But tax cuts, NASCAR, and sugarless chewing gum are widely
endorsed, too. That fact hardly determines the value of those things. Even if
the curriculum and other policies educators choose to emphasize are neutral
in the sense of being widely endorsed, they are not neutral in their impact on
students, teachers, and society. What we choose to emphasize and de-emphasize
will shape people's conceptions of prudential value and the opportunities they
have to enact them.[6] Governments and communities make decisions about "the
good" all the time and in the face of dissent. These policies can be perfectly
appropriate. If that is true, the issue must not be that judgments of what is good
cannot guide public policy but that perfectionists must require some sort of
unjustifiable processes or policies.

What exactly does perfectionism demand or imply politically? How, within a perfectionist framework, can we protect freedom, justice, and other liberal values? Liberals argue that the state must be neutral (more or less) about the good. Before getting into the case for perfectionism, let's consider what neutrality might entail.

## POLITICAL NEUTRALITY

We might contend that neutrality requires that all reference to goods or ideals be excluded from political deliberations.[7] Whether some conception of the good is true or false, reasonable or unreasonable, is no concern for the state and its agents. Instead, the state should do what it should to help satisfy people's wants. The wants might be silly or ill-advised, but that has no bearing so far as political action is concerned. If the want is identified in some fair and accurate way, a school could institute it and still be appropriately neutral, taking no position on the value of the want.

This is the sort of view taken by advocates of a market approach to value. The idea is that what people value, prefer, desire, and so on will be formed through a competition among possibilities. The things that "sell" will be the things people value, or, if we admit that the "best sellers" might not give us a completely accurate picture of people's values, at least they provide the proper neutral basis for state action.[8]

Given the subject-relativity of well-being, educators, indeed, should be sensitive to individuals' wants. However, proper regard for individual freedoms and democratic processes does not require excluding conceptions of the good and well-being from political deliberation.

We have already considered one reason to question the exclusion of goods. Well-being does not consist of having wants satisfied but experiencing things that genuinely are good. People do not want to just believe or hope they are doing well; they want to truly do well. Maybe there can be times and reasons for being content with false beliefs, but usually people do not want to live in a world of make-believe, and it is not in their interest to do so.

However, if it is undesirable to exclude conceptions of the good from political deliberations, we might still want the state to be neutral in some other way. For example, the state might encourage particular goods, but only those about which an "overlapping consensus" can be achieved.[9] By furthering those goods the state is not giving an advantage to any particular conception of the good and so is neutral in that sense. For some liberals, this is the sort of response needed in the face of intractable disagreements about the good. The neutrality liberals seek need not be "pure"; neutrality is a matter of degree.[10] Clearly, Rawls does not advocate exclusion of ideals. He says that in justice there is an integration of the right and the good.[11] The liberal concern is that deliberation and policies be neutral enough about the good, or neutral in an appropriate way.

As I will argue, perfectionists can endorse some sort of political neutrality. Clearly, they will not countenance exclusion of ideals; but there are other sorts or degrees of neutrality. Here let's turn to the exploration of perfectionist politics.

## DELIBERATION AND ADJUDICATION

I'll start by dividing the political process into two different aspects. One aspect is deliberation. One fault Rawls sees in perfectionism is that it is destructive of fair and productive deliberation. I will dispute Rawls's claim, but we do have reason to wonder whether public debates about policy are a good venue for such a wide-ranging and complex issue as well-being.[12] Greenawalt imagines political debates leading to "acrimony, a hardening of lines, and less fruitful interchange about . . . comprehensive views."[13] It might be more productive to restrict discussion of comprehensive views to other venues or times — over coffee at the local diner — when action on particular policies is not at stake. We can see the sense in Greenawalt's point. For instance, if debate about laws restricting or outlawing gay marriage is carried on in terms of comprehensive views such as religious views, we can easily see how acrimony can arise; it has arisen. I imagine many of us shudder at the thought of legislators defending or attacking policies on the basis of what they claim their religion demands of them, excusing their parochial, self-righteous actions by passing them off as taking a "moral" stance.

There is another component of politics, also. Politics is not only about talking. Decisions have to be made, policies enacted, and actions taken. As Strike states the problem with perfectionism:

> At the end of the day, after we have debated what is good, perfectionists will want a collective and reasonable decision about whose view of the good is to prevail. For liberals of a Rawlsian sort, that there are dissenters is a reason why we should avoid such decisions. Society is characterized by durable pluralism. No perfectionist view will be big-tented enough to accommodate this diversity and no amount of talk will produce consensus. Perfectionists will wish to decide what the moral basis of our fundamental institutions is to be despite this durable disagreement.[14]

The supposed problem is that even if perfectionist political deliberation is fair, at the end of the day deliberation will not produce consensus; however, perfectionists will want to enact particular policies despite the fact that there is durable disagreement about them. The gist of the criticism is that perfectionists underrate the persistence and significance of moral diversity, with the result that they will assume or seek to establish a "moral basis of our fundamental institutions" that is illegitimate and destructive because it excludes or marginalizes some people in the political process due to their dissent from the conception of good or well-being that serves as the basis of institutions. When a conception of the good is imposed on people, their dignity is at stake, respect for them as free, self-determining agents. The danger is singularly acute when the imposition is exercised or supported by the coercive power of the state.

Strike is right that perfectionists are not content just to talk about issues. They will see adjudication as a legitimate and important political activity. That is, they will make discriminations between better and worse conceptions of good and well-being and work to see that the better ones are instituted and the worse ones eliminated or discouraged. So the question becomes how this can be done without violating principles of freedom and justice and prompting destructive acrimony. Here, too, I believe perfectionists have strong responses. In the remainder of this chapter I will examine political deliberation. Adjudication is the focus of the next chapter.

## THE AIMS OF PERFECTIONIST DELIBERATION

To begin, I respond to two statements Strike makes about perfectionist aims in the passage given earlier. That will help us understand the perfectionist politics I offer.

First, Strike supposes that perfectionists want to decide "the moral basis of our fundamental institutions," where that basis is skewed toward some particular conception of a good life. However, there is considerable ambiguity in that charge, in what sort of "basis" this might be and what a "fundamental institution" is. One fundamental institution to consider, and one that Rawls is especially concerned about, is the "constitution," the statement of fundamental civil rights, governmental procedures, and so forth. Liberals argue that the constitution should be neutral regarding conceptions of the good.

However, neutrality can apply at two different political levels.[15] On one hand, we could propose that politics must be neutral through and through; not only must the constitution be neutral but also political deliberation must be neutral. On the other hand, though, politics need not be neutral through

and through. Politics could be neutral in the sense that constitutional fundamentals are neutral regarding the good but that some conceptions of the good
still can come to be favored in and through the political process. Again, there
are examples where this occurs. One is Griffin's example of trees planted along
Parisian boulevards. In that case, aesthetic values are favored over other possible
values, like traffic safety. Federal support for the arts and municipal support
for public libraries and mass transit are other examples. Some people might
object to promoting these goods at the expense of others, but at least part of
the justification for favoring such goods is that they were determined through
a fair political process. The neutrality of the process might be guaranteed by the
constitution, but it is acceptable that the outcome of the process is non-neutral
regarding certain goods.

Perfectionists need not be concerned to decide the moral basis of fundamental institutions if that means particular conceptions of the good and well-being
must be privileged at the constitutional level — say, that being a Christian or
an atheist is required to hold public office. In fact, as I will explain shortly,
perfectionists have reason to support constitutional neutrality. However, perfectionists still could insist on a constitution that allows for state support for
particular goods, but it is unclear that asks for anything beyond the sorts of
support that exist already and for support that is inappropriately non-neutral.

We might wonder, however, whether this separation between politics at the
constitutional level and at the broader deliberative level really can be maintained.
Similar to what Longino describes for the conduct of science, we should not
think that values constitutive of science, the principles that define the practice
of science, are immune to the influence of external social and political currents
and demands.[16] Those trends can affect what is deemed good science.

Along the same lines, we should not be complacent about the separation
between the values constitutive of liberal democracy, as embodied in the constitution, and the broader political milieu. Perhaps one obvious and crass example
in the United States is the attempt to build a definition of marriage into state
and federal constitutions. Of course, constitutions provide for amendments,
so there is nothing wrong *per se* with constitutional changes. The issue is what
changes are made and how those changes are made, whether conceptions of
the good can play a legitimate part.

Also, there is a difference between deliberation leading to formation of social
policy and to enshrining particular policies in the constitution. Defining marriage is not a constitutional issue. Of course, there are people who deny that,
but, again, it seems to me the best reply to them needs to incorporate reasons
of good and well-being as well as liberal appeals to rights.

Yet, we still might have doubts. This brings me to the second statement Strike makes, that perfectionists will want to dictate "whose conception of the good will prevail." Simply phrasing the issue as "whose" conception of the good will prevail distorts the issue in two ways. First, it implies that the aim is for one conception of the good to dominate all others. Strike compares perfectionism to a theocracy.[17] As I have suggested already and will explain further later, perfectionists can value a plurality of conceptions of good and well-being and support people's freedom to choose from among those conceptions.[18]

The second, related distortion is that the "whose" conception language implies that perfectionists must be parochial and suggests deliberation must be a battle over "whose" conceptions of the good will win out. Rawls, too, writes consistently as if perfectionists must be concerned to institute particular — that is, their own — conceptions of well-being. However, human capabilities are values that do not belong to anyone in particular. The question is "what" conception or conceptions of the good will prevail, not "whose."

My response might seem rather too slick. There will be disputes about the value of particular putative goods, particular conceptions of well-being, particular manifestations of the capabilities. There, "whose" values might be a more legitimate issue. Even so, if perfectionists are true to perfectionist aims they will not endorse conceptions of the good only because they are, at the moment, theirs; they will endorse them because they have reason to believe the conceptions genuinely are good. So, perfectionists have an interest in impartiality or neutrality that has at least some affinity with what liberals seek. Perfectionists can agree that principles of justice should not favor particular conceptions of the good, conceptions that might be erroneous or not exhaust the good lives that are possible.

In political deliberations perfectionists can recognize that different conceptions of well-being all might have a legitimate claim to being genuinely good conceptions. The aim of deliberation then need not be to eliminate conceptions that differ from one's own but to learn something from them.

Also, if by "conception of the good" we mean a comprehensive conception of what is good or what a good life entails, then Strike's description of perfectionism is at least somewhat off target, because perfectionists need not be concerned to pass judgment on whole conceptions of a good life. Perfectionists are concerned about comprehensive conceptions of a good life in the sense of conceptions that capture a wide range of elements of human life; the human capabilities approach aims to do that. But perfectionists can be more concerned that human capabilities are developed and less concerned how the capabilities are manifested and the priority particular ones are given.

That isn't to say that when goods are disputed perfectionists won't aim to have certain conceptions of good and well-being, or aspects of conceptions, prevail. (I'll say more about that in the next chapter.) But it is difficult to see how that must be inappropriate. For example, as discussed in Chapter 1, some people might doubt that play is a good or important aspect of schooling. However, there are strong reasons to believe that play should be an important activity in schools. People might continue to disagree, but it is difficult to see why the mere fact of disagreement must prevent implementation of well-justified policies.

Of course, there could be issues much more controversial than the value of play; for example, whether the capability of health requires that youth know how to use contraception. However, to consider the wisdom of premarital sex and contraception hardly necessitates claims that either abstinence or pre-marital sex makes an entire life good or bad. Or if homophobes persist in their opposition to gay marriage for religious reasons or other reasons we need not condemn their entire religious way of life. The reply to their opposition is that religion does not provide adequate reasons for condemning homosexuality; but that does not imply a religious life cannot be good. We can endorse the care, commitment, and other goods that exist in any good marriage, homosexual or heterosexual, goods that many religions espouse.

To this point, I have sketched some of the basics of my perfectionist politics. I have suggested that perfectionist deliberation is desirable, but I must do a good deal more to make the argument for that. For example, a pluralist perfectionism implies some degree of openness, but it is not clear just how far that openness goes. Before pursuing the desirability question further, though, let's ask a "practical" question: Even if perfectionist deliberation were desirable, is it workable?[19]

## IS PERFECTIONIST POLITICAL DELIBERATION WORKABLE?

Rawls charges that applying perfectionist principles

> tends to be politically unworkable. For if the elaborate theoretical calculations involved in applying their principles are publicly admitted in questions of political justice, the highly speculative nature and enormous complexity of these calculations are bound to make citizens with opposing views and interests highly suspicious of one another's arguments . . . The information they presuppose is difficult if not impossible to obtain, and often there are insuperable problems in reaching an objective and agreed assessment.[20]

But deliberation about goods and well-being is not as difficult as Rawls supposes. If the perfectionist aim were to encourage only those conceptions of the good that are best in the relative sense, then perhaps fine-grained, complex calculations would be needed. However, working with what we have called the absolute sense of good, perfectionists need no more than some modest ordinal ranking of "best," "good but less than the best," and "not good." There might be some difficult cases at the margins of these categories, but most judgments need not be highly elaborate. That people might disagree about specific rankings within the broad categories does not preclude agreement on what belongs in the categories. For example, the fine arts have had a hard time finding a place in school curricula lately. I think we would be hard-pressed, though, to find people who deny that the arts are part of a best life, even as they believe other things have to be ranked higher in terms of education priorities. Where agreement about what is best or good does not exist, perfectionists can acknowledge that and the limitations it puts on implementing public policies. (I will say more about that later.)

It is also unclear that the human capabilities of bodily integrity, affiliation, and so on are "highly speculative." Again, deliberation can be about more or less specific values, such as human capabilities, rather than whole conceptions of well-being. Greenawalt's concerns, presented earlier, were about debates regarding comprehensive views such as religious views, but deliberation need not be aimed at passing judgment on whole ways of life.

## POLITICAL STABILITY

However, we also have Rawls's claim, noted at the beginning of this chapter, that deliberation at this level of comprehensive views is destabilizing. Wong presents a similar claim that

> [d]isagreement with others on the level of the most general and comprehensive principles may be radical, while on the more concrete levels where we consider what can be done now, given the present circumstances, and given what has already happened, disagreement may be less severe because everyone's options have been narrowed.[21]

So, Wong's advice is that disagreements on the level of general and comprehensive principles should be avoided. His concern is similar to Rawls's concern about comprehensive religious, philosophical, and moral doctrines that are incompatible.

We can acknowledge the value of such a move. And it is consistent with inquiry into comprehensive views of well-being that is our ultimate concern. The contribution is not direct, but if "concrete" bits of life can be implemented and tested, what we learn can be accumulated and might do much to provide insight into conceptions of well-being that embody them.

Still, it is not clear that the move toward the concrete must be the preferred move. For instance, if sex education is being debated, a move to a "concrete" issue — whether schools should provide contraception — might result in consensus, but it is not difficult to imagine how that particular issue could cause more controversy rather than less. It is possible that a move to greater generality would reduce the severity of disagreement. In Chapter 5 we encountered Taylor's point that disputes are resolved on the basis of issues and values disputants accept. For example, in education there might be conflict between perspectives that emphasize teacher authority in students' well-being and perspectives that emphasize student freedom. Disputants still might be able to agree or remember that their shared concern is student well-being; controversy is not the same thing as conflict of interests.[22] Disputants still might be able to agree on the value of practical reason, for instance, even as they disagree on the role of teacher authority and student freedom in its realization. Or if, for instance, some people appeal to religious reasons for emphasizing teacher authority, that perspective might well add to the richness and civility of the discussion. (Another claim that gets more attention later.)

Charles Larmore endorses a similar move.[23] Larmore's view is that to achieve proper neutrality in the face of disagreement, each disputant "should prescind from the beliefs that the other rejects."[24] This move need not be toward the concrete but simply toward whatever beliefs the disputants might share. This does not require one be neutral in the sense of doubting the truth of one's own view on the contested belief; one simply sets that belief aside in order to keep conversation going or to seek reasons that can persuade the other party.[25] Perfectionists can endorse this sort of neutrality; it is simply a principle of reasonable public deliberation.

Granted, finding common ground at some more or less general level leaves the concrete issues of education policy and instruction to be resolved. But a move toward generality is not just dodging important issues but can serve to focus attention on the fundamental issue — well-being. Disputants need to argue for their views, not just based on their predilection for authority, freedom, sexual abstinence, or whatever, but based on how those things do or do not serve students' well-being. Indeed, there would be no conflict if disputants did not acknowledge they were debating the same issue. Conflict in the strong sense of logical incompatibility requires that disputants see that they are talking about the same thing.[26]

If that is true, though, we might wonder just how far it gets us. After all, we still would be left with disagreements, perhaps deep disagreements. Later in this chapter I will say more about perfectionist responses in the face of disagreement, but our issues here are the workability and desirability of perfectionist deliberation, and at least we have seen the possibility that in perfectionist deliberations and debates we are not condemned to acrimony and people talking past one another.

At this point let me recap the conception of deliberation I have been constructing. I do not propose that perfectionist political deliberation will eliminate disagreement and acrimony. Yet my conception of political deliberation imagines people concerned to live lives that genuinely are good, so they welcome differences and challenges from which they can learn, even if it means altering their current conceptions of their well-being. Or if for some individuals their allegiance to some way of life is essential to their well-being, those people still can come to respect other ways of life. Also, my conception imagines people willing to take a small-scale approach to pursuing well-being. There are pragmatic reasons for that, but there are ethical reasons as well. One implication is that people are willing to see well-being as a complicated matter that cannot be reduced to one or a few decisive values; for example, that because a religion proscribes premarital sex that the lives of sexually precocious youth must be bad, or that because governance of a school is less than strongly democratic, faculty and students must be suffering. Surely, religious and democratic values are relevant and important, but the concern need not be to decide the merits of a religious or democratic life broadly considered. The concern is with how the well-being of people is affected.

However, this prompts another workability question, a psychological question: Why should we think people could and would adopt such a political stance? My conception would seem to demand a lot from people. It expects an attitude that welcomes disagreements and challenges. It expects people to take a step or two away from values central to their own lives for the sake of a multidimensional examination and evaluation of elements of their and other people's welfare. Are those reasonable expectations?

## THE PSYCHOLOGICAL DEMANDS OF
## PERFECTIONIST DELIBERATION

First, let's consider why we might be skeptical that people would adopt the perspective I have described. Rawls presumes particular attitudes in his construction of the "original position."[27] In Rawls's original position, the imagined participants who are determining constitutional fundamentals are ignorant of their particular conceptions of their well-being. Rawls includes this aspect in the belief that reasonable people, while attempting to determine basic principles of justice, would not want constitutional essentials to favor particular conceptions of well-being, because their own conceptions might not be the favored ones. That premise is reasonable. However, Rawls takes it a step further. He supposes that people above all would want to maximize the odds of their own conceptions of well-being surviving the political process. They do not want the constitution to be biased against possible conceptions of their well-being, but, even more, they do not want conceptions of well-being to enter into a political competition at all. The attitude assumed is that people would prefer to develop and live their own conceptions of their lives, even if mistaken, rather than have their own conception losing out to a different, better conception. However, it is unclear why we should assume reasonable human beings would adopt that position. As I proposed before, reasonable people can desire appropriate constitutional neutrality while also desiring that the constitution allow for some conceptions of well-being to gain prominence through a fair political process. Perhaps what my conception suggests is that reasonable people can be willing to trade some freedom for the sake of increasing their chances of living a life genuinely good for them.[28]

Like Rawls, I make no claims about the nature of human beings, selfish or altruistic, individualistic or cooperative. I do believe, though, that reasonable people can take, and would prefer, an attitude toward disagreement that differs from what Rawls envisions. As Nietzsche states the relevant attitude, "You should seek your enemy, you should wage your war — a war for your opinions. And if your opinion is defeated, your honesty should still cry triumph over that!"[29] The point is that people need not be most concerned to protect the conception of their well-being they happen to have but rather to live lives that are really worthwhile and satisfying. Thus, they can have an interest in having a political process that aims to separate the genuinely good from what is only apparently good, even if it means their own current conceptions are put at a disadvantage somehow.

Nietzsche's statement is disturbing, though. He writes of people "at war" with "enemies." He is writing metaphorically and ironically, but many people would see the disputes I have been talking about literally as wars: physicians who perform abortions deserve to be shot, clinics should be bombed, Holocaust museums should be attacked. As Rawls does, we might fear that perfectionism encourages the attitude that certain conceptions of well-being have to be defeated. We should think more about how perfectionism can contribute to political deliberation that is cooperative and constructive rather than adversarial and destructive.

One aim of the foregoing discussion was to show that, in political deliberations, perfectionists can acknowledge and encourage a wide range of possibilities for good lives. Nevertheless, we might wonder just how open and productive deliberation can be when people have fundamental disagreements about what a good life entails. We need to think about the terms in which the deliberation is carried on. For example, it might be that well-intentioned people want to give a fair hearing to differing goods and lives, but maybe some of those appear so weird that people cannot really understand them and so cannot give them a fair hearing.

## RECIPROCITY

Rawls offers a conception of public reason that includes a duty of reciprocity: people must "be able to explain to one another on those fundamental questions how the principles and policies they advocate and vote for can be supported by the political values of public reason."[30] The point behind "public reason" is that rather than appeal to parochial principles that might be inaccessible or incomprehensible to some people, in public deliberations citizens should appeal to reasons that all citizens can recognize as legitimate. So, for instance, to argue for prayer in public schools because one's Christian conception of welfare demands it does not show reciprocity, because one cannot reasonably expect other people to agree that dictates of particular religions provide reasons for them.

There is an issue of just how broad the scope of reciprocity must be. It is possible that, under certain conditions, reasonable people could accept coercion or imposition based on reasons inaccessible to them.[31] An example that at least approaches such a situation is our common reliance on experts in particular arcane fields. We might accept an expert's opinion on the healthiness of some food or drug because we recognize "she is an expert" as a legitimate reason when we ourselves do not have the requisite knowledge. Furthermore, the reasons why the expert even should be deemed an expert could be too specialized and technical to be accessible to us. Of course, we have reason to be cautious about "the cult of the expert" that yields to experts too great a role in policy decisions. However, to grant experts authority in some areas is consistent with proper public caution and oversight.

Surely reciprocity is an important and widely relevant principle. It implies that in public deliberation participants — experts included — actually try to connect with other people and communicate in ways that all can understand and accept as bases for discussion and persuasion even as they disagree about the weightiness of those bases and the decisions they imply. That is a reasonable expectation. However, it still can be demanding. Let's consider religion again. Religion is a major part of many people's well-being, yet people have different religions, and some people might give religion little if any place in their well-being. Can we debate well-being meaningfully if some people do not recognize religious reasons as reasons for education policy while other people insist religious reasons are relevant and even primary? What does reciprocity demand in such a case?

I will begin by questioning just how well some liberal theories serve reciprocity in this domain. Amy Gutmann and Dennis Thompson discuss the 1983 incident where some Hawkins County, Tennessee, parents objected on religious grounds to several features of a reading series adopted by the local public schools.[32] For example, the parents objected to "a passage describing a central idea of the Renaissance as 'a belief in the dignity and worth of human beings,' because such a belief is incompatible with true religious faith."[33]

Gutmann and Thompson argue that the parents' reasons do not pass the reciprocity test: "The parents' reasoning appeals to values that can and should be rejected by citizens of a pluralist society committed to protecting the basic liberties and opportunities of all citizens."[34] If well-being is our concern, we do have to defend the principle of the worth and dignity of human beings. If we did not honor people's dignity as human beings, why would we be concerned about their welfare? However, we need to be careful how we analyze the situation Gutmann and Thompson describe. To attack the parents' rejection of the worth of human beings can be construed as an attack on their conclusions and not on their reasons. What I mean is that if at the base of the parents' reasoning is appeal to "true religious faith," that is a reason accessible to people as a reason. Reasonable people can recognize the legitimacy of religion as a reason for action even if it is not a reason they themselves act upon. We have examples, such as Dr. Martin Luther King Jr. and Mahatma Gandhi, who used religion powerfully as a basis for their struggles for freedom and justice. The problem with the Hawkins County parents' argument is what they conclude about the demands of faith. At least, religions have differing attitudes about the worth of human beings; surely, not all religious faiths require that one deny the worth of human beings.

It might seem that I'm talking about a difference that makes no difference: whether the parents' denial of the worth of human beings is considered a reason for their actions or as an outcome of their deliberation, their attitude is hostile to the project of serving people's well-being.

I do believe there is an important difference between the analyses. The parents can be criticized for offering an argument that does not establish their conclusions about human beings, but the point of reciprocity is not to talk only with people who offer sound arguments but to make productive argument possible. The distinction between reasons and conclusions can be slippery, of course. Even so, the example suggests that if the point of reciprocity is to connect with persons on the level of reasons, we need to keep in mind the degrees of freedom we have in that project. If we cannot connect on beliefs about the worth of human beings, perhaps we can at least credit the parents' appeal to religious faith and establish some common basis for dialogue.

We might wonder, though, just how accessible to nonreligious people, or even some religious people, is these parents' appeal to faith? Perhaps their claim is intelligible, but that is not the same as being accessible in the sense that other people are "in a position to evaluate and credit the insights drawn from the experience."[35] That is, some people do not have the experience of religious revelation or profound faith, and so it could be difficult if not impossible for them to credit claims to insight through faith and revelation. Those claims might be intelligible, comprehensible, but without the religious experience, people are not able to access the force of the purported reasons. Even so, people can have sufficient access — through people like King and Gandhi — of evidence of "the fruits of conviction," the benefits religious experience has provided the people who have undergone it, and benefits conferred directly or indirectly on others.[36]

However, a different situation arises when adherents of a faith or some other doctrine deny other people can have access to relevant experiences or insist on particular reasons that are inaccessible to others. For example, the parents described could insist that their reasoning was sound: their religion requires exactly what they said it does; they did not make a mistake in reasoning. My optimistic scenario imagined that they might be willing to think about religion more broadly. Some people are not willing to do that. For example, Noddings writes of an incident during which a speaker stated the values his religious group espoused. Noddings pointed out to him that the values were widely shared. Noddings found, though, that, "For him and those who share his religious perspective, the values we share are *secondary*. What counts most is the worldview that sustains and justifies the values."[37] This seems to be a clear case of reciprocity being absent; the speaker insists on what separates him from people rather than looking for commonalities that might exist. The speaker need not change his belief that "worldview" is primary in some sense. However, for the sake of deliberation, the shared values could be the starting point.

Of course, people like Noddings's speaker might not go along. So, acrimony arises, or an impasse, at least. However, I do not see how neutralism in such circumstances must offer a better response than perfectionism. If people insist their particular religious (or other) beliefs provide good reasons for or against some policy or action, the proper response would be to dispute that claim rather than say that, for neutralist reasons, the claim cannot be disputed or must be accommodated. At least, to exclude reasons people deem important seems just as likely to engender discord as does debating those reasons. Even if some people are not open to such debate, political deliberation should not be held hostage by a small group of ideologues. They might not be persuaded, but they will be accorded due respect, and perhaps other people will better understand them and their beliefs.

My claim is not that perfectionism demands no restraint or compromise in people's appeals to aspects of their well-being in public deliberation. However, I believe that the proper restraint is not so tight as some liberals, such as Gutmann and Thompson, contend they are. I am not saying perfectionists must disagree with Gutmann and Thompson that the Hawkins County parents' proposals should be opposed. As noted before, concern for well-being implies belief in the worth of human beings. The perfectionist point regards the nature of the deliberation and/or opposition. Parties to the deliberation need to address the reasons people offer, not only in terms of liberal political values but also in terms of the good (religious and otherwise) and well-being. All the parties have an obligation to try to offer reasons accessible to one another. People like the Hawkins County parents might reject the religious reasons others offer. It is not clear, though, that their objections must be any stronger than the objections they have to a secular political grounding. It is possible that their objections actually would be less strong if the opposition they get is in terms of good and well-being, because at least this sort of opposition would appear to better fit their own conception of the kind of reasons suitable to public deliberation, especially if the grounds include religious grounds.

There is another issue to consider, however. I have argued that perfectionist public deliberation can be inclusive in several ways. However, inclusion is not the only relevant concern. There is also the issue of differential power.

## DIFFERENTIAL POWER IN PUBLIC DELIBERATION

People might be included in public debates, but they still can lack power relative to other people, so their interests do not get a fair hearing. This problem is especially salient for individuals and groups who already are underserved or at particular risk. Perfectionists have been accused of exacerbating the problem. Will Kymlicka charges:

> [S]tate perfectionism . . . dictates a time and place — political deliberation over state policy — in which minorities are most vulnerable. State neutrality, on the other hand, gives culturally disadvantaged groups a greater ability to choose the time and place in which they will confront majority sensitivities and to choose an audience with whom they are most comfortable.[38]

State perfectionism, embodied in teachers' activities and education policy generally, does imply that times and places are made for dialogue and deliberation about well-being. People's interests are at stake when a school budget or bond issue is being considered, and it can be important for people to participate in deliberations in order to protect their interests. Yet we all know that there are times to "show your hand" and times to be cautious. However, it is unclear how state perfectionism must create more danger than state neutrality. State policies need to be debated in any event. Again, the concern must be that state perfectionism dictates the content of state policies and the nature of the deliberative process so as to present an exceptional risk. For example, maybe the fear is that disadvantaged groups will have their cultural identities on the line, somehow. Perhaps illegal immigrants could risk their status becoming known. But, as I have argued, perfectionism does not require entire ways of life be exposed and judged in that way. Illegal immigrants, or their advocates, could focus their arguments on cultural and political interests that are not directly connected to their resident status.

It also is unclear that perfectionist deliberation limits vulnerable individuals' and groups' choices to the extent Kymlicka suggests. People can and should have the freedom to decline involvement. Granted, this could be merely a formal freedom because, as a practical matter, those at a disadvantage simply could not afford to forgo participation. But that would appear to be the case whether public policies were perfectionist or not. Also, there are ways to reduce the risks. Certainly perfectionists can endorse and pursue conditions of fair and safe debate. Kymlicka believes a better strategy is to keep the relevant issues out of the political arena in the first place. However, in reply to that, it seems to me that when repression and discrimination really are the majority's aims, often the latter's strategy is to assert the political irrelevance of perfectionist claims for minority recognition.

However, even if the time and place of perfectionist political debate were not a problem, Kymlicka raises questions about the process itself. He argues:

> [W]here there is state perfectionism, the minority must immediately aim at persuading the majority, and so they will describe their practices in such a way as to be palatable to the majority, even if that misdescribes the real meaning and value of the practice, which often arose precisely in opposition to dominant practices.[39]

Kymlicka has a point. Debate about well-being can lead to conflict, where there are winners and losers. So, we should acknowledge the urgency that can be behind people's defense of their conceptions of their welfare when they see them threatened by state policies and educators' actions. They might have to aim at immediate persuasion. Again, though, why must perfectionism present a greater danger than a neutral or "rights" approach? Imagine some minority group — illegal immigrants, say — agitate to have their interests and experiences represented in history, economics, and political science classes, in opposition to dominant curriculum practices and community attitudes. If the immigrants were to assert their wishes in terms of rights rather than goods, I do not see why that would be any less dangerous or controversial. In the political climate that exists as I write this, asserting rights likely would be less productive, because many people in dominant groups are willing to acknowledge few if any meaningful rights for illegal immigrants. Of course, such people are unlikely to listen to arguments based in the goods due any human being either, but those are ethically powerful arguments, and, in any event, again I do not see why those arguments are bound to be more dangerous for the minority. Perhaps they are more likely to foster compassion.

Nor is it clear that in a perfectionist climate the minority always must immediately aim to persuade the majority. Perfectionism is consistent with a number of political responses not aimed directly at persuading, at least not in the sense of persuasion Kymlicka appears to hold. Protest and civil disobedience are possibilities, for instance. Once again, there could be practical concerns such that more or less immediate persuasion is needed, but that would seem to be true in the case of rights as well as goods. Still, at some point the aim is to persuade through deliberative means.

If that is the case, how should we respond to Kymlicka's "distortion" point? He is correct that people might distort their views in order to make them palatable to people who oppose them. However, the matter is complicated. For one thing, it is not clear that "distorting" views must be to the disadvantage of vulnerable groups. Of course we would wish that conditions were such that distortion wasn't necessary; but given conditions as they sometimes exist, making views palatable to others can be an effective, even if not ideal, strategy. In addition, offering a description of a practice alien to others in such a way as to make it accessible and understandable to them (which is not the same as "palatable") need not be an ethical or political failure, nor need it be a misdescription.

Determining the "real meaning and value of a practice" is tricky. As we have seen, the meaning and value of practices, experiences, and so on typically are not univocal; there might be some number of differing yet correct or acceptable descriptions of a practice. For example, how might we describe "the real meaning and value" of immigrants' attempts to have their values and interests represented in school curriculum? Is the aim increased political power? Tolerance and understanding between them and others? Preserving their history and culture for their children? The value and meaning could be in these things and others; I do not see why one or another must be truer. Perhaps one would be more palatable to the majority, and therefore would be politically wise to emphasize, but that need not be to the detriment of the minority.

Surely, it's possible to distort people's conceptions of their well-being. Dominant conceptions of good might work against some people. Consider the prostitutes of Calcutta again. It is easy to imagine them thinking, "I'm no good," because that is what their society keeps telling them. Attempts to better their plight by appeal to goods thus are likely to be distorted by the dominant conceptions of good. Prostitutes might describe to researchers the "happiness" they experience. Perhaps the prostitutes would be honest and accurate regarding the emotions they feel. However, it's not a stretch to say that's a distortion of their situation and their own conceptions of their well-being, if they were shown other possibilities. Similarly, if the women described their situation as a choice they made, I imagine that would be at most a half-truth that would be palatable to people who would rather blame the women than blame a society that created and maintained conditions that pushed women into prostitution.

Once again, though, why would perfectionism be more likely to force a merely palatable description from the women? Perhaps palatability is not all bad; at least people might be more inclined to listen if what they heard was palatable to them. But if the aim really is to improve the lot of disadvantaged persons, perfectionist language, language that brought real issues of welfare to the foreground, would be an advantage rather than a disadvantage. It is difficult for people to advocate for their rights if they do not first have a sense of their worth as human beings and individuals. Besides, who knows, maybe there would be people with the insight and compassion to see beyond what was merely palatable to them.


## CONCLUSION

In this chapter I have tried to show how perfectionists can endorse open, fair, pluralistic, productive deliberation regarding education and well-being. I have argued that productive public deliberation is workable. I hope it's clear that I don't claim the process is easy or success inevitable. Part of my argument is premised on the possibility that people will see value in being confronted by differing or conflicting conceptions of well-being and will sustain one another in their struggles to live a good life. I grant that is asking a lot and might go against dominant political and cultural trends. Nonetheless, I think education can increase the odds of the possibility being realized.

However, as yet we haven't squarely faced the issue of actually making decisions about well-being and education policy and practice. As noted before, perfectionists are not content just to discuss issues; deliberation should lead to action, and that includes making distinctions between better and worse policies and practices. And when we consider that, the issues we have discussed arise all over again. In the next chapter I move to the adjudication issue, how we are to move beyond deliberation and make judgments about the quality of differing goods and lives.

*Chapter 8*

# Judging Well-Being

In this chapter the issue is how to move beyond deliberating about well-being to adjudicating, judging which conceptions of well-being are good or the best and which are not, which parts of a life should be encouraged or discouraged. One question is why we must make the move to adjudication at all. For example, if there is robust public deliberation where alternatives for well-being are adequately debated, why not leave it at that and leave it to people to make their own decisions? One might agree with the value of perfectionist deliberation while resisting the idea that the deliberation should result in decisions about the quality of goods and lives. Arguments for this view could appeal again to the values of political stability and interpersonal relationships. Wong argues that our principal concern should be "with repairing the rupture of human relationship rather than deciding the rights and wrongs of the parties."[1]

## ADJUDICATION AND INTERPERSONAL RELATIONS

In the passage just mentioned, Wong worries that deciding rights and wrongs, what I am calling adjudication, will create, maintain, or exacerbate ruptures in human relations. So, for example, even though a student is wrong about her conception of a good life, maybe a teacher's main concern should be preserving relationship with the student and not for judging the student's conception of her welfare.

Indeed, we should be ready to set aside questions of right and wrong for the sake of preserving or repairing human relationships. Certainly, "relationship" is a value perfectionists can recognize and encourage (as with Nussbaum's "affiliation"). However, adjudication is not the problem Wong thinks it is.

Trying to avoid disputes can be as destabilizing as confronting them, if not

more so. Recently, there have been plenty of public figures, on cable news chan-
nels for instance, who are more than willing to associate citizenship with being
Christian, heterosexual, English-speaking, unthinkingly "patriotic," and such.
It seems clear that those people have done a good deal to encourage divisiveness in the United States. But rather than show we should avoid debate at this
level, this shows that "dividers" need to be challenged. At least, it would be an
improvement if the "discussion" were broadened to include serious exploration
of the comprehensive values central to people's well-being, beyond the mere
spouting of narrow and narrow-minded ideologies.

Another problem is that if consensus becomes the overriding concern, the
result can be conceptions of the good that are exceptionally weak. For example,
Cuban offers three criteria a good school should meet: "Are parents, staff, and
students satisfied with what occurs in the school?" "Is the school achieving the
explicit goals that it has set for itself?" and "Are democratic behaviors, values,
and attitudes evident in the students?"[2] While such an approach might make
sense in some circumstances, we should recognize how limited it is. Just because
things get done and people are satisfied with them, it does not follow that the
school is doing things that really are good. Cuban believes we must keep goals
weak (not his word) because people disagree about the good.

Furthermore, we should ask just how important consensus is. Wong contends that, other things being equal, one should "minimize the opportunity
for serious disagreement."[3] Disagreement can be destructive, but why must
the priority be to minimize it rather than to learn how to live with it and use
it productively? Indeed, why shouldn't we say that, other things being equal,
we should minimize the opportunity for serious *agreement*? The dangers of
agreement have been a common theme for postmodernists who believe that
the real threat is not from disruption but from consensus that "normalizes"
people. For example, William Connolly says something like this in his "politics
of discordance."[4] I do not propose that we give priority to discord; rather than
privilege one extreme or another we are better-off taking a "both/and" attitude
toward concord and discord.[5]

Of course, we cannot use the value of discord as an excuse to ride roughshod
over people with whom we disagree. Yet the aim is not to avoid disagreement
but maintain conditions where policies can be effectively criticized, deliberated,
and changed if need be. The debate might not turn out well, but that is not a
criticism of perfectionist adjudication; it is a reason for caution.[6]

Another part of Wong's argument we should question is that adjudication is radically different in its divisiveness compared with accommodation.
Adjudication need not be divisive; it can show positive respect for people.

Regard for others is required for adjudication, at least insofar as we seek evaluations based on full and accurate knowledge of other people and their conceptions of well-being. Bernstein gets at this point in his distinction between adversarial and dialogical argumentation that I mentioned in the Introduction. In the latter, one strives to understand others' views in their strongest form, even to the point of strengthening them oneself. To consider a challenge to one's own conception of well-being, to the point of adducing the strongest reasons in favor of the challenge, might sharpen and enlarge the disagreement, but that can show readiness to take the challenge and the challenger seriously.

It is not clear we should avoid questions of right and wrong if we aim to establish or preserve the sort of interpersonal regard Wong values. Wong argues that appropriate regard requires recognition that "other communities have something worthwhile."[7] Acknowledging this worth and attempting to learn from others manifests a deeper sense of respect than simple toleration. However, the issue of worth presents the need for adjudication, unless we simply are to assume worthiness. In the Kantian sense of respecting persons, we should assume the worth of persons; but we are not talking about the worth of persons here but rather the worth of their conceptions of well-being and how they are living them out. If we aim for some strong regard for other persons, because we have regard for them as persons and for the possibility that we have something to learn from their conceptions of well-being, then it is reasonable that something be done to show the worth of those conceptions, for their sake as well as our own. This does not mean worth has to be demonstrated before people and their views are admitted into public deliberations. Similar to Sumner's view that individuals' conceptions of their welfare are authoritative yet defeasible, Taylor argues that others' ways of life are owed a presumption of worth but might, upon examination, be shown not to be worthy, or less worthy than was presumed.[8] But for Taylor this is no mere test of worth in terms of one's own present standards; one must be prepared to transform one's own standards of prudential value and other values in order to exercise good judgment. As we saw with Gadamer, understanding some subject matter, including value and well-being, requires a "fusion of horizons," a transformation of participants. Here, too, we can see a sort of accommodation among people realized in adjudication and not opposed to it.

For these reasons, we should question the opposition between adjudication and accommodation, between the search for lives that are genuinely good and respect for the diversity of good lives. However, we should take a closer look at this claim. What does this "respect" amount to in terms of space for individual freedom? It would seem possible for a person to say something like this to another person: "I respect your conception of your well-being, and I have learned something from it; but the way you live your life still is not good, all things considered, and should be discouraged."

Let us first remember the sort of goods being advocated. The capabilities we have considered leave plenty of room for people to determine their own conceptions of their welfare. From this perspective, if a capability is being adequately developed or exercised, one has limited grounds for opposing the particular way it is developed.

However, when we considered the need to function and not just have capabilities, I offered a few controversial examples. As accommodating as we might try to be, we should admit that inevitably there will be some people who do not buy into conceptions of the good that guide education policy and practice or even into the general aim of human well-being, and that some ways of developing and exercising capabilities are not good and need to be discouraged or opposed. Those sorts of disagreement might be troublesome, but I do not see perfectionists having any more of a problem with them than neutralists.

Perfectionists don't advocate oppression and exclusion any more than liberals; in Chapter 7 I argued how perfectionists can be even more inclusive. In addition, people are inclined to resist imposition of ways of life upon them. Perfectionists realize that pushing too hard against such resistance likely would be counterproductive. Even if a person's life is less than the best, perfectionists will be wary of imposing a better life because self-determination is itself a good.

Also, the perfectionist aim is to help people live lives that genuinely are good, but, in terms of the capability of practical reason, that implies some amount of self-confidence in one's ability to form a conception of well-being. If exposing students' shortcomings is the primary concern, it is unlikely they will achieve the requisite self-confidence. Of course, students need to be made aware of their errors at times, but that need not be the primary aim.[9]

Still, perfectionist tolerance for conceptions of the good is limited. Conceptions of the good can be mistaken, and those conceptions require some sort of response. This takes me back to the sort of pluralism perfectionists can support.

## PLURALIST PERFECTIONISM REVISITED

We should not be glib about what pluralism implies. Griffin, for example, suggests that pluralists need not be more tolerant than monists.[10] One might grant that there is a plurality of values yet claim they fall into a rigid hierarchy where one or more values are always and clearly superior to others. If this is not a monism strictly speaking, we could call it a monism of emphasis.[11]

Just how broad is perfectionist pluralism? Even if one agreed that there is a plurality of worthwhile lives, one could insist that worthwhile lives are confined to a more or less narrow range of possibilities. However, perfectionism need not take a narrow, elitist form but can be wide enough to include values all or nearly all human beings can attain, a position Arneson calls "egalitarian perfectionism."[12] Consider the capacity for practical reason, for example. Nussbaum describes this as "[b]eing able to form a conception of the good and to engage in critical reflection about the planning of one's life."[13] We need not give this capacity a privileged place in a hierarchy of human capabilities. People can lead good, satisfying lives without giving practical reason a privileged role in their lives, and without their critical reflection being especially sophisticated. Still, if we are concerned for people's well-being it is important that people have the ability to form at least an adequate conception of their well-being and how to pursue it.

So, perfectionists have reasons to be tolerant and respectful of a broad range of good lives. However, despite all the plurality, tolerance, and respect perfectionism implies, we have to face squarely that the tolerance and respect have limits; perfectionism holds that some values might be higher than others, "higher" values being those that represent what is best in human beings, compared with "lower" values. That is a difficult, and perhaps scary, claim; it merits further attention.

If people can lead good and satisfying lives without extensive or sophisticated use of their practical reason or other capabilities, the conclusion still could be that their lives should be deemed to have lesser quality than lives where practical reason has a more substantial place; their lives could be good but still less than the best. Arneson defends the antielitist merits of wide, egalitarian perfectionism, but his defense is that

> [t]he "wider" a perfectionist doctrine, the more it values goods that virtually all humans can reach, and the smaller the gap between the value assigned to these lower goods compared to the value assigned to the higher goods that few can attain.[14]

Arneson aims to close the gap between higher and lower goods, yet he maintains that there is a gap. In her reply to Arneson, Nussbaum rightly is concerned about the language of higher and lower goods, that scientific activity, for example, has more "intrinsic value" than the activity of a farmer, mother, or street sweeper.[15] However, there is ambiguity in talking about the activity of a farmer, mother, or street sweeper and the intrinsic value of the activity. Here we confront the ambiguity in the idea of "what is good for its own sake" for a person.

Although the trend is by no means clear or absolute, we do have some tendency — despite our instrumentalism — to deem things good for their own sake superior to those that are only good as a means to something else. For example, we might think that an artist who produces campy art for the sake of making money has demeaned art and herself. Art should be done for its own sake. On the other hand, that attitude can lead to snobbery. And it might be noble for an artist to produce works she cannot sell, but at some point that moves from nobility to something more like foolishness. At least, doing something to put food on her table and a roof over her head are perfectly legitimate parts of a good life.

I set aside the question whether people should prefer things good in themselves to things that have only instrumental value; the problem is not instrumental thinking but the dominance of such thinking. However, it is helpful to think a bit more about the meaning of "good in itself" or "good for its own sake." Doing so will not eliminate the gap between higher and lower goods — I don't propose that it is desirable to eliminate it (although I do not subscribe to Arneson's suggestion that widely attainable goods are therefore "lower") — but it will help us understand the gap better and feel less threatened by it.

Following Korsgaard, something is intrinsically good if it "has its goodness in itself."[16] That is one way for something to be good for its own sake. Its goodness is unconditional, independent of circumstances, because the good is "in" the thing. Extrinsic goodness, in contrast, is conditional; the thing's goodness depends on certain conditions being met. In light of that distinction, debate over what does or does not have intrinsic value is not terribly productive, because many or most life activities do not possess intrinsic value or have value that is purely intrinsic. The value of scientific activity or art depends at least in part on the conditions under which they are undertaken: if they serve good rather than evil purposes, say, or aim to challenge dogmatism rather than support it. The situation is similar with farming. Nothing says farming must be a low-value activity, yet its value does depend on circumstances. The value of farming is lessened if the farmer is poisoned by insecticides or develops skin cancer from long exposure to the sun.

Nussbaum's capabilities can be thought of as some of the conditions on which extrinsic goods depend, and also thought of as extrinsic goods whose value is conditional. For example, a farmer's well-being is conditioned by whether he is capable of protecting his health and using his practical reason to make his own decisions about what crops to plant. Or, to return to the person who is not sophisticated in practical reason or does not give it a central place in her life, that presents no problem under certain conditions — say, because practical reason has an appropriate fit with other of her prudential values. The importance of practical reason could be greater if conditions were different, perhaps if the person were denied opportunities to develop her practical reason adequately.

Also, even if some occupations or activities — like counting the hairs on the back of your hand — do little to manifest significant capabilities and so are lower activities, that alone is not decisive, because judgments of individual well-being are aggregate judgments.[17] That is, well-being is constituted by many aspects of life and the constellation in which they fit. Doing poorly in some part of life can be offset by doing well in another aspect of life. Hence, again, the limited value in dwelling on isolated "intrinsically" higher or lower lives and activities.

Perhaps the concern for intrinsic value gets traction if there are some activities that by their nature preclude or maximize exercise of human capabilities. For example, it is pretty easy to conclude that slavery is intrinsically bad because it denies slaves control over their bodies, environment, and other essential aspects of their lives. Or as was said in *Schindler's List*, perhaps the list was an absolute good, reflecting some of the best of humanity amidst humanity at its worst.

However, and here is Korsgaard's essential point, something need not be good intrinsically in order for it to be good for its own sake. The intrinsic/extrinsic distinction does not map onto the ends/means distinction.[18] This provides another way to describe the view of value and prudential value I have been advocating. Watching a beautiful sunset can be an end in itself; its value need not lie in it being a means to something else, like getting your date in a romantic mood. Yet its value is extrinsic, dependent on certain conditions being present, such as one's attitudinal set and the absence of mosquitoes.

Arneson might not agree with my interpretation of his statement that "what is good for its own sake for a person is fixed independently of her attitudes and opinions toward it," but I believe my discussion shows how we can preserve the independent prudential significance of values while still being consistent with the subjectivity of well-being. Accomplishment, for instance, is good for its own sake for a person; it is, or can be, an end in itself. In the relevant sense, its prudential value is independent of the person's attitudes. Yet the value of accomplishment is extrinsic, dependent on circumstances. "Accomplishment," although prudentially good for its own sake, need not benefit an individual if conditions are wrong. As I said before, people do not achieve "accomplishment"; they accomplish particular things, and the actual prudential benefit depends on the particular accomplishments and the individual's attitudes toward them.

The conditionality and particularity of value also suggest a way to think again about the objectivity of values, and a reason to "think small" as advocated before. Korsgaard argues that a good can be good objectively even if its goodness is conditional.

> "[G]ood objectively" is a judgment applying to real particulars; this woman's knowledge, this man's happiness, and so on. To say of a thing that it is good objectively is not to say that it is the type of thing that is usually good (a good kind of thing like knowledge or happiness) but that it contributes to the actual goodness of the world: here and now the world is a better place for *this*.[19]

So, objectivity is not the same as universality. The near universality of goods does not imply those are objective goods. Just because something — like great art or homemaking — is usually good and satisfying, that does not imply it will contribute to the goodness of the world or for a particular person in the here and now. If we construe objectivity the way Korsgaard does, making value comparisons among broad activities such as science, parenting, farming, or art are difficult and largely unhelpful because the value of all these things is conditional, dependent on the who, when, and where. The point about particularity is reinforced if we go with egalitarian perfectionism and value things within most people's reach. It is difficult for many of us to be "pure." Frailty is much more in our grasp. But as we considered with Rose and Charlie from *The African Queen*, "frailty" can be an objectively good thing.

I believe the discussion shows judgments of "higher" and "lower" should be treated cautiously yet need not be overly threatening. There is a point in retaining the higher/lower distinction, if it is used appropriately. Perseverance, say, might be a wonderful thing by and large, but persevering at counting the hairs on the back of your hand is a lower activity than persevering at athletic training. Counting hairs might be an accomplishment of some sort, but it is not the sort of activity that merits praise, other things being equal. At least, we should retain the perfectionist principle that lives and activities can be compared and judged better and worse. If we are to provide conditions where people can seriously examine their lives and make good judgments about their quality, we have to believe that there are differences in quality in activities and lives.

However, if some goods and lives are better than others, what can be done to ensure that people will be treated fairly and equally? What is to stop perfectionists from being excessively punitive with people who adopt undesirable conceptions of their well-being, or from disrespecting people's right to make mistakes? Even if we genuinely are respectful of differing good lives, that does not eliminate the possibility that we should favor lives that are more "excellent" or more essential than others. For instance, it could be that certain individuals should be favored— say, for their contributions to society. We cannot prevent unreasonable biases and bad judgment, but we need to think more about what perfectionism implies regarding distributive justice and interpersonal comparisons of well-being.

## DISTRIBUTIVE JUSTICE AND INTERPERSONAL COMPARISONS OF WELL-BEING

In Chapter 5 we focused on how to judge the quality of individual lives, but we cannot be concerned with individuals only. Educators have responsibility to society as well as to individuals. The welfare of an individual could conflict with society's well-being; the "expensive tastes" issue is an example. The well-being of one individual might compete with the well-being of another individual. How are we to distribute resources justly?

Let's start with the individual-society scenario. What makes a society "excellent" from a perfectionist point of view? Excellence can be thought of in aggregate social terms as well as in individual terms. In other words, the perfectionist aim could be to increase overall excellence in a society, or it could be to maximize "peaks" of excellence represented by individuals. Rawls uses his second moral power as a basis for equality: all normal persons should be understood to have the capacity for a conception of the good.[20] Can perfectionists take a similar view on equality? I propose a perfectionist version of Rawls's moral power: all normal persons should be understood to have the capacity for a *truly good* conception of their well-being. That is a stronger claim for equality than Rawls's. It might appear more empirically problematic therefore, but if we understand "truly good" in the inclusive egalitarian way we have considered, the claim becomes more plausible. And if the principle is more demanding normatively — for example, in calling for greater expenditure of public resources to more fully develop all persons' capacity for identifying what is genuinely good — then perfectionism could provide even stronger grounds for equality, and a more substantial sense of equality, than Rawls provides.

Consistent with my pluralism, I do not say the group necessarily must come before individuals or vice versa. The point is that perfectionist public policy does not preclude concern for excellence in the aggregate social sense; it need not be concerned for individuals only. However, Rawls presents a challenge to that claim by denying the principle of diminishing marginal utility. He argues:

> There is little reason to suppose that, in general, rights and resources allocated to encourage and to cultivate highly talented persons contribute less and less to the

total beyond some point in the relevant range. To the contrary, this contribution
may grow (or stay constant) indefinitely.[21]

Rawls's challenge here is that perfectionist concern for excellence must lead us
to favor talented individuals whose contributions are especially valuable to the
group, and these contributions might grow indefinitely, or at least stay constant. If that is true, then perfectionists have no nonarbitrary grounds to divert
resources away from talented persons to persons who lack basic goods or whose
contributions are less valuable. Rawls's claim is not clearly true, though.

First, perfectionists need not see much advantage in open-ended cultivation.
Given the absolute conception of "best" with which we are working, once a
person has achieved some best way of life there is diminished value in carrying
that even further. Even if such a person were able to achieve a life that was better
somehow, the advance likely would be marginal, and perfectionist gains would
be greater if another person were able to achieve a best life he did not have
before. Furthermore, it is likely that any gains open to a person who has already
achieved a best life are relatively inexpensive. Initial high costs for education,
for instance, need not continue. Finally, the greatest excellences probably are
more likely to be achieved in a cooperative environment where all persons are
appropriately encouraged and supported in their efforts at excellence, compared
with an adversarial one. Perfectionists certainly can see the merit in Rawls's
conception of society as a fair system of social cooperation.

However, the comparisons needed are not only between individual well-
being and societal well-being; often, we have to make comparisons between
individuals, and that is complicated, too. Imagine two people, pursuing their
well-being in different ways, equally distant from equivalent levels of well-
being. For one, music is central to her welfare, so there is cost for an instrument,
lessons, and so forth. For the other person, the costs of achieving well-being are
not as great for some reason. Do we treat these people as equally in need because
they are equidistant from their states of well-being, so that whatever resources
we have are allotted equally to the people? Or should the aspiring musician
receive more, needing more resources in order to progress in her well-being to
a degree similar to the person whose progress costs less?

Furthermore, the status "better-off" or "worse-off" might not be the only
relevant concern. For example, what if a person initially better-off would use
additional resources much more productively and efficiently than the person
initially less well-off? Or what if the better-off person is studying for a vocation
desperately needed by society whereas the less well-off person is not? My point
in all of this is not to support one or another course of action but to show, if

it isn't obvious already, that what is just or fair or wise in comparing people's well-being and distributing resources is a complicated task. Nonetheless, the discussion shows that perfectionists have principled reasons to support fairness and equality in distributing resources.

We are left, though, with the question of how to make fair decisions about resources. In the face of the complexity, we might conclude that judgments of justice and well-being can or should only be made at a general level. Many theories of justice take a broad view, not being concerned for offering answers to particular questions of justice. For example, as we have seen, Rawls is concerned to establish basic principles for the just governance of a society.[22] In his "difference principle" he tells us that principles of justice should favor the least advantaged. Such broad theories can be important for education policy, for example for civil rights and school desegregation. These theories might not tell us how to desegregate yet provide a strong case that justice requires desegregation. We might abandon attempts to make fine-grained judgments of individuals' well-being and turn to grosser measures such as gross national product, per capita income, or expenditure per student in some school or school district.

Broad principles and policies of justice can be important and legitimate. However, that does not change the fact that teachers and others constantly are confronted by decisions regarding particular individuals' welfare. Such decisions are made all the time — for example, in deciding who will get an organ transplant or be admitted into a college.[23] Often, we are concerned for "local justice," and, in practice, local justice is "a messy business."[24] It is messy because typically there are a number of different and conflicting criteria at work in deliberation. I have noted some examples. On the one hand, we are concerned for the level of persons' well-being, so that if a person is doing more poorly than another, we have reason to raise the former person's level of well-being. On the other hand, we are concerned for efficient use of limited resources and perhaps increments of well-being, so that if the well-being of some person can be raised substantially while the well-being of a person somewhat poorer-off will not be raised, or raised only marginally, we might have reason to favor the former person. Plus, we are concerned not only for the well-being of individuals but also for the society at large, so that people who already are well-off might be favored if it is to the advantage of society somehow. Compassion and efficiency, both legitimate concerns, might pull us in different directions.[25]

The problem of local justice and local judgments of well-being will be my concern here. Supposing that teachers should make local judgments about individuals' welfare, what are the proper bases for those judgments?

## BASES FOR JUDGING AND COMPARING WELL-BEING

We already have encountered one basic issue — the problem of incommensu-rability. There may be no one neutral standard by which to evaluate differing lives. A move toward the more concrete and specific could be helpful, such as reference to human capabilities. Judgment does not take a deductive form, where a "thick but vague" conception of welfare somehow provides a neutral commensurating ground. Rather, the process would be to

> [s]how that each of the initially clashing conceptions of the good differently specifies or particularizes the constructed (or discovered) common ground. Resolution of the conflict between incommensurable conceptions of the good becomes possible on the basis of an appeal not to a "higher" impartial authority . . . but rather to a given specification's superior ability to accommodate the detailed concerns addressed by each vague value.[26]

The better conception shows itself better able than its rival to explain the "detailed concerns" in question. Say a "vague value" at issue is practical reason. A teacher knows a high school senior, Colin, plans to join a cult after gradua-tion. In the cult, little if any of his practical reason will be used or encouraged; he will be expected to obey the cult's strictures. The teacher also has a senior student, Sara, who has made bad decisions in the course of her life but is now trying to make better use of her practical reason and make better decisions.

The students have clashing conceptions of their lives. "Practical reason" is a value common to both cases, but it does not serve as an impartial "authority." So, we look at the "detailed concerns" involved. For example, a concern is that the students make reasonable judgments about their lives. Sara seems to aim for that more so than Colin. But the case isn't straightforward. Colin could argue he is using his practical reason. He has thought about his decision. He knows that, in some sense, once he joins the cult he will surrender his freedom to exercise his practical reason; but in return he will get other goods, such as affiliation.

I will not pursue the example further. To arrive at a good judgment about the case, we would need more detailed information. I do think we would have grounds to think our aspiring cultist needs our help, perhaps more than Sara. There are a number of ways to have fulfilling affiliations, for example, and with his move Colin might lose affiliations as well as gain some, and get into relationships that are not beneficial for him. We need not try to impose some point of view on him but ask him if he is informed about his decision and if his plan really fits well with other aspects of his own conception of his well-being.

Perhaps we would have to conclude that both students are doing well, or at least well enough that we would have no right to intervene further. My point here is not to show what direction judgment must take, but how it can proceed without some neutral commensurating criterion. Rather, we look at our concerns — such as practical reason and affiliation — and see how different conceptions of well-being specify those concerns and how those specifications fit into a whole constellation of concerns.

Essentially, this is the process discussed in Chapter 5 as the process of scientific progress. In science, competing theories are evaluated, in part, by how well they account for the "detailed concerns" that arise as theories are explored and anomalies encountered. The "superior ability" still will be based on standards of particular conceptions of well-being, but as MacIntyre argues, this does not preclude nonrelativistic judgments of the superiority of "alien" traditions.[27] And if we are concerned for objectivity in our judgments, we need to recall Korsgaard's depiction of objectivity, in which the question is the benefits to particular persons, at particular times, and in particular places.

So far in this chapter I have presented conceptions of value, equality, judgment, and so on that perfectionist teachers could bring to bear in their decisions. To get the process going, though, how do we get a sense for how people are faring? In Chapter 9 we will see how, through dialogue and other activities, students can be seduced to explore, discover, and express their well-being. Still, teachers have to be able to figure out what students' expressions mean.

Because of the difficulties in judging a person's well-being, we might have to admit we cannot judge it directly. Instead, we might have to rely on an "operational proxy" — that is, some observable feature of well-being.[28] If we go that route, we admit that the proxy does not give the full story of a person's well-being, but, practically, it is the best we can do. For example, the limits of our own experience and empathy might make it difficult to feel what others feel about some experience, and so we do not have a good sense of what their feelings are and how their feelings affect their well-being. Yet their actions and expressions of satisfaction and dissatisfaction surely can provide some legitimate and helpful "proxy" that provides insights. For example, for the life of me, I cannot understand the kick people get out of NASCAR. I cannot tell for sure how well their lives are going, but the attention and passion they give to auto racing, and the enjoyment they get from watching it, provide some indicators.

Human capabilities can be considered proxies in this sense. We admit there is more to well-being than these capabilities, but they are vital abilities that can be observed at least to some extent. We can get a sense of a child's capability for affiliation, for instance, by observing whether or how he has friends among his classmates. However, satisfaction is part of well-being, too; outward appearances might not tell us a lot about the satisfaction people do or do not experience. So let's return to the notion of self-reports.

Because of the subject-relativity of well-being and the fact that even young people have some idea of their well-being, teachers simply might ask students if they are doing well. But as we have noted many times, we cannot always trust people's self-reports and outward behavior. Or, people might be tempted to exaggerate their needs in order to get more resources. Some people might be more inclined to express dissatisfaction compared with other people. Because of such problems, Scanlon concludes that a person's expression of satisfaction and dissatisfaction "by itself carries no moral weight: We don't yet know whether [the person's] preferences should be given special weight or whether he is simply more demanding."[29]

Scanlon is right to caution us about judging people's well-being only on the basis of their expressions of satisfaction and dissatisfaction. Even so, it is unjustified to conclude that such expressions must carry no moral weight.

First of all, if by "more demanding" we mean that people are asking for "mere wants" rather than what they really "need," we still can have moral grounds for serving those demands. Noddings asks, "Must a want rise to the level of need before it is satisfied? Warm, loving families respond generously to many wants that are not needs. Indeed, we might say that everyone has a need to have at least some wants (non-needs) satisfied."[30] We need not model schooling on families to think that there can be benefit in "satisfying mere likes or preferences or even whims"[31] and that educators can have reasons to satisfy individuals' wants. A want can be very important to a child. I remember as a child desperately wanting to write on the chalkboard (there were no whiteboards back then). It is difficult to describe writing on the board as a need, and allowing students to write on the board probably creates more trouble for a teacher rather than less, but it is important for children to experience adults listening to them, even for, or maybe especially for, the "little things."

However, even if this is true, we might think it should be the exception rather than the rule. After all, good parents do not give in to their children's every want. Scanlon's concern is the basis for judgments about possible lives, and the question people need to ask is not just "What do I/you/they prefer?" but also "*Why* should I/you/they prefer this to that? What makes the one better than the other?"[32] Teachers should make comparisons on the basis of good reasons, and preferences can be unreliable as reasons.

The difficulty with Scanlon's argument is not that judgments about well-being should be based on reasons but what he considers good reasons to be. As

I argued in Part One, the sort of emotional expressions Scanlon distrusts can themselves be reasons for choice and action. Thinking back to Evelyn Couch, her emotional "outburst" likely shows, compared with whatever minimal understanding she had previously, that she had come to a clearer and more accurate sense of why she should prefer "Towanda" to continuing to be a "good girl." If conditions exist such that we cannot trust people's expressions, then we should change those conditions rather than merely ignore the expressions. Emotions can be educated so that they provide awareness and insight and reasons for action.

I suppose all teachers have had students, colleagues, parents, and others express dissatisfaction (or satisfaction) that merits little if any weight or response. People are merely whining (or brown-nosing) rather than expressing something weighty regarding their well-being. Yet even if expressions are whines, if we are to educate emotions educators must be prepared to respond to them. Whines provide something to negotiate, such as issues of individual and social welfare and authority. If the origin of the whine is in some misunderstanding between teacher and student, that can get explicit attention so that understanding can be achieved.

However, while I am inclined to reject Scanlon's claim that emotions and preferences have no moral weight, we should not err at the other extreme and make those emotions and expressions decisive. Even if we arrive at a place where we can trust people's emotions and self-reports to be honest and based on at least some degree of understanding, our ethical obligations do not end there. However unlikely, I suppose it's possible that there are "happy" prostitutes who really understand and accept their condition. That hardly relieves us of the responsibility to improve their lives.

So, people's self-reports and emotional expressions, perhaps even their whines, can have moral weight. They can tell us a good deal. As I have proposed, we should treat people's self-reports as authoritative. Yet we also should treat them as defeasible; they cannot substitute for educators' wisdom and judgment.

Educators have norms for well-being and access to evidence of people's well-being. There is another factor to consider, though. The subjectivity of well-being could suggest that educators should do as much as they can to see other people's well-being from those people's point of view. I have a hard time seeing the value of cults and NASCAR, but maybe I need to do more to see things from others' points of view.

"Point of view" is an ambiguous notion, though. In particular, there is a difference between "point of view" in the sense of the perspective a person actually happens to have, and "point of view" in the sense of the stance a person would take if she had more information and better understanding. The current point of view might not be the authentic point of view. With the latter sense in mind, a proponent of a capabilities approach to well-being plausibly can claim to take another individual's point of view even while disagreeing with that person regarding her current welfare. So, even if a "happy" prostitute sees no particular value in protecting the integrity of her body or controlling her environment, trying to persuade her otherwise need not be an imposition; she could come to see the prudential value of those things; that would be her real point of view.

Obviously, we have to be careful with such claims. Given the subject-relativity of well-being and concern for freedom we have to give some place to an individual's actual values, desires, and so on, even if we believe them mistaken. For example, consider Noddings's ideas of "engrossment" and "motivational displacement," which are essential elements of care, in her view.[33] Engrossment and motivational displacement ask educators to make students' aims and interests their fundamental guides. This does not mean caring teachers cannot challenge students or even coerce them at times. But doing so requires work to maintain or reestablish a good relationship.[34]

However, this does not adequately explain the notion of taking another's point of view. Literally, an individual can never take another's point of view, and it is not necessary to do so in order to judge responsibly. Now, I am not saying there is no legitimate and helpful way that people cannot see, or try to see, from others' points of view.[35] I might not be a good example, but in this book I have tried to do that when I criticize people like Griffin and Rawls and try to understand people like Tevye and Evelyn Couch.

Nevertheless, literally, people cannot put themselves in other people's places, and it is ethically important for us to realize that. As popular as it is to think one should "walk a mile in others' shoes" before judging their lives, perception and truth claims might actually work in the other direction. Merleau-Ponty says the process involves

> a kind of demand that what I see be seen by [the other person] also . . . It is thus necessary that, in the perception of another, I find myself in relation with another "myself," who is, in principle, open to the same truths as I am, in relation to the same being that I am.[36]

If I hope to persuade another person to see his life differently, I certainly want to be open to his perspective, and, for Gadamer, openness requires that "I myself must accept some things that are against me, even though no one else forces me to do so."[37] Nevertheless, "[o]nly by being given full play is [our own prejudice] able to experience the other's claim to truth and make it possible for him to have full play himself."[38] If I give "full play" to my prejudices, my prejudices could be altered, but that helps me in forming the truth I perceive, which I then work to have my dialogical partner see as well.

Also, there is something ethically suspect in the idea that one can adopt another person's point of view; it risks misunderstanding if not arrogance about what someone can know about another person or group. Also, it can just be a cop out; educators cannot, and should not, escape their own conceptions of a good life as they make judgments about others' lives.[39] Having determined a justified conception of a good life, an educator should not deprive students of whatever experience and wisdom the educator has to share. But that experience and wisdom comes from educators living their own lives. Ultimately, they have no other context for judging well-being; no one can live another person's life.

That might appear to be a surprising suggestion given the subjectivity of well-being. It requires more explanation. First of all, there are several ways we might compare possible lives and judge some better than others. Some comparisons rely relatively little on particular conceptions of a good life. People can make mistakes because they do not have adequate information or misconstrue the information they have. Or, there can be contradictions internal to a person's conception, aspects of the person's constellation that are mutually exclusive or at least fit poorly together. A person who claims to make health central to his well-being, yet drinks heavily and stays out late most nights, really has something he ought to sort out. He is erring or unwise based on what he himself deems important for himself. Correcting these sorts of mistakes would allow educators to be appropriately neutral regarding the quality of other persons' conceptions of their well-being. They merely ask students to gather more information or show them they should think more about their own conception of their well-being.

However, this approach is trickier than it might appear at first. We have considered before that gathering more information is an activity reasonable persons could reject because it competes with other activities they deem more important. So, we appear unable to escape subject-relativity even in the seemingly innocuous activity of encouraging self-examination and learning.

Much depends on what we construe learning to be. There are legitimate educational avenues of correction and persuasion and even coercion. Some of those will be explored in Chapter 9. But how can criticism and correction be appropriate if we always judge from our own point of view ultimately?

## EXPERIENCE AND COMPETENCE IN JUDGMENT

Ortuño-Ortin and Roemer offer a model for interpersonal rankings of actual or possible states of affairs as to their prudential value.[40] This model uses the notion of "local expertise" to describe the competence required. There are two principal features of this local expertise. One is that an individual can develop empathy for others because during her own life she has been a person of different types. Educators cannot literally put themselves in others' shoes, but through the experiences of their lives they can come close, having been the "type" of person others are at the current time. The idea is not that to judge the value of a student's desire to hitchhike through South America one must have done so oneself. Yet the judge can be the same type of person, having taken adventures of one sort or another, experienced the joys and fears of being self-reliant with meager means at her disposal.

Experiences and types will be more or less similar, so competence or justification for judgment is a matter of degree. It is possible for one's experience to be too far from another's. The persons might differ too much in type.[41] Or the experiences two people have could differ radically even though they are similar sorts of persons. For example, two people might be risk-takers but the experience of risking one's life as a seaside lifeguard is rather different than risking a few bucks in the football pool. So, any particular individual might not be a competent judge in some situations.

But this leads to the second principal feature of the model, which is that judgment is not a solitary activity but a matter of combining individual judgments. Ortuño-Ortin and Roemer show that a unique (though perhaps partial) ordering of states of affairs can be achieved by combining individual judgments. We should be clear what that means. The claim is not that the judgments of incompetent judges somehow will converge on the correct ordering. The point is that a group of competent judges can order some range of possible lives. So, perhaps a group of competent educators together can offer their students a reliable picture of the relative prudential value of various possible lives.

In addition, similar to my earlier response to Scanlon, if our limited experience makes it difficult to empathize with others, or if we cannot trust the honesty of people's claims about their well-being, we can work on establishing conditions so that we are better able to empathize with other people and to trust what they say about their welfare. If students do not portray their well-being accurately, educators can examine the conditions that encourage them to be inarticulate or dishonest, and work to give them the knowledge and skills to be articulate and accurate. Or, if educators' own experiences are limited, they can expand and deepen them. The challenges never can be totally eliminated, but I do think that there is much that educators can do to deal with them well.

## CONCLUSION

In this chapter I have argued that judging the quality of lives or aspects of lives need not result in destructive discord; rather, it can be a way to express and cultivate understanding and respect for persons and their conceptions of their welfare. We cannot be glib about the intellectual and emotional demands of good judgment and fair distribution of resources. However, if students and educators educate themselves and one another, and work together, we can increase the likelihood of accurate and helpful judgments. Experienced educators can reach legitimate assessments of others' well-being, even though they cannot literally take others' points of view.

Educators cannot avoid the responsibility to make judgments about the quality of people's lives. But their responsibility is not only to pass judgment on people. Educators also are responsible to help people develop good conceptions of their well-being and live satisfying lives. The next chapter begins to sketch out possible conditions for that to occur, in terms of classroom interactions and seductions.

*Chapter 9*

# Seducing Souls

In this chapter I give attention to "seducing souls" as an aim for education for human well-being. Essentially, the goal is to draw students into experiences where they can begin to discover, reveal, and elevate their selves, transform their being in the world so as to achieve the vision that is the essence of living well. Talk of "seduction" can be disturbing, implying manipulation that conflicts with the sort of student freedom and judgment needed if students are to learn to see and live well. The burden of this chapter is to explain this seduction, its value, and its justification.

To begin, I consider the subject matter conducive to self-transformation. Self-elevation is not contentless; it occurs through experience with a subject matter of some sort. Perhaps this also begins to allay some fears about seduction, because it is subject matter primarily, and not teachers, that seduces students. I describe the relevant subject matter as "spiritual exercises."

## SPIRITUAL EXERCISES

By "spiritual exercises" I mean activities aimed at the sort of transformations we saw in Evelyn and Tevye and hypothesized for Private Branham. "Spiritual exercises" might conjure up images of sitting on a mountaintop with a yogi, or participating in séances. However, we can conceive spiritual exercises more broadly to include any project of self-examination and elevation that attempts to connect the individual to something cosmic or universal. Hadot sees this as the basic project of ancient, "therapeutic" philosophy and sees Socrates as a paradigmatic example.[1]

As Hadot sees it, Socrates did not intend to teach his colleagues anything, but, rather, to "put *themselves* into question, forcing them to pay attention to and take care of themselves."[2] We can see this at work in *The Republic*, for example. Socrates worked from his partners' ideas and questions; he urged them to put themselves "out there." Socrates's insistence on not knowing was no mere ploy (although there could be some deception in it, as we will get to shortly); he aimed to keep his students' attention focused on their self-examination rather than give them the easy way out of getting answers from him.

Later in this chapter I will emphasize the dialogical nature of spiritual exercises. For now I will suggest two sorts of exercise: writing and reading.

What is the relationship between writing and reading (and other spiritual exercises, such as art) and care for self and well-being?[3] To explore that question I turn to Michel Foucault, who devotes a good deal of thought to writing as a spiritual exercise.

Foucault emphasizes "concern for self as a practice of freedom," and proposes "self writing" is one of those practices.[4] Writing is one way to create the sort of artistic self Foucault desires. Taking a similar view, David Schaafsma says:

> When students . . . write, they do not "discover" themselves or get in touch with or express their "true" selves . . . [We should view] self as multiple — voices/subjectivities — discursively and interactively and contradictorily constituted, open to shifts and changes as discourse shifts.[5]

As noted earlier, Hadot argues that care for the self includes putting oneself in question, and to that extent his view is similar to Foucault's and Schaafsma's. Yet Hadot also argues that one does not write oneself, nor does writing constitute the self. Rather, writing and other spiritual exercises change "the level of the self, and universalizes it."[6] We have considered how this elevation of the self can be experienced. Writing can be an experience of that sort. When a person writes she feels as if she is being watched, feels that she is part of "the silently present human community."[7] Taylor argues that the agenda of some of the greatest twentieth-century writers "is not the self but something beyond."[8] As we have seen, this attention to something beyond the self does not deny the importance of the self; it is a sort of "self-forgetting" that ultimately serves the self and well-being.

Urging students to write toward the universal is not asking them to ignore or devalue their everyday lives. Their day-to-day lives might be good things to write about. A particular attitude toward their writing and their selves is needed, however. For example, Foucault discusses letter writing as a spiritual exercise. He analyzes one of Marcus Aurelius's letters and how Marcus details all the "unimportant" things he did (like chatting with his mother) that actually are the important things, because they are him, what he felt and thought.[9]

The "unimportant," everyday details of a person's life can, indeed, be important, but they are *not* the person. Persons are also constituted by elements of broader horizons, sometimes extending to what is universal. The resonance we have sought within human beings comes when people see themselves as part of nature, or as a reasoning being, or as having some other universal experience, an experience that is or can be within every individual. Far from ignoring the present, "in the enjoyment of the pure present [one] discovers the mystery and splendor of existence."[10]

But, one might object, for many people existence isn't especially splendid and enjoyable. Yet perhaps it is important to help young people see splendor in life even if their lives also include a good deal of suffering. That is one function for reading. Nussbaum cites a passage from *David Copperfield* where David says that amid his childhood miseries, his dead father's books became "a glorious host, to keep me company. They kept alive my fancy, and my hope of something beyond that time and place."[11]

We see that happen in the movies we have talked about and in literary fiction such as Hurston's *Their Eyes Were Watching God*. The story follows Janie's day-to-day life, full of the humiliations and sorrows of a young black woman. But Janie comes to see her self and the world in new, more encompassing and fulfilling ways. The novel ends with Janie reflecting:

> Of course [her lover Tea Cake] wasn't dead. He could never be dead until she herself had finished feeling and thinking. The kiss of his memory made pictures of love and light against the wall. Here was peace. She pulled in her horizon like a great fish-net. Pulled it from around the waist of the world and draped it over her shoulder.[12]

Hoping for and remembering something beyond can be mere escapism, but hope and fancy can be good things, too. Even if the aim of reading and writing is not to engender hope and splendor, if we are to help people understand the meaning of their circumstances, the injustices and other suffering they endure, they, just as anyone, need to understand the broader ethical horizon so that they can orient themselves in it. This horizon is no distant abstraction; one can "drape it over her shoulder."

Of course, as with other things, to see reading and writing as spiritual exercises would require changes in dominant attitudes. On one hand, there is the view that the lessons gained from literature should be aesthetic, not ethical.[13] That is, literature should be read for its style, character development, and similar features. For Hadot, this indicates "we have forgotten *how* to read: how to pause, liberate ourselves from our worries, return into ourselves, and leave aside our search for subtlety and originality, in order to meditate calmly, ruminate, and let the text speak to us."[14]

The aim of reading is not just to practice deciphering language or to analyze the subtleties of character development. Good writers write to tell us something. We need to be open to the lessons. As Socrates did for his compatriots, we must allow the text to dialogue with us to prompt inner dialogue, self-reflection, a "battle" with ourselves.[15]

On the other hand, the sort of spiritual exercises I am suggesting can be attacked by subjectivists, such as some postmodernists, who advocate the non-rationality, or at least the unhelpfulness, of judging the quality of different lives, "voices," values, and so forth. Schaafsma expresses that view when he says we should view self "as multiple — voices/subjectivities — discursively and inter-actively and contradictorily constituted, open to shifts and changes as discourse shifts."[16] Yes, self is not static, but not all "voices and subjectivities" need serve persons well. Suppose a child hears her "voice" say, "I am a capable person," and the contradictory voice say, "I am not capable." We all are complex creatures capable at some things but not others, but that is not what Schaafsma endorses; he endorses "contradictorily constituted" selves. It is difficult to see how any child or other person would benefit from living with contradictions like "I am capable and I am not capable." If persons are unsure about their capabilities, they try to make sense of what they can and cannot do and not just live with contradictions. Recalling Dewey's point about the connection between meaning and unity, multiplying voices and subjectivities is more likely to be confusing than helpful.

We should see the self as something in motion, something that "happens," so, indeed, we should be suspicious about claims to have discovered someone's true self. And as we explored with Private Branham, Evelyn Couch, and Tevye, people certainly can be complicated admixtures of attitudes, emotions, beliefs, and other things. We could see how Evelyn and Tevye were torn in various ways. They had to live with that to some extent, for some time. But they also sought to resolve the tensions. Even if the resolutions of their "contradictions" were not perfect, we found reasons to think that Evelyn and Tevye arrived at a state that was not just different but also better. Also, while they were open to shifts, we should not overestimate the ease with which that can and should occur. Stubbornness is not a vice necessarily, nor a surrender of freedom. Indeed, if a person shifts whenever discourse shifts, that might well indicate a lack of freedom; one is just a victim of the pushes and pulls around her.

One might object, though, that the way to serve commitments like justice is to encourage the clash of differing perspectives; urging students to achieve a universal view is more likely to limit freedom and discussion than encourage them. For instance, David Blacker opposes the notion of "the 'universal intellectual' . . . who claims to speak for the collective consciousness. The 'universal' figure claims to stand outside power."[17] I choose this passage because it directly challenges the universality I argue is essential to the pursuit of well-being. Contra Blacker, helping people through spiritual exercises to become "universal intellectuals" is exactly what educators need to do.

First, the universal intellectuals I hope educators and students can be do not claim to stand outside power if that means to stand in some completely neutral place. Such a sense of truth or transcendence is illusory. But there is also a sense of truth and transcendence that is innocuous.[18] We know that language can be used to manipulate people and what passes for truth; we cannot escape language and in that sense we do not stand outside power. Yet that in no way implies that truths cannot be achieved within those limits. After all, postmodernists claim to uncover and identify the workings of power, so they must think language allows for accurate criticism. If postmodernists insist that their criticisms are not "true" because those criticisms are themselves subject to criticism, that appears to suppose that truth must be certain and non-revisable. But that is an implausibly demanding conception of truth.

We know that truths are partial and fallible; nonetheless, we are justified in talking in terms of truth as an "idea of reason." As Thomas McCarthy puts it:

> While we have no idea of standards of truth wholly independent of particular languages and practices, "truth" nevertheless functions as an "idea of reason" with respect to which we can criticize not only particular claims within our language but also the very standards of truth that we have inherited . . . We can and typically do make contextually conditioned and fallible claims to unconditional truth (as I have just done). It is this moment of unconditionality that opens us up to criticism from other points of view.[19]

That brings me to the point about the universal intellectual speaking for the collective consciousness. Blacker supposes that is a criticism, whereas it need not be. On one hand, to claim to speak for others can be unjustified and arrogant — say, when the speaker is just ignorant and spouts biases. But, on the other hand, speaking for the collective consciousness is precisely what one does when one speaks unconditional truth claims. If one really is interested in the truth and not merely in expressing oneself, one strives to perceive and act as a human being receptive to aspects of a world that is a reality for, and accessible to, all human beings. By attempting to speak for the collective in this way, one is not trying to decide issues for other people but to put before them some part of that world for shared exploration. Hadot argues:

> Writing . . . takes the place of other people's eyes. A person writing feels he is being watched; he is no longer alone, but is a part of the silently present human community. When one formulates one's personal acts in writing, one is taken up by the machinery of reason, logic, and universality. What was confused and subjective becomes thereby objective.[20]

Writing of painting, Merleau-Ponty makes a similar point:

> The actions most proper to [the painter] seem to emanate from the things themselves, like the patterns of the constellations. Inevitably the roles between him and the visible are reversed. That is why so many painters have said that things look at them.[21]

And an artwork is no mere object; it offers us an opportunity to wander and see anew: "I would be at great pains to say *where* is the painting I am looking at. For I do not look at it as a thing; I do not fix it in its place. My gaze wanders in it as in the halos of Being. It is more accurate to say that I see according to it, or with it, than I *see it*."[22]

Students' writing and other artwork need to be more than "things." They are media for things to look back at students and help them and others see with it, to invite them to "wander in the halos of Being." Of course, writing and art need not achieve what Hadot and Merleau-Ponty contend it does. They are talking about using them as spiritual exercises, as transformative experiences. As with learning how to experience in general, people need to be guided and educated for and in spiritual exercises.

At this point I move away from curriculum to look more closely at teachers and their activities and how they might guide students. Just like everyone else, teachers cannot make silk purses out of sows' ears. Teachers can be talented and caring and yet be thwarted by conditions around them. Still, teachers are the people face-to-face with students day-to-day. They make day-to-day decisions about "local justice" and students' welfare. In the next several sections we will consider further how teachers might guide students toward and through spiritual exercises and other experiences in ways consistent with well-being and proper freedom.

## QUESTIONING AND UNDERSTANDING IN DIALOGUE

The perfectionist concern for openness and deliberation implies that questioning will be a major activity in schools that promote well-being: "What is the point of this?" "What good is that?" "Shouldn't that have been done differently?" Such questions have to be welcomed and openly pondered — through writing, reading, drawing, drama, talking, and other means — if students are to develop a sense that such questions are legitimate, develop a sense of prudential value, and develop the perception needed for good decisions about value.

Shortly I will add a few examples of questions to the ones offered here, but my main objective is not to give a list of possible questions.[23] My focus is on what teachers do with questions, how they might encourage and guide questioning in dialogue with students.

First, let us consider further why questions and dialogue are so important. A central theme for Gadamer is that coming to an understanding of some subject matter is a task for dialogue among people. Of course, many educators think talking with students once in a while is a good idea. However, for Gadamer dialogue is not just one among various avenues for achieving understanding; dialogue is more than a nice break from lectures or independent study. For Gadamer reaching an understanding *means* reaching an agreement about the subject matter through dialogue. Lectures might accomplish something, but the mere transfer of information from teacher to student does not imply understanding.

This raises the question of just what sort of understanding we are talking about. If a history teacher says to her students, "The American Civil War began in April 1861. Do you understand?" and the students replied (truthfully), "Yes," we have no particular reason to doubt that teacher and students have a legitimate sense of "understanding" in mind. However, paralleling our earlier discussion of meaning, we have here an understanding that essentially is confined to comprehension of the teacher's statement. We saw before that there are other and deeper senses of meaning, and the same holds true of understanding.

To get a better sense of Gadamer's point let's identify the sort of questions that are relevant here. All questions are not alike; to ask questions and give replies is not necessarily to engage in dialogue. Gadamer distinguishes between "true" questions and "apparent" questions.[24] True questions are open questions. They are open because, for all the participants in dialogue, the answer is not known or not clear. In contrast, one type of apparent question is the pedagogical question. Pedagogical questions are not true questions because there is no questioner. That is, the poser of the "question" has no question himself. Teachers do this sort of thing all the time: "When did the American Civil War begin?" "What is the product of 2 and 4?" "What is the shortest highway route from Des Moines to Moline?" These sorts of questions are not open; the idea is that students will arrive at the answer the teacher already knows or could know. The teacher is not looking to gain knowledge for herself (beyond knowing whether the students have the answers, that is).

Another type of apparent question is the rhetorical question. A rhetorical question has neither questioner nor object. Not only does the questioner have no question but also he offers no subject matter for students to think about. These "questions," too, are common: "Children, should we stab our neighbors with our pencils?" "What do we do when it's time to clean up?" "How should we walk in the hallway?" These "questions" do not ask anything; they make or imply propositions or commands in question-like form. They are intended to reinforce or remind students of things they already know, or are expected to know.

Pedagogical and rhetorical questions might have a proper place in teaching, but we need to recognize them for what they are. Dialogue requires open questions, questions for which neither teachers nor students have the final answers. The aim of dialogue is to make headway on answering these questions by reaching a common understanding about the issues raised.

The cycle of question and answer forms the basic structure of dialogue. We already noted Gadamer's claim that "the structure of the question is implicit in all experience."[25] But questioning has a particularly vital role in the experience of learning and understanding. Gadamer says: "Discourse that is intended to reveal something requires that that thing be broken open by the question. For this reason, dialectic proceeds by way of question and answer or, rather, the path of all knowledge leads through the question."[26] We need to be clear, too, what this aim "knowledge" is. It easily could be agreed that questions are a, or the, path to knowledge. However, the aim could be the end of questioning, a sense of knowledge where questions finally have been answered. From this not uncommon point of view, having questions implies lack of knowledge. Gadamer presents a different view: "Only a person who has questions can have knowledge."[27]

Gadamer's claim might seem odd at first, but I imagine many of us have had the experience that the more we know the more we know we don't know. We become ever more cognizant of the complexity of issues and the limits of our knowledge. And along with that, we become suspicious of people who have no questions, who claim to have "the answers." The certainties these people expound take on the character of dogma rather than knowledge. Using Gadamer's distinction, people might be confident in their "opinions," but opinions do not constitute knowledge: "Knowledge always means, precisely, considering opposites. Its superiority over preconceived opinion consists in the fact that it is able to conceive of possibilities as possibilities."[28] As we considered before, for Evelyn-Towanda to know that her new life is superior to her old life, she had to consider differing possibilities for her life. She did that. Ninny's stories brought home that a different life was not just a castle in the sky but was a possibility that *was* a possibility.

Making dialogue central to teaching does not imply that dialogue is the only appropriate mode for learning. Hermeneutic experience is an adventure and as such cannot occur constantly. Similarly with the dialogue and understanding proper to experience. Teachers' non-dialogical acts (cajoling students, simply dispensing information, unilaterally setting parameters for dialogue) can be consistent with the aim of dialogue. Pursuing experience and dialogue does not straightforwardly imply particular acts. However, if well-being is the aim, experience and dialogue provide standards against which teachers' actions must be judged. Teachers must be able to justify departures from those standards.

If people are to conceive and pursue their well-being, they need to understand what their beliefs and actions mean: Is this science project an accomplishment? What does "accomplishment" mean? They need to understand their purposes: Do I do this because it is something important to me? What am I trying to achieve? And typically, these are open questions: meanings are complex and uncertain; our purposes might not be clear to us. Heidegger suggests, a person "does not have control over unconcealment itself, in which at any given time the real shows itself or withdraws."[29] However, although teachers might not control unconcealment, there are ways to facilitate it through spiritual exercises and dialogue. For example, Socrates took on his students' personae in a sense, when he said things like, "Now, what you're saying is this, right?" That way he confronted his partners with themselves, mirrored them back to themselves. When his interlocutors question Socrates they question themselves.

Through dialogue students begin to reveal who they are, in terms of what they value, where they locate themselves in value frameworks. For teachers, this revealing has dual value. First, it is valuable for students to start to understand who they are. Second, it is valuable for teachers to begin to understand who students are in order to help guide them toward a genuinely worthwhile and satisfying life.

Teachers often are told they need to know their students and give them opportunities for self-reflection. However, Gadamer's analysis of dialogue has significant implications for how one should conceive such things as teacher authority, classroom instruction, teacher knowledge, and school subject matter. It does much to challenge traditional and contemporary images of teaching that emphasize the teacher's responsibility to set objectives for learning and otherwise manage students' experiences. The challenge is not only to those who deny the importance of dialogue and student freedom. There is the cliché that a teacher "should guide from the side" and not be a "sage on the stage." As with most slogans, this might sound appealing; but we should not suppose that experience and understanding will occur just because teachers guide from "offstage." Nor should we suppose that being "onstage" cannot facilitate students' experiences. Teaching for understanding and experience cannot be reduced to simple formulae.

I have more to say about the importance and nature of dialogue, but before getting to that, I will address two common objections that arise when talking about dialogue, open questions, and so on. I have opened the door to these already when I say that dialogue is not always appropriate. The objections are that dialogue is appropriate only to particular subject matters and only to students of a particular age or ability.

We might think there are differences between subject matters so far as their openness. In arithmetic, for example, the sum of 3 and 6 is pretty definite (so long as we're clear about the number base we're working in). Of course, many teachers believe that students should not only memorize addition facts but also understand the logic behind addition and other arithmetic operations. But there, too, the issue would not seem to be open. Addition is logically prior to multiplication, because the latter is merely shorthand for the former. Arithmetic teachers surely should help students see the logic, explain things to them and entertain their questions, but it is less clear why they should dialogue with them about it. It could be perfectly appropriate for arithmetic teachers to have more or less firm goals in mind, toward which they direct their students.

There is nothing to object to in those ideas. However, we need to be careful not to construe the subject matter too narrowly. It is one thing to understand arithmetic in the sense that "2 × 3" is arithmetically equivalent to "3 + 3," but such does not exhaust the understandings relevant to arithmetic. Subject matters such as arithmetic are to be understood for their contributions (or lack thereof) to a satisfying life. For understanding of that sort, dialogue and other spiritual exercises are needed.

Let's consider the other objection, though. One might point out that the stage of students' development is relevant here. We might suppose that older students are capable of the dialogue we are talking about and are less in need of teachers'

firm direction, but that is not the case for younger children. Perhaps the objector would appeal to Piaget's distinction between "concrete" and "abstract" stages
of thinking.

Surely, teachers should be sensitive to their students' maturity and ability.
However, we also have to be careful not to underestimate the abilities of even
young persons. Even if Piaget is correct about concrete and abstract stages of
development, nothing says meaningful dialogue has to be abstract.[30] To ponder
with young children the prudential value of history, for instance, we need not
appeal to pithy but abstract notions like being doomed to repeat history if we
do not know it. They can explore living history embodied in parents and grand-
parents or other older people about them. Even young children are interested
in "Where did I come from?" and "How did I get here?" which are, in part,
historical questions. (And a handy diversion if you don't want to get into the
"birds and bees" part.)

There is significant evidence that even young children are interested in,
and able to fruitfully discuss, "big questions" of human life.[31] And if we must
conclude that young people and their ideas are in some sense "immature," we
should heed Dewey's admonition that immaturity is not a deficit.[32]

The upshot is that while I stick to my point that dialogue might not be
appropriate always, its appropriateness cannot be neatly categorized according
to subject matter or stage of student development (or anything else, I'd hazard
to say). There can be times when dialogue is objectively appropriate or not, but
here I'm using the sense of "objective" introduced before; the objective value
depends on particular circumstances.

At this point I turn to look further at the process of dialogue. A perfectionist
conception of well-being and teaching holds that teachers should guide students
toward good conceptions of well-being. How might a teacher participate and
guide through dialogue, particularly while avoiding improper influence or
coercion? A central principle is that the teacher's role is passive primarily.

## DIALOGUE AND PASSIVITY

Gadamer argues, "To conduct a conversation means to allow oneself to be con-
ducted by the subject matter to which the partners in the dialogue are oriented."[33]
So, participation is "not something active but something passive (*pathos*),
namely being totally involved in and carried away" by the subject matter.[34]

I do not want to overstate the case, for teachers surely are actively judging
and helping in dialogue, but there is a sort of passivity that in a significant sense
calls upon teachers to yield their authority and guidance. The exploration of

well-being becomes an open question, sustained by the whole classroom community. The notion of passivity runs counter to typical ideas about a teacher's role, so I will start by anticipating some objections to the notion.

In Part One we explored experience and learning and the notion of "being totally involved and carried away." Still, I imagine there are at least a couple of ideas here that might be bothersome. One is the prospect of teacher and students getting "carried away" by subject matter. Sure, sometimes we admire teachers and students who really get caught up in what they are doing. But being carried away implies loss of control, which can be frowned upon, as when one might criticize Evelyn Couch for getting carried away in the parking lot, or criticize a teacher for getting carried away and forgetting about some of the day's learning goals his lesson plan contained.

Of course, when Gadamer talks about getting carried away he is not saying, "Go crazy." (Although, as the example of Evelyn Couch challenges, maybe there is a place for going crazy.) He is talking about the sort of total involvement a ballplayer undergoes in experiencing a ball game. In experience one gets carried away in the sense of being seduced into forgetting one's self.

Another troublesome suggestion, though, is that participants are passive in this process. We have hinted at this issue in earlier discussion of receptivity in experience. Receptivity suggests some release of control. However, it is worth our while here to explore this idea in more detail.

Dewey, for example, makes strong statements against passivity:

> Perception is an act of the going-out of energy in order to receive, not a withholding of energy. To steep ourselves in a subject-matter we have first to plunge into it. When we are only passive to a scene, it overwhelms us and, for lack of answering activity, we do not perceive that which bears us down. We must summon energy and pitch it at a responsive key in order to *take* in . . . For to perceive, a beholder must *create* his own experience.[35]

Here Dewey aims to counter the idea that the world simply "impresses" itself upon us. Events have to be interpreted; meanings have to be discerned. Conceptual schemes must be brought to bear, and to that extent there must be a "going-out of energy." And to have experience, of a ball game say, certainly one must "plunge" into it and not withhold energy, intellect, and emotion. So, much in Dewey's statements accords with the conception of perception and experience I have advocated.

However, Gadamer gives us reason to refine or add to Dewey's claims about activity, passivity, and "creating" experience. I am not sure how much I am diverging from Dewey, but there is an important ambiguity in the notion of "creating" experience, and exploring that will help show how passivity is appropriate to experience.

Gadamer argues that a question "'occurs' to us . . . 'arises' or 'presents itself' more than that we raise it or present it."[36] Here Gadamer describes an important sense in which a beholder does not create his own experience, at least if we are concerned about the experience of dialogue and understanding. People must plunge into experience to be present with it, and questions have to be perceived as questions; yet, for people present to experience, questions arise less from conscious effort than from the demands of dialogue as it uncovers what is questionable. In that sense participants have to be passive in the face of the unfolding dialogue and its subject matter. It is the sense in which Socrates was passive when he said the next question to consider was the one that came next.

With Gadamer's depiction of dialogue and the example of Socrates, we have a basis to see how teachers can make perfectionist decisions and guide students without inappropriately limiting freedom. Teachers need to have the wherewithal to know when questions of well-being present themselves and how to follow the course of inquiry the questions imply. But they are not there simply to impose their opinions on students; they are there to bring everyone, including themselves, to understanding.

That does not mean teachers are unconcerned for truth and guidance. The point is that truth does not reside exclusively with the teacher. For Gadamer, in dialogue,

[w]hat emerges in its truth is the logos, which is neither mine nor yours and hence so far transcends the interlocutors' subjective opinions that even the person leading the conversation knows that he does not know.[37]

Truth is no mere matter of opinion — a belief that is yours or mine — but neither is it something graspable independent of human understanding. Ultimately, claims to truth can only be redeemed through dialogue among human beings, in the exchange of people's "opinions"; but the truth is in the "logos" we follow even as we know we don't know where it will take us.

An example might help make the point. What if a teacher were to pose, as a true question and not just a rhetorical one, "Should we accept cultural differences?"[38] We could look for truth in the sense of a "yes" or "no" answer. But open questions are open just because simple "yes" or "no" answers are inadequate. An objective answer depends on circumstances. The truth that can be exposed is the logos of the subject matter. If we were to treat the question seriously, what would need to be explored? Among other things, exposing the truth would require exploring what's meant by "culture," "difference," and "acceptance." It would require exploring possible justifications for one response or another; for example, ones based in respect for other people and ones based on respect or loyalty to one's own culture(s). One truth of the logos that might become clearer for people is that the question really is open. All these topics are logical parts of the subject matter.

The logos of the subject matter is not just anything, although it surely is complex. Discussion might not lead to consensus on a "yes" or "no" answer to the question. There might be consensus that some differences should be accepted and others not. Understanding the subject matter is the aim in Gadamer's dialogue, not a particular view about it. Maybe that seems woefully inadequate when one thinks about the intolerance for cultural differences that exists. But as we should worry about dogmatic intolerance, we should worry about dogmatic tolerance, which can lead to injustice, as when someone would pass off a culture's caste system as "just their way of doing things."

This dialogue — in science, ethics, and other areas — is not concerned merely with opinions in the sense of assertions blurted out without the benefit of evidence and other justification. Yes, the logos must be articulated through people's expressions; there is no other way to go about it. But the aim of dialogue is to unfold the logic of the *subject matter*, to uncover the truth of it, and not just to express one's personal opinions about it. If people are present in and with the dialogue, at some point individual beliefs are transcended. What they express is a question or response that "presents itself" in the flow of the dialogue. People are mouthpieces for expressions, but the expressions are not theirs. The expressions cannot be theirs because they do not know what to believe; they only know that they do not know.

In this way, the subject matter is open, but the openness is limited in important ways. Although the subject matter need not dictate the specific course dialogue should take, it does provide some boundaries. Certainly it is possible for dialogue to get off the subject. That is not to say, though, that one should never get "off task." As dialogue proceeds, it might show that the subject matter is not what participants initially thought it was. Participants have to be ready to follow the logos where it takes them. Even if shifts are necessary, however, they are necessary because of the logic of the subject matter, and not simply the subjective thinking or beliefs of individuals. Participants have to be passive in the sense of opening themselves to the unfolding of the subject matter. That is the essence of the dialogical experience.

The upshot is that while the logic of the subject matter, student development, and perhaps other factors put some constraint upon the course of dialogue, these constraints are wider and more fluid than might commonly be believed. Teachers must remain open to the need for their passivity; the boundaries of their subject matter cannot be firmly fixed ahead of time, nor can the particular path of dialogue within those boundaries. Judgments about the course of dialogue might need to be made among participants and not by the teacher alone.

But this claim prompts us to look more closely at the teacher's authority in dialogue.

## TEACHER AUTHORITY IN DIALOGUE

Even if we grant that teachers do not have all the answers and that there is some presumption of equality between teacher and students, teachers still have a responsibility to guide students by virtue of the teachers' experience and wisdom. In dialogue the aim is "unfolding what consistently follows from the subject matter itself."[39] As shown by the example of Socrates, some people might be more adept than others when it comes to helping the subject matter unfold.

However, we should consider the authority the teacher has in dialogue. The connection Gadamer makes between understanding and application is helpful here. Gadamer argues that the sort of understanding we seek always involves application of the subject matter; understanding and application are not two separate processes. Individuals necessarily understand from some particular personal, sociohistorical vantage points. For me to understand arithmetic beyond its mere technical aspects, I know how it "applies" to me, what it means for me and my world now and for my future, what it can and cannot contribute to a worthwhile life for me and other persons. This connection between understanding and application challenges the common belief that teachers are in possession of understanding that students first must learn and then apply, or that it is sufficient for teachers to know content without understanding its relevance to life.

Of course, educators have been concerned about understanding and application. Thus, arithmetic texts do not just give lists of computation exercises; they even have some story problems that supposedly help students apply the computational skills they acquire. But this sort of application does not go nearly far enough. Students (and other relevant persons) must themselves be participants in the dialogue that hammers out the meaning of school subject matter. If students are to understand, they must, with guidance, make their own connections between subject matter and life, not just be informed of the connections others see or project for them.

We considered an example of this before, when we imagined how a student might not see her work as an accomplishment. Before, we analyzed this in terms of the experience the student had with her work. In language we are using now, the student's situation can be described as an experience where application is lacking.

A teacher could work to help the child see the application to her life. But the teacher would lack the competence and authority to do so if he could not speak from experience, as the type of person the student is and from an understanding of how the subject matter can apply to the student.

However, the teacher's task is not only to lead students to the sort of experience he has had. Gadamer says, "To reach an understanding in a dialogue is not merely a matter of putting oneself forward and successfully asserting one's own point of view, but being transformed into a communion in which we do not remain what we were."[40] Maybe it is not shocking to think that students should be transformed through encounters with teachers and subject matter; we might think that learning necessarily constitutes some sort of transformation. However, Gadamer's statement presents three other points that could be more surprising. One regards "asserting one's own point of view." We should think about just how much teaching comes down to teachers asserting their own point of view, not that that cannot be warranted. There is no particular problem with a teacher asserting that $2 + 3 = 5$ or that the American Civil War began in 1861 (at least, that's when the real shooting began). As we have seen, though, such points of view constitute only a portion of the understanding students need.

I imagine many teachers already are cautious about asserting their own point of view. But notice that Gadamer does not suggest teachers should not assert their own points of view. He says that is not all they should do, that the ultimate aim is a "communion." It is difficult to see how teachers can form a communion with their students if they refuse to offer their points of view in appropriate ways and at appropriate times.[41]

Obviously, there are dangers. There might not be a genuine communion; students might merely be seduced to the teacher's point of view because of the teacher's overwhelming charisma. However, there are ways of avoiding the danger that do not require teachers to avoid meaningful dialogue. There are things teachers can do to foster an environment where real questions can be presented and constructively explored, such as being open about their own uncertainties. And if students change their points of view, there is nothing wrong with that necessarily. Indeed, Gadamer proposes that there is a transformation in every genuine experience of understanding.

But what sort of transformation is Gadamer talking about? Earlier we considered that learning is a sort of transformation, which seems unexceptional. However, transformation might conjure up images of schools molding students, which could be scary, especially if the aim is that students should not remain what they were. Recalling the authenticity issue, do we really want to transform students into something they are not?

On one hand, yes, we do want to do that, when it is called for. The ultimate aim of therapeutic philosophy and dialogue is to persuade and not just reveal the truth. We want students actually to move toward lives that are genuinely worthwhile and satisfying. Persuasion is not the same thing as coercion, but there might even be times when coercion is justified: we don't leave it up to a child to decide if she will step in front of a speeding car. Perhaps even more disturbing, we have to entertain the possibility that souls need to be "seduced."[42] So, we turn to the issue of whether the aim of well-being justifies deceit and other seductions.

## SEDUCING SOULS

In Chapter 7 we saw Gadamer's doubts about the power of reason compared with "affections" and his point about the reasonableness of rhetoric, even if it appeals to people's feelings. However, even if appealing to feelings is reasonable, we might have some discomfort about that, especially because I have been stressing the importance of truth. For example, it would appear to follow from Gadamer's point that a teacher could be justified in inflaming students' passions in order to seduce them into doing an activity or to see a point. At least at first blush, it might be difficult to see how that is consistent with the passivity and communion with students I have advocated for teachers. I will argue that it is consistent, but first of all let's admit that there might be an element of deception and manipulation in teachers' dialogical actions.[43]

Hadot describes Socrates as deceptive, putting on a mask, in his dialogues.[44] Socrates pretends to be puzzled about issues. He acts as if he is identifying with his interlocutors' views, while actually he merely uses those views to seduce his partners to identify with the dialogical project.[45]

That might sound pretty fishy, but let's think about it more. Recall the example of the softball player. We might say she was seduced by the game. The difference between seduction as exploitation and seduction in spiritual exercises is that the participant gives consent to be part of the exercise.[46] We might wonder how sincere or authentic that consent is. Often, though, we simply are seduced by things attractive to us. We might say Evelyn Couch was seduced by Ninny's stories. Her consent might not have been a decision, but we would be disappointed if she hadn't opened herself to the stories. They were seductive; something would be amiss if she wasn't seduced but, rather, resisted their pull.

Or, returning to the example of our ballplayer, we might say she was seduced into being present with the game; she was transformed from her "normal" self to a person engaged in the adventure of experience. But that is not a bad thing. She was transformed in the sense of forgetting her self and being present to experience. However, this sort of change is consistent with personal identity and authenticity; identities develop.

Similarly, perhaps a teacher has to play a role in order to keep dialogue going, to ease students' frustrations by saying he's frustrated, too, for example. Perhaps it is deceptive in a way when a teacher does not say what he thinks but, rather, what he takes the logos to require. Perhaps he needs to inflame or feign passion to keep dominant opinions from closing down dialogue. We have to view these seductions and deceits (if we want to call them that) in terms of their purpose and results. The aim is not merely to trick students but to draw them into experience and better understanding of themselves and their welfare.

Certainly, teachers should be careful with their seductive powers. But the transformations aimed for need not involve the impositions liberals fear. Seducing students to experience baseball during physical education class does not condemn them to switch their career ambitions from music to baseball. If anything, it would appear to enable their choices to be even more autonomous and authentic just because they have experienced a variety of possibilities. I imagine we would want school experiences to be seductive rather than bland.

If we are concerned about the idea that students are seduced into the transformation and communion Gadamer advocates, we should also recall his idea of a fusion of horizons that we encountered before. Fusing horizons does not require one to become like another person or even to change one's beliefs. What it requires is that beliefs be explored and understood in light of other possibilities. These other possibilities might represent challenges to current beliefs, but that does not mean current beliefs must be changed. It means one must respond to the challenges so as to broaden one's horizon and give one's beliefs greater warrant.[47] Even if some beliefs go unchanged, our perspective is transformed.

And Gadamer does not suggest that it's only the students who must be seduced and transformed. Maybe we see some affinity with this in the not uncommon idea that teachers should be students and their students teachers; both groups can learn from each other. But bidirectional learning does not imply communion and transformation. A teacher teaches *Macbeth* to her students; the students teach her hip-hop songs. Or, students teach their teacher that his approach to teaching science isn't working; he responds and so teaches the students that he's willing to listen to them and be flexible. Both examples show teacher-student and student-teacher in action, and both may show valuable interactions. Yet, in neither example is communion clearly manifested. For instance, in neither example are people asking why they're doing what they're doing. The one teacher still will teach *Macbeth*, the other still will teach the science lesson, even if in a different way. Teachers, too, need to allow the subject matter to seduce them.

Even if teachers must be passive for this seduction to happen, it does not follow that seduction and understanding happen by themselves. If understanding, experience, and elevation of the soul are to happen, teachers need skills. What might those skills be?

## SKILL IN TEACHING

Teaching skill is not achieved by loading teachers up with "tools" they utilize in classrooms, contrary to dominant conceptions of teaching and teacher education. Regarding questioning, for instance, Gadamer argues, "There is no such thing as a method of learning to ask questions, of learning to see what is questionable. On the contrary, the example of Socrates teaches that the important thing is the knowledge that one does not know."[48]

To illustrate, recall Dewey's point about plunging into subject matter. Dewey does not say there is a "method" to perception, but he does talk in terms of a "method" of intelligence or inquiry. When he talks about method he is not talking about a recipe or formula. Still, as I did earlier, I question Dewey's analysis. I suppose we all can imagine or recall people who plunge into subject matter "intelligently," with great seriousness and diligence but with a predisposition to look for particular things. Thus, they end up seeing what they were looking for. They miss what might be novel or disconcerting. They have no sense that there might be complications, important issues that they have missed. They might create their experience in some sense, but the experience is limited.[49] And likely it would not help much to tell them to look harder. We return to another point made earlier: there might come a time when you have to change yourself rather than just gather more information.

I am not sure I am diverging dramatically from Dewey here, but there is a difference between emphasizing the operations of intelligence compared with emphasizing one's ignorance, knowing that you do not know. There is no method for perceiving what is questionable. However, with experience can come the requisite openness, sensitivity, and responsiveness.

However, one might dispute the idea that there is no method here. After all, I have claimed that there are a number of things teachers can do to help students have experiences: by reading books, watching movies, writing, being seductive. But it's easy to imagine students reading a good book or watching a provocative movie and getting little out of it. Even if those can be helpful activities, they cannot be applied as methods that will yield the desired results.

Gadamer does write of questioning and dialogue as a skill or art: "A person skilled in the 'art' of questioning is a person who can prevent questions from being suppressed by the dominant opinion. A person who possesses this art will himself search for everything in favor of an opinion."[50] Contrast Gadamer's scenario with what often happens in classroom discussions. Students give their opinions about one thing and another in a free-floating, nonjudgmental conversation. That might seem to be an exemplar of non-suppression, but consider further. In such a conversation, opinions might not be suppressed, but questions are. Perhaps there is no one opinion that dominates, but opinion still dominates.

Let's return to Socrates for an alternative. Socrates's interlocutors expressed all sorts of opinions, but Socrates didn't let them get away with just that. He prodded them to explain their views, to draw out their implications, to justify them in the face of counterexamples. Of course, Socrates had his own views that he thought should dominate (because they were better justified than others), but, putting on his "mask," he did not let his views suppress questions. He encouraged questions. He helped his partners search for things in favor of their opinions. Granted, there were times, as with Thrasymachus, when Socrates could not do much to help. Some opinions simply aren't very good, so considering everything in favor of them might not take long. Still, Socrates's attitude was much different than the "everyone-has-their-own-opinion-and-let's-leave-it-at-that" attitude.

But to take classroom interactions beyond that latter scenario is no mere matter of applying techniques. To search for everything in favor of an opinion requires a sense of one's fallibility — I know I do not know — and wisdom and experience that cannot be reduced to skillful application of tools.

However, we need to remember that a big factor in Socrates's success was that he was engaged in a community whose members shared essential values and purposes. If the constitution of the group were different — composed of the people who ultimately condemned Socrates — no amount of Socrates's skill, and certainly no technique, could achieve much.

## CONCLUSION

In this chapter we have begun to get an idea of what it means to be a teacher whose aims are well-being, experience, and elevation of the self. We can offer students freedom and choices, but teachers are in a position to help those things be meaningful, to help students discover and live their selves and their well-being.

One essential characteristic is experience, so that the teacher can embody and bring to the classroom different "types" of persons, to help judge students' well-being. Another is knowledge of students and prudential value so that the teacher can see what is questionable in dialogue regarding well-being. Another is ability to be seductive, to facilitate students' engagement with spiritual exercises and dialogue that can elevate the selves of all people involved. Another is willingness and ability to be part of a communion where possibilities are explored and choices made. We have also seen, though, that there is no method to the requisite experience and understanding.

This brings me to the end of my arguments. We have covered a lot of territory regarding the nature of well-being, of value, of perfectionist political processes, and of classroom dialogue and seduction. A more or less constant theme has been the complexity of these issues. If individual well-being is subject-relative, and if pluralism is an appropriate perspective on value and politics, it could seem that we have little to conclude beyond the notion that we face complex issues.

In the brief Epilogue that follows, I remind us of some "constants" needed if teachers are to serve persons' well-being, and offer one way to think of a common goal for all educators: educating for philosophy as a way of life.

*Epilogue*

# Philosophy as a Way of Life

I began this book with Aristotle's claim that living well is the highest of practical goods and the aim of politics, and that education, as a practical and political endeavor, should aim high and strive to serve people's well-being. This book represents an extended argument for why that aim is vital and how it can be pursued.

Along the way, I have been cautious about offering prescriptions for education policy and action because of the individual, philosophical, and political complexities inherent in the pursuit of human well-being. However, in this brief Epilogue, what I want to review and emphasize are not all the reasons for caution but, rather, some of the fundamental commitments educators and others must take up if we are to, with a straight face, claim to be seriously interested in human well-being. In particular, I propose that there might be some center of gravity for the constellations we form as individuals and communities as we endeavor to achieve well-being for ourselves and other human beings — philosophy as a way of life.[1]

First of all, though, let's ask if we have any reasons for optimism that well-being can in fact become a meaningful aim in education.

## OPTIMISM AND POLITICAL ACTION

In education and the broader culture, we are faced with policies and attitudes largely apathetic, and even hostile, to human well-being. Many people would see little if anything especially seductive about the sort of experiences I have advocated. We should not underestimate the obstacles to achieving education

197

aimed at human well-being. However, alternatives and resistance do exist. People find comfort in certainty, simplicity, and control; but we have also considered the very human yearning for meaning, joy, and elevation of self. Human history is full of attempts to constrict, repress, and destroy human life, mind, body, and spirit; but it is also full of human beings' attempts to open themselves to and dwell with great universal, existential questions and ideas through philosophy, religion, myth, art, and other avenues.[2]

This suggests that educators must commit themselves to political action. I do not say educators must set out to change the world; however, one can be in the world as a political being, aware and ready to engage as circumstances and practical wisdom demand. This includes pushing out the horizon of political concerns beyond what is the case typically. Teachers might see some reason to participate in local politics of school and school district, but they also have a place to try to affect the larger culture of education. For example, I have often heard that educators and education students should become wise consumers of research. However, if education research is in the condition I fear it is, educators cannot only pick and choose from the "findings" offered them but need to encourage, even demand, from researchers the sort of research and theory that would aid educators in their quest for well-being. Teachers and teachers-to-be can demand from colleges of education that they offer and credit experiences conducive to practical wisdom and practice.

Obviously, teachers cannot effect sweeping changes on their own. Education for human well-being likely would imply changes in how we think about such things as school choice, curriculum, and teacher education. I have used words like spirituality, soul, and reverence, words that are not part of the common education vocabulary, and likely would be ridiculed by more scientistically-minded people. But we have to resist the temptation to throw up our hands and say nothing can be done. Serious public deliberation about good and well-being is possible, and it need not be divisive. People might find common ground in common meanings such as the importance of human capabilities, even as they might disagree about their proper manifestations. We can reach a point where we move beyond debates over first principles to communal explorations about those principles.[3]

Even if productive large-scale deliberation does not happen, from small solidarities, larger solidarities might grow. And there is a good deal individual teachers can do to advance the welfare of students, their colleagues, and themselves, or at least ameliorate the pain they might have to endure.

If this is to happen, one essential thing teachers must bring to bear is sight. It is worthwhile to return to, and reemphasize, that idea.

## BEING AND SEEING

I have talked about sight as a central element of well-being, as with McDowell's point that "there is nothing for a correct conception of doing well to be apart from [the] capacity to read situations correctly." I have to think that experienced teachers (where experience is not measured by time on the job, necessarily) who have, and strive to develop, the ability to read situations well will see and take advantage of opportunities as they present themselves. The opportunities might be maddeningly infrequent. As we have seen, though, meaningful experiences need not be, and should not be, constant. Genuine experience is an adventure, the effects of which ripple out and put people in a place to see their whole life in clearer, deeper ways. And the activities need not be "deep" in the sense people often think. A student need not write with the world looking over her shoulder in order to exercise "higher" human capabilities and experience elevation of her soul. A student intrigued with small engines can push his horizon toward the universal if he can see the things behind the immediate thing. He can marvel, childlike, at the human ingenuity that brought technology to this stage of development and ponder the broader value, and disvalue, of technology. He can appreciate the aesthetics of a well-running machine that requires the harmonious functioning of dozens of parts. He can ponder what the joy he finds in his presence to his experience tells him about his self (even if his next class is literature, which he hates).

It can be difficult for any one teacher to see or understand the possibilities in different activities, even if the teacher has been different types of person during her life. That is one reason why community is so important. But we should remember Nussbaum's exhortation:

> We live amid bewildering complexities. Obtuseness and refusal of vision are our besetting vices. Responsible lucidity can be wrested from that darkness only by painful, vigilant effort, the intense scrutiny of particulars. Our highest and hardest task is to make ourselves people "on whom nothing is lost."[4]

Our vision never will be perfect, but we can try to be people on whom nothing is lost. And that is a philosophical task, at root.

## PHILOSOPHY AS A WAY OF LIFE

Certainly, conceptualizing, judging, promoting, and living good lives require philosophy. But philosophy is central to experience broadly considered, as well.

If, as Gadamer argues, experience always involves a judgment about the situation or event being this or that, meaningful experience requires some degree of philosophical understanding of the nature of those things, the nature of their existence and their prudential significance. And if experience results in or makes possible the self transcendence we have talked about, it is because the individual can live a life of philosophical imagination that keeps him or her in touch with and open to the universality of human existence that provides a horizon of value.

However, if philosophy becomes just one more tool or technique or class to use we will miss its significance. We don't want to confuse philosophy with discourse about philosophy.[5] Merely raising and talking about philosophical issues is unlikely to go anywhere if teachers do not have a sense of what is questionable. And while there is skill and artistry — and maybe even some deceit and seduction — in fostering fruitful spiritual exercises and dialogue, that cannot be reduced to applying technologies.

That is one reason why I speak of philosophy as a way of life. Philosophy is a human capability, but it is not only a capability; it is a mode of being that is virtually inescapable for human beings. When we use our sight or other senses to get around in the world, we might not have any particular purpose in mind, we might not be looking for anything in particular, we might not see very well; yet we do see (and/or feel, hear, smell, and taste) and judge situations as this or that.

Of course, I am not saying philosophy as a way of life means making every part of our lives into a philosophical dilemma. The ancients encourage us to live in the present, to be happy now, because if we wait life will pass us by.[6] I have advocated something similar when I say education should be no mere preparation for well-being: education should be an experience of well-being for students and educators.

At the same time, though, we also are told that for the ancients, "philosophy was a mode of existing-in-the-world, which had to be practiced at each instant, the goal being to transform the whole of the individual's life."[7] That sounds like a terrific burden. But to practice philosophy at each instant does not require it be practiced self-consciously. We practice philosophy at each instant by existing in the world in a particular way, with a particular sort of vision. If it is not "natural," it can become "second nature."[8] And if transforming the whole of a life sounds challenging — which it is — transformation does not mean creating a whole new persona for oneself. Transformation is transcendence, lifting the level of one's self. What greater opportunity is there for doing that than education, people being together in joyfully experiencing universal questions of the human condition? Philosophy is a way of life, not only for individuals but also for communities of practice that keep those questions alive.

So, I encourage educators and others who strive to promote the well-being of all human beings to live philosophically, aiming for experience, practical wisdom, and communal practice. There is more to a good life than philosophy, of course, but the ability to read situations well is the essence of a correct conception of well-being.

I will conclude as Charles Taylor concludes his *Sources of the Self*. As I hope has been clear, we should recognize the dangers and obstacles in undertaking the way of life and being I have portrayed in this book. We should look at these things as challenges, though, and not as inescapable traps. Even noble causes come at a cost, so there might be a point in playing it safe, cutting back on our ambitions at times. But if that is the course we should take, "we deceive ourselves if we pretend that nothing is denied thereby of our humanity."[9]

# Notes

*Introduction*

1 Aristotle, *Nicomachean Ethics*, 1095a7-28 (trans. J. A. K. Thomson [New York: Penguin Books, 1953], p. 66).

2 That language is Charles Taylor's (*The Ethics of Authenticity* [Cambridge, MA: Harvard University Press, 1991]).

3 For other criticisms of No Child Left Behind, see Deborah Meier and George Woods, eds., *Many Children Left Behind* (Boston: Beacon Press, 2004).

4 It's popular to suppose that colleges and public schools are failing. The evidence for these supposed failures is far from conclusive or even persuasive. For example, see Deborah Meier's defense of public schools in her *The Power of Their Ideas* (Boston: Beacon Press, 1995), especially her chapter, "Myths, Lies, and Other Dangers," pp. 67–83.

5 Although the report is over 25 years old by now, *A Nation at Risk* continues to exert its influence (The National Commission on Excellence in Education, *A Nation at Risk* [Washington, DC: US Government Printing Office, 1983]). For instance, in her article "Lessons from Locke" (*Newsweek*, August 11, 2008, p. 47) Donna Foote cites the *A Nation at Risk* claim of "a rising tide of mediocrity" in schools and asserts, "The tide is in." Unfortunately, the notions of educational "excellence" espoused in *A Nation at Risk* have taken hold and persist in the mass media and more broadly. Regarding No Child Left Behind, if the influence isn't direct, there's an ancestral connection with *A Nation at Risk*, for example, in their assumptions about the subject matters that are "basic."

6 See John Kekes, *The Morality of Pluralism* (Princeton, NJ: Princeton University Press, 1993). Kekes proposes that our morality is in some sense disintegrating, but he explains this not as the disintegration of morality but as disintegration of monistic conceptions of morality. To monists, the plurality of legitimate conceptions of value shows the destructive creep of relativism into our society

and culture. However, as we will explore later, plurality in value is not the same thing as relativism.

Frequently, one hears charges that "relativists" are leading us into a society "where anything goes." But it is not in pluralistic societies that "anything goes." It is in societies and groups like Nazi Germany, Stalinist Russia, and religious extremists that "anything goes," where even murder supposedly is justified by awful certainty in a singular, narrow vision of the "moral" society. Tolerance, compassion, and respect for different people are not signs of moral weakness or degeneracy.

7   Richard J. Bernstein, *The Restructuring of Social and Political Theory* (Philadelphia: University of Pennsylvania Press, 1976), p. xiii.

8   Ibid., p. 233.

9   Ibid., p. 236.

10  I follow James Griffin in referring to this class of values as prudential values. See his *Well-Being* (Oxford: Oxford University Press, Clarendon Press, 1986).

11  Martha Nussbaum frames the aim of higher education (quoting Seneca) by saying: "[w]hile we are among human beings, let us cultivate our humanity," and she describes institutions and faculty that are trying to achieve that aim (Martha C. Nussbaum, *Cultivating Humanity* [Cambridge, MA: Harvard University Press, 1997]).

12  Perhaps we should not think in terms of a "line" between rigor and accessibility but, rather, a sort of rigor. Michael Tanner proposes, "What is needed is a recognition that there are other modes of rigor and precision than quasi-formal ones, and ways of being profound that do not require near-unintelligibility" (quoted in Martha Nussbaum, *Love's Knowledge* [Oxford: Oxford University Press, 1990], p. 20, note 33). Here Tanner and Nussbaum are criticizing the form writing too often takes when professionals are writing for other professionals. I do not know how profound the present book is, but I hope it will be intelligible while also being rigorous.

13  Richard J. Bernstein makes this distinction in his *The New Constellation: The Ethical-Political Horizons of Modernity/Postmodernity* (Cambridge, MA: MIT Press, 1991), pp. 337–8.

14  That is a claim made in Foote, "Lessons from Locke," p. 47.

15  One reason, which we are especially prone to ignore, is the poverty in which youth and families live. See David C. Berliner, "Our Impoverished View of Educational Reform," *TC Record*, August 2, 2005, available online at: www.tcrecord.org/content.asp?contentid=12106 (accessed on March 7, 2010).

16  Nel Noddings, *Happiness and Education* (New York: Cambridge University Press, 2003), p. 68.

17  The idea of institutionalizing regret comes from Benjamin Barber, *Strong Democracy* (Berkeley: University of California Press, 1984), pp. 258–9.

*Chapter 1: Basics of Well-Being*

1   L. W. Sumner argues for the subject-relativity of well-being in his *Welfare, Happiness, and Ethics* (Oxford: Oxford University Press, 1996).

2   James Griffin introduces the idea of prudential value in his *Well-Being* (Oxford: Oxford University Press, Clarendon Press, 1986). Later I argue that Griffin's notion of prudential value is importantly ambiguous. For the present it serves to distinguish values that contribute to a person's well-being from other sorts of values: ethical, aesthetic, and so on. This does not mean these various sorts of value are distinct, though. An aesthetic value such as beauty can also have prudential value. An ethical value such as generosity can also have prudential value.

3   Martha Nussbaum, *Women and Human Development* (Cambridge: Cambridge University Press, 2000), p. 71.

4   Sumner, *Welfare, Happiness, and Ethics*, p. 38.

5   The latter is Nussbaum's principal concern. A conception of well-being for individuals, which is the aim of Part One, is different from a political conception of well-being appropriate to guiding public policy. The distinction will be addressed in Chapter 6.

6   Sumner, *Welfare, Happiness, and Ethics*, p. 171.

7   Helen E. Longino, *Science as Social Knowledge* (Princeton, NJ: Princeton University Press, 1990), p. 54. Longino makes this point in the context of discussing Thomas Kuhn's unfortunate talk of people living in different worlds and seeing different things. In Longino's analysis, people can see the same things but attach differential significance to them. Or, they will focus on different aspects of a common world.

    Making a similar point, Charles Taylor says, "If the historiography of the Roman Empire in twenty-fifth-century China is different from our own, this will not be because what we can identify as the same propositions will have different truth values. The difference will be rather that different questions will be asked, different issues raised, different features will stand out as remarkable, and so forth" ("Understanding the Other: A Gadamerian View on Conceptual Schemes," in Jeff Malpas, Ulrich Arnswald, and Jens Kertscher, eds., *Gadamer's Century* [Cambridge, MA: MIT Press, 2002], p. 288).

8   Griffin, *Well-Being*, p. 69.

9   This is the approach Griffin takes. See ibid, pp. 24–6. Griffin says, for example: "Simply to rule out irrational desires would . . . go too far. A compulsive hand-washer's desire is irrational, but its fulfillment affects his utility. So since irrational desires cannot be excluded wholesale, why not let them in, and if their fulfillment is sometimes morally intolerable, look to other moral matters besides utility to block it" (p. 25).

10  Richard Rorty, *Contingency, Irony, and Solidarity* (Cambridge: Cambridge University Press, 1989), p. 89. There can be other costs as well. For instance, Joseph Raz notes that an increase in affluence among poor people can come

at the expense of dislocation in neighborhoods and work communities (*Ethics in the Public Domain*, rev. ed. [Oxford: Oxford University Press, Clarendon Press, 1994], p. 28).

11   Sumner, *Welfare, Happiness, and Ethics*, p. 43.

12   Temple Grandin, *Thinking in Pictures: My Life with Autism* (New York: Random House, Vintage, 2006), p. 105. Grandin also presents the important question of whether Asperger's Syndrome and more extreme forms of autism really are disabilities (p. 218). It is only because of some "disabilities" that autistic people are gifted in other areas; certain "normal" brain functions can be obstacles (p. 220). Grandin herself believes her successful life and career have been facilitated by her "abnormality" (p. 217). The point is applicable to all people: Is every abnormality a disability that has to be fixed?

13   Griffin, *Well-Being*, p. 82.

14   Plato, *The Republic*, trans. Benjamin Jowett (Buffalo, NY: Prometheus, 1986), Book IV, 424, pp. 134–5. (I give the standard pagination, then the pages from the Jowett translation.)

15   Nel Noddings, *The Challenge to Care in Schools* (New York: Teachers College Press, 1992).

16   Nel Noddings, *Happiness and Education* (New York: Cambridge University Press, 2003), p. 88.

17   Of course, often the rationale for teaching more science and math is not that it does students all that much good but that more scientists and mathematicians are needed to maintain our nation's global economic and political power, or clean up the messes their elders have created. I have to wonder just how short we are of scientists and mathematicians, though, if we have enough of them to develop things like longer-lasting air fresheners and more absorbent toilet tissue.

18   Nussbaum offers an "objective" approach that will occupy us in Chapter 6.

19   For a list of recently published self-help books, see Darrin M. McMahon, *Happiness: A History* (New York: Atlantic Monthly Press, 2006), pp. 471–2.

20   Jonathan Haidt, *The Happiness Hypothesis* (New York: Basic Books, 2006), p. 104. Psychological work, in general, tends to equate well-being with happiness, where the latter is reduced to what is pleasant or satisfying to people. See, for example, Daniel Kahneman, Ed Diener, and Norbert Schwarz, eds., *Well-Being: The Foundations of Hedonic Psychology* (New York: Russell Sage Foundation, 1999).

21   Haidt, *The Happiness Hypothesis*, p. 104.

22   Friedrich Nietzsche, *Twilight of the Idols*, trans. R. J. Hollingdale (New York: Penguin Books, 1968), p. 23; emphasis in the original.

23   Jeremy Bentham, "An Introduction to the Principles of Morals and Legislation," in *The Utilitarians* (Garden City, NY: Anchor Books, 1973), p. 18.

24   It is interesting, though, that in *The Matrix* one character, Cypher, escapes the machine world only to choose to be plugged in again; the struggles of the real world were not worth it for him, or so he thought. Also, at another point

in the movie, an agent of "the system" explains that there had been an earlier version of the Matrix in which every person was to have been happy; that version was a failure. The agent's belief is that the program failed because human beings define their lives by misery. It seems clear that the movie intends us to see these beliefs as mistaken; both Cypher and the agent are evil. But perhaps there are some inconvenient truths embodied in their beliefs.

25  Friedrich Nietzsche, *Thus Spoke Zarathustra*, trans. R. J. Hollingdale (New York: Penguin Books, 1969), p. 211.

26  Friedrich Nietzsche, *The Gay Science*, trans. Walter Kaufmann (New York: Vintage Books, 1974), p. 258. Probably, we should be skeptical about Nietzsche's claim that thinkers are particularly, or necessarily, happy.

27  John Dewey, *Philosophy of Education* (Ames, IA: Littlefield, Adams, 1956), p. 269. Originally published as *Problems of Men* (Philosophical Library, 1946).

28  Aristotle, *Nicomachean Ethics*, 1175a10–31 (trans. J. A. K. Thomson [New York: Penguin, 1953], p. 322).

29  John Dewey, *Human Nature and Conduct* (Carbondale: Southern Illinois University Press, 1988/1922), p. 110.

30  This attitude has a long history; for instance, Aristotle believed that "'Play to work harder' seems to be on the right lines" (*Nicomachean Ethics*, 1176b15–1177a5 [p. 327]).

31  John Dewey, *Democracy and Education* (New York: Free Press, 1916), pp. 202–3 emphasis in the original. Deborah Meier has a similar attitude and lists playfulness as one characteristic of an educated person. See her *The Power of Their Ideas* (Boston: Beacon Press, 1995), p. 170.

32  Dewey argues, "Work which remains permeated with the play attitude is art — in quality if not in conventional designation" (*Democracy and Education*, p. 206).

33  Dewey, *Human Nature and Conduct*, p. 111.

34  Ibid., p. 112.

35  Ibid. How beneficial it would be if we did more to remember and accept the child in us. As Cora Diamond describes Ebenezer Scrooge's transformation, he "is touched by human childhood, the vulnerability of children, the intensity of their hopes, the depths of their fears and pains, their pleasures in their play, their joy in following stories," and he accepts "the Scrooge-child" in himself ("The Importance of Being Human," in David Cockburn, ed., *Human Beings* [Cambridge: Cambridge University Press, 1991], pp. 42–3). Diamond notes that the first thing the newly aware Scrooge does is laugh (p. 49).

36  John Dewey, *Moral Principles in Education* (Carbondale: Southern Illinois University Press, 1909), p. 56.

37  Ibid.

38  Martha Nussbaum, *Love's Knowledge* (Oxford: Oxford University Press, 1990), p. 211.

39  Ibid., p. 213.

40   John Dewey, *Experience and Nature* (Chicago: Open Court, 1926), p. 78.

41   Catherine Lutz, *Unnatural Emotions* (Chicago: University of Chicago Press, 1988).

42   Ibid., p. 167.

43   Dewey, *Experience and Nature*, p. 80.

44   See Sumner, *Welfare, Happiness, and Ethics*, p. 149.

45   Richard Kraut, for example, equates welfare with flourishing: "[w]hat is good for human beings is to flourish as human beings" (*What Is Good and Why: The Ethics of Well-Being* [Cambridge, MA: Harvard University Press, 2007], p. 131, note 1). Later, I will consider problems with that conception of well-being.

46   Immanuel Kant, "The Metaphysics of Morals," in *Kant's Ethical Philosophy*, trans. James W. Ellington (Indianapolis, IN: Hackett, 1983), p. 44; p. 387 in the Akademie edition.

47   Raz uses the idea of self-respect to make a similar point, arguing that persons can see their lives as flawed while still maintaining self-respect (*Ethics in the Public Domain*, p. 25). However, Raz also rejects the idea that an attitude of contentment or satisfaction with one's life is necessary for well-being (for example, ibid., p. 6, note 3). Similar to Kraut, Raz equates well-being with living a good life, an equation I deny.

48   Haidt, *The Happiness Hypothesis*, p. 219.

49   Temple Grandin is an example. See her *Thinking in Pictures*, p. 24.

50   Kant, "The Metaphysics of Morals," p. 149; p. 481 in the Akademie edition.

51   See Noddings, *Happiness and Education*, and McMahon, *Happiness: A History*, for discussion of connections made between happiness and suffering.

52   Dewey, *Experience and Nature*, p. 45.

53   Haidt, *The Happiness Hypothesis*, p. 118.

54   Martha Nussbaum, *The Fragility of Goodness* (Cambridge: Cambridge University Press, 1986).

55   Martha Nussbaum, *Upheavals of Thought* (Cambridge: Cambridge University Press, 2001), p. 197.

56   Michael Stocker, *Plural and Conflicting Values* (New York: Oxford University Press, 1990), p. 331. See also Stocker's "Abstract and Concrete Value: Plurality, Conflict, and Maximization," in Ruth Chang, ed., *Incommensurability, Incomparability, and Practical Reason* (Cambridge, MA: Harvard University Press, 1997), pp. 196–214.

  Kraut appears to assume a "relative" sense of good and welfare when he says things like, "Of course, someone who forgoes travel, gourmet food, and opera is living less well than he might be" (*What Is Good and Why*, p. 50). First, it is not clear that the things Kraut mentions — travel, gourmet food, and so on — must contribute to persons' welfare. Second, even if a person's well-being would be bettered by experiencing those things, it is unclear why one must strive to live a better life if her life is a best sort of life already.

57   McMahon, *Happiness: A History*, p. 473.

58  Ibid., p. 333.

59  Dewey, *Democracy and Education*, p. 104.

60  Dewey, *Human Nature and Conduct*, p. 147.

61  Ibid., p. 146. Dewey also says, "Learning, in the proper sense, is not learning things, but the *meanings* of things" (*How We Think* [Boston: D. C. Heath, 1910], p. 176; emphasis in the original).

62  Dewey, *Experience and Nature*, p. 132.

63  John Dewey, *Experience and Education* (New York: Collier, 1938), p. 44.

64  Ibid., p. 35.

65  Dewey, *Democracy and Education*, p. 202; emphasis in the original.

66  Dewey, *Human Nature and Conduct*, p. 146.

67  Much depends on who is "lashing back." Anticipating an issue that will occupy us at length later, there is a difference between an experienced teacher or student acting "impulsively" compared with a teacher or student who really is merely reacting to events beyond their understanding. To act in seemingly impulsive ways does not mean one's acts are unintelligent or meaningless.

68  This is a point Dewey clearly agrees with, for example, in his point about the "collateral learning" that occurs along with intended learning (Dewey, *Experience and Education*, p. 48).

69  Haidt, *The Happiness Hypothesis*, p. 23. Haidt endorses the idea.


*Chapter 2: Experience, Desire, and Well-Being*

1  L. W. Sumner, *Welfare, Happiness, and Ethics* (Oxford: Oxford University Press, 1996), p. 122.

2  James Griffin, *Well-Being* (Oxford: Oxford University Press, Clarendon Press, 1986), p. 20.

3  Ibid., pp. 18–19.

4  Ibid., p. 23.

5  Our bonds to other human beings do not depend only on the capacities those people have. For Cora Diamond, "The sense of mystery surrounding our lives, the feeling of solidarity in mysterious origin and uncertain fate: this binds us to each other, and the binding meant includes the dead and the unborn, and those who bear on their faces 'a look of blank idiocy,' those who lack all power of speech, those behind whose vacant eyes their [*sic*] lurks a 'soul in mute eclipse'" (Cora Diamond, "The Importance of Being Human," in David Cockburn, ed., *Human Beings* [Cambridge: Cambridge University Press, 1991], p. 55). For a person unable to exercise characteristic human capacities, "A human life *without* the exercise of those capacities is *his* human life" (p. 59, note 48; emphasis in the original).

6  Some parents might not react that way but rather withhold sympathy so that the child will "be tough." Perhaps that is warranted at times. But Martha Nussbaum shows the dangers in teaching children to be "ashamed of

neediness" (*Upheavals of Thought* [Cambridge: Cambridge University Press, 2001], p. 196 and *passim*).

7   Griffin, *Well-Being*, p. 19.

8   Haidt, *The Happiness Hypothesis* (New York: Basic Books, 2006), p. 239. As I noted before, Haidt claims allegiance to the "no reality" view, but much of his argument appeals to "reality" of one sort or another.

9   Griffin, *Well-Being*, p. 14. See also Sumner's criticism, *Welfare, Happiness, and Ethics*, p. 128.

10  Catherine Lutz, *Unnatural Emotions* (Chicago: University of Chicago Press, 1988), pp. 40–1.

11  Nussbaum, *Upheavals of Thought*, p. 31. See also Martha Nussbaum, *The Therapy of Desire* (Princeton, NJ: Princeton University Press, 1994). The notion of emotional intelligence has caught on in the field of moral education, but perhaps not in the most desirable way. For discussion and Aristotelian critique of current trends, see Kristján Kristjánsson, "'Emotional Intelligence' in the Classroom? An Aristotelian Critique," *Educational Theory* 56 (2006): 39–56.

12  Nussbaum, *Upheavals of Thought*, p. 321.

13  Ibid., p. 31.

14  Ibid., p. 325.

15  Ibid., p. 326.

16  Haidt, *The Happiness Hypothesis*, p. 31.

17  Ibid.

18  Nussbaum, *Upheavals of Thought*, p. 130.

19  Ibid., p. 132.

20  Ibid., pp. 130, 133.

21  Perhaps Nussbaum would argue that if "gloom" is triggered by a particular event, has a particular object, we are not really talking about gloom but an emotion like grief. I would concede the point; I am not especially interested in how we categorize what I have called "emotion-like" phenomena. My point is that if people are disposed to have gloomy dispositions that seem not to have any particular identifiable source, that does not mean they simply create a gloomy "reality" for themselves. Short of their gloom being pathological, while their gloom might dispose them to perceive particular aspects of the world in particular ways, that does not preclude cognition of and sensitivity to realities in the world.

22  Nussbaum, *Upheavals of Thought*, p. 54.

23  Ibid., p. 55.

24  Martha Nussbaum, *Love's Knowledge* (Oxford: Oxford University Press, 1990), p. 79; emphasis in the original.

25  Stephen E. Ambrose, *D-Day* (New York: Simon and Schuster, 1994), p. 582.

26  Griffin, *Well-Being*, p. 22.

27  Ibid., p. 27.

28  Ibid., p. 315, note 19.

29  Sumner, *Welfare, Happiness, and Ethics*, p. 131.
30  Ibid., p. 132.
31  Griffin, *Well-Being*, p. 14.
32  Sumner, *Welfare, Happiness, and Ethics*, p. 133.
33  Griffin, *Well-Being*, p. 27.
34  Ibid., p. 30.
35  Ibid., p. 31.
36  Similarly, Jonathan Dancy argues that Griffin attempts to "blur" the distinc-
    tion between "recognition and reaction" but maintains the distinction, and so
    does not carry the project far enough. See Jonathan Dancy, "Recognition and
    Reaction," in Roger Crisp and Brad Hooker, eds., *Well-Being and Morality:
    Essays in Honour of James Griffin* (Oxford: Oxford University Press, Clarendon
    Press, 2000), pp. 39–52. In his response to Dancy, Griffin insists that he aims
    to do more than blur the distinction; "recognition and reaction" are "mutu-
    ally intertwined" and "inseparably mixed" (James Griffin, "Recognition
    and Reaction," in *Well-Being and Morality*, p. 290). However, this is an
    inadequate response to Dancy's criticism. Even if recognition of value and
    reaction to it (desire for it) are not separable, Griffin continues to maintain
    the distinction.
37  I say "particular sort of understanding," because talk of "priority" implies a
    separation of understanding from desire that I aim to deny. Griffin criticizes
    John McDowell for making understanding prior to desire (*Well-Being*, p. 322,
    note 19). McDowell's work will have a central place in my argument regarding
    understanding, desire, experience, and other related issues.

*Chapter 3: Attunement, Motivation, and Reasons*

1  Charles Taylor, *Sources of the Self* (Cambridge, MA: Harvard University Press,
   1989), p. 510.
2  Martin Heidegger argues that modern technology "has the character of a
   setting-upon, in the sense of a challenging-forth" (*Basic Writings*, David Krell,
   ed. [New York: Harper and Row, 1977], p. 297). The issue is not whether
   humans can get things from the world but how: through brute force and
   "setting-upon" or with some respect for what the world is prepared to yield.
      See also Stephen R. Kellert and Timothy J. Farnham, eds., *The Good in
   Nature and Humanity* (Washington, DC: Island Press, 2002), where a central
   aim is to develop an environmental ethic that shows the importance of the
   natural world for human well-being and therefore humans' responsibilities
   to care for that world.
3  Hans-Georg Gadamer, *Philosophical Hermeneutics*, trans. David E. Linge
   (Berkeley: University of California Press, 1976), p. 4.
4  Taylor, *Sources of the Self*, p. 510. My view is very much like Taylor's, although
   he does not emphasize prudential values. See also Stanley Cavell, *The Claim*

*of Reason* (New York: Oxford University Press, 1979) for how people can be attuned with one another in language.

I feel obligated to try to be explicit about the view of value I am proposing, or at least about some of its basics.

My talk of attunement to the world entails a sort of value naturalism and endorsement of the supervenience principle. That is, the evaluative features of something supervene on its natural features. In itself, that is not terribly enlightening, because supervenience is an ambiguous notion. Employing Jaegwon Kim's analysis, I will focus on two aspects of supervenience: dependency and non-reducibility (*Supervenience and Mind* [Cambridge: Cambridge University Press, 1993], p. 140). The beauty of a sunset, say, depends on its natural features, the brightness and hues of its colors, for instance. Yet, beauty cannot be reduced to those features. We human beings have to make our own contribution. But then neither can beauty be reduced to the physiology and anthropology of human beings. We can ask things like, "Why do the colors make the thing beautiful?" or "Why is beauty so important?" Yet at some point we can only say something like, "Beauty simply is a good thing," which is an evaluative claim. For additional discussion, see Michael Smith, "Does the Evaluative Supervene on the Natural?" and Griffin's response, "The Supervenience of the Evaluative on the Natural," both in Roger Crisp and Brad Hooker, eds., *Well-Being and Morality: Essays in Honour of James Griffin* (Oxford: Oxford University Press, Clarendon Press, 2000), pp. 91–114 and pp. 296–303, respectively.

This also implies a sort of value realism. This goes beyond scientific realism and its propositional truths. Some truths can only be known by direct acquaintance, which goes beyond bare sensory perception. This is the sort of truth Dewey and Gadamer refer to with the notions of "direct grasp" and being "overwhelmed" in the experience of art, beauty, and other things. For discussion of the affinity of Gadamer's hermeneutics with realism, see Roderick M. Chisholm, "Gadamer and Realism: Reaching an Understanding," in Lewis Edwin Hahn, ed., *The Philosophy of Hans-Georg Gadamer* (Chicago: Open Court, 1997), pp. 99–108, and Gadamer's reply to Chisholm, "Reply to Roderick M. Chisholm" in the same volume, pp. 109–10. See also John McDowell, *Mind, Value, and Reality* (Cambridge, MA: Harvard University Press, 1998), which includes several essays on ethical naturalism, realism, and supervenience.

Values such as beauty are not brute facts; human perception and conceptualization are needed to comprehend them. Perhaps that presents a problem, though. Using the sort of fanciful example philosophers are so enamored with, imagine an extraterrestrial being is visiting Earth, and you take it outside to experience the beauty of an earthly sunset. You discover, however, that because of its sense organs and/or conceptual repertoire, your visitor does not agree with your exclamation, "Isn't that beautiful!" (The creature might have no conception of beauty, or everything we call "beautiful" it calls "ugly.") We might conclude, then, that there is no fact about the beauty of sunsets, or that beauty is species-relative.

However, it is unclear why we must conclude from this scenario that there are no facts about values. Even if we would say beauty is species-relative, the issue is how we human beings live our lives. To say an extraterrestrial does not see beauty when looking at sunsets is no more disturbing than saying we cannot see viruses without electron microscopes. Our perceptual and conceptual abilities enable us to see things an extraterrestrial might not, but rather than conclude we do not discern real values, we might feel sorry for our extraterrestrial friend that cannot experience what we can. In technical terms, I am endorsing weak rather than strong covariance (see Kim, *Supervenience and Mind*). That is, light with certain intensity and wavelength might not be beautiful in all possible worlds. So, that sort of light isn't necessarily beautiful, in that sense. But sunsets really can be beautiful in this world, even if they are not necessarily beautiful across the universe.

5  Pierre Hadot, *Philosophy as a Way of Life*, Arnold I. Davidson, ed. (Oxford: Blackwell, 1995), pp. 210–11.

6  Hans-Georg Gadamer, *Truth and Method*, 2nd rev. ed., trans. Joel Weinsheimer and Donald G. Marshall (New York: Continuum, 1989), p. 379.

7  To be clear, I am using "seeing" metaphorically and not literally. People can be perceptive and discerning without eyesight.

8  John Dewey, *Experience and Nature* (Chicago: Open Court, 1926), pp. 18–19; emphasis in the original.

9  John Dewey, *Human Nature and Conduct* (Carbondale: Southern Illinois University Press, 1922), p. 39.

10  I balk at Dewey's "conceptualization" claim because, as we will see with McDowell in Chapter 4, the sort of receptivity I take Dewey to be describing always involves concepts. I can agree with Dewey to the extent that one cannot *fully* understand the good of food until one has experienced the good of food. But experiencing the good of food comes through a history of experiences and the concepts of good and bad employed in previous experiences. For example, the good of food might include some sense of comfort, which would be a concept likely brought to bear in a number of contexts and for a number of different things — the comfort of a fuzzy teddy bear, a quiet room, a soothing word from a parent, and so on.

If Dewey's point about "conceptualizing" regards the process of "intellectualizing" the good of an experience, we surely can see the value of that process, but that's what I'd call "specification" or "analysis."

11  People who suffer from depression present a potential counterexample. Their difficulty need not be lack of understanding or experience of accomplishment but that they do not feel the satisfaction that comes with the experience. But this does little to support Griffin's perspective. Depressed persons who desire and achieve accomplishment can still be depressed; it's difficult to see how they are doing well. Nor does the example count against my claim that the

experience of prudential value comes with the experience of accomplishment. For a depressed person, the joy of accomplishment does not get through, but that is a special case of a possibility we all face. All human beings need to be in a position to receive the prudential value of experiences.

12  This is not a criticism, necessarily. Temple Grandin acknowledges that, due to her autism, while she "knows" intellectually that sunsets are beautiful, she doesn't feel it (*Thinking in Pictures: My Life with Autism* [New York: Random House, Vintage, 2006], p. 91). Grandin writes of having emotions, but they are few and basic (p. 164). She has lived a good life even without the sort of emotional life many people have and desire. Yet she also makes a point about how emotions are important for making good decisions, and so autistic people can have difficulty making good decisions (p. 158).

13  John White, *Education and the Good Life* (New York: Teachers College Press, 1991), p. 56.

14  Dewey, *Human Nature and Conduct*, p. 84.

15  Ibid.

16  White, *Education and the Good Life*, p. 56.

17  Robert Audi, "Moral Judgment and Reasons for Action," in Garret Cullity and Berys Gaut, eds., *Ethics and Practical Reason* (Oxford: Oxford University Press, Clarendon Press, 1997), pp. 125–59.

18  White, *Education and the Good Life*, p. 34.

19  Dewey, *Moral Principles in Education* (Carbondale: Southern Illinois University Press, 1909), p. 1.

20  Gadamer, *Truth and Method*, p. 462.

21  White, *Education and the Good Life*, p. 32.

22  Dewey, *Moral Principles in Education*, p. 47.

23  George Sher, *Beyond Neutrality* (Cambridge: Cambridge University Press, 1997), pp. 197–8; emphasis in the original. Griffin is a target of Sher's criticisms, but that is a mistake. Sher is right to criticize subjectivist views he describes, but, as we have seen, Griffin sees the desire-value relation as bidirectional; he clearly does not argue that desire "confers" value on objects.

24  White, *Education and the Good Life*, p. 33.

25  Audi, "Moral Judgment and Reasons for Action," pp. 153–4; emphasis in the original.

26  Ibid., p. 159. See also Martha Nussbaum's discussion of Aristotle's views on emotions as "guides to ethical truth" (*The Therapy of Desire* [Princeton, NJ: Princeton University Press, 1994], p. 97 and *passim*).

27  Dewey, *Moral Principles in Education*, p. 58.

*Chapter 4: Perceiving and Valuing in Hermeneutic Experience*

1  John Dewey, *Experience and Nature* (Chicago: Open Court, 1926), p. 96. Such qualities are described (and sometimes discredited) as being mere "secondary"

qualities. With color, for instance, something might appear red, but its redness need not be an essential feature of the thing (an apple might be red, but redness isn't necessary for something to be an apple), or the apparent color might change in different circumstances, different lighting, perhaps. The inclination, then, is to say these qualities are mere "projections" upon the world.

John McDowell challenges that idea: "Values are not brutely there — not there independent of our sensibility — any more than colours are: though, as with colours, this does not prevent us from supposing that they are there independently of any particular apparent experience of them" (*Mind, Value, and Reality* [Cambridge, MA: Harvard University Press, 1998], p. 146).

2   John Dewey, *Philosophy of Education* (Ames, IA: Littlefield, Adams, 1956). Originally published as *Problems of Men* (Philosophical Library, 1946), p. 253.

3   Ibid., p. 270.

4   James Griffin, *Well-Being* (Oxford: Oxford University Press, Clarendon Press, 1986), pp. 18–19.

5   John McDowell, *Mind and World* (Cambridge, MA: Harvard University Press, 1996), p. 112.

6   Ibid., p. 113.

7   Ibid., p. 26; emphasis in the original.

8   Hans-Georg Gadamer, *Philosophical Hermeneutics*, trans. David E. Linge (Berkeley: University of California Press, 1976), p. 15.

9   Ibid.

10   Hans-Georg Gadamer, *Truth and Method*, 2nd rev. ed., trans. Joel Weinsheimer and Donald G. Marshall (New York: Continuum, 1989), p. 355.

11   Ibid., p. 126.

12   Gadamer, *Philosophical Hermeneutics*, p. 55.

13   Gadamer, *Truth and Method*, pp. 101–10 and *passim*.

14   Gadamer, *Philosophical Hermeneutics*, p. 53.

15   Gadamer, *Truth and Method*, 104.

16   Gadamer, *Philosophical Hermeneutics*, p. 55.

17   Ibid.

18   Maurice Merleau-Ponty, *The Primacy of Perception*, James M. Edie, ed. (Evanston, IL: Northwestern University Press, 1964), p. 186.

19   Gadamer, *Truth and Method*, p. 461.

20   Ibid., p. 388.

21   Temple Grandin found that "inclusion" did not work well for her schooling. She found her belonging with people who shared her interests (*Thinking in Pictures: My Life with Autism* [New York: Random House, Vintage, 2006], pp. 162–3).

22   This does not deny that Socrates is using irony and some amount of deception. We will explore that more when we get to teacher-student dialogue and seduction in Chapter 9.

23 McDowell, *Mind and World*, p. 9; emphasis in the original. We should be clear that concepts need not be held through language. For Temple Grandin and other autistic persons, thinking is done in pictures; words are a second language (*Thinking in Pictures*, p. 3). Abstract concepts — such as peace or "getting along" with people — can be understood, but the concepts are learned through symbols. For instance, Grandin grasped the concept "getting along" by visualizing it as a jammed sliding glass door that had to be approached and handled carefully because it could break (p. 20).

    In his work, McDowell draws a good deal from Gadamer. See McDowell, *Mind and World* and his "Gadamer and Davidson on Understanding and Relativism," in Jeff Malpas, Ulrich Arnswald, and Jens Kertscher, eds., *Gadamer's Century* (Cambridge, MA: MIT Press, 2002) pp. 173–93.

24 Hans-Georg Gadamer, *Truth and Method*, p. 355.

25 Dewey, *Experience and Nature*, p. 133.

26 Dewey, *Philosophy of Education*, p. 269.

27 John Dewey, *The Quest for Certainty* (New York: Perigree, 1929), p. 258.

28 Gary Klein, *Sources of Power: How People Make Decisions* (Cambridge, MA: MIT Press, 1998), p. 3.

29 Ibid., p. 11.

30 Ibid., p. 21. John Dewey takes the opposite view, proposing that skilled practitioners aim to "prevent the acceptance of the first suggestions that arise" (*How We Think* [Boston: D. C. Heath, 1910], p. 74).

31 John Dewey, "Moral Judgment and Knowledge," in *The Essential Dewey*, vol. 2, Larry A. Hickman and Thomas M. Alexander, eds., *Ethics, Logic, Psychology* (Bloomington: Indiana University Press, 1998), p. 333.

32 Gadamer, *Truth and Method*, p. 362.

33 John Dewey and James Tufts, *Ethics* (New York: Henry Holt, 1909), p. 418. We might wonder if Klein's work really challenges Dewey's depiction of valuing and reflection. It could be that if a rescue worker has to make judgments about how to treat a seriously injured person, that does not include reflection on aims; the aim — saving a life — is not at issue. But if that is true on occasion, it is not always the case. Surely a rescue worker can face questions of aims. If there are several people who are seriously injured there might have to be judgments about who is treated first; that is what triage is all about. Even in the case of a single individual, there can be questions about aims. Is the aim to save the person's life or to just ease his pain — say, if there is little chance of saving the person, or if what is needed to save the life might risk additional injury? Such questions can be answered well through experience, analogies, and the other elements of judgment Klein describes.

34 Dewey, *Experience and Education* (New York: Collier), p. 69.

35 Aristotle, *Nicomachean Ethics*, 1116b33–1117b6 (trans. J. A. K. Thomson. [New York: Penguin Books, 1953], pp. 133–4).

36 John McDowell, "Deliberation and Moral Development in Aristotle's Ethics," in Stephen Engstrom and Jennifer Whiting, eds., *Aristotle, Kant, and the*

*Stoics: Rethinking Happiness and Duty* (New York: Cambridge University Press, 1996), p. 26.

37 For people unfamiliar with the movie, "Towanda" is the battle cry used by Idgie, one of the characters in the stories Ninny tells Evelyn, when she challenges conventions and people. Evelyn whispers "Towanda" to herself right before she crunches the girls' car and continues to use it, for example, in reply to her husband's refusal to have Ninny stay in their home.

38 In Nussbaum's view, "Perception, we might say, is a process of loving conversation between rules and concrete responses, general conceptions and unique cases, in which the general articulates the particular and is in turn further articulated by it" (*Love's Knowledge* [Oxford: Oxford University Press, 1990], p. 95). We might wonder how much love was going on when Evelyn rammed the car, but, arguably, she had a conversation between the general values she treasured — her dignity, friendships, freedom — and the particulars her unique case presented her. She certainly felt joy at what she did. She surely perceived the particulars in a way she would not have before. She was receptive to them. Perhaps we could say she loved them, or at least loved what they revealed for her.

39 Catherine Lutz, *Unnatural Emotions* (Chicago: University of Chicago Press, 1988), p. 157.

40 Ibid., p. 181.

41 Gadamer, *Truth and Method*, p. 322.

42 Charles Taylor, "Interpretation and the Sciences of Man," reprinted in Eric Bredo and Walter Feinberg, eds., *Knowledge and Values in Social and Educational Research* (Philadelphia: Temple University Press, 1982), p. 182.

43 Michel Foucault, *The Essential Works of Foucault, 1954–1984*, vol. 1, Paul Rabinow, ed., *Ethics* (New York: New Press, 1997), p. 262.

44 Pierre Hadot, *Philosophy as a Way of Life*, Arnold I. Davidson, ed. (Oxford: Blackwell, 1995), p. 102.

45 Perhaps John Steinbeck was saying something like that when he insisted he was a writer, not an author. See Jackson J. Benson, *John Steinbeck, Writer* (New York: Penguin, 1984).

46 Thomas Kuhn, *The Structure of Scientific Revolutions*, 2nd ed. (Chicago: University of Chicago Press, 1970). I make no claims about the accuracy of Kuhn's depiction of science.

47 See Helen E. Longino, *Science as Social Knowledge* (Princeton, NJ: Princeton University Press, 1990).

48 John McDowell, "Eudaimonism and Realism in Aristotle's Ethics," in Robert Heinaman, ed., *Aristotle and Moral Realism* (Boulder, CO: Westview Press, 1995), p. 213; emphasis in the original.

49 John McDowell, "Deliberation and Moral Development in Aristotle's Ethics," p. 31.

50 Stanley Cavell, *The Claim of Reason* (New York: Oxford University Press, 1979), p. 268; emphasis in the original.

51 This is the sort of question Dewey associates with valuing. Again, my dispute with Dewey does not regard the importance of this sort of valuing but his claim that perception is distinct from evaluating or making value judgments.

52 James Griffin, *Well-Being* (Oxford: Oxford University Press, Clarendon Press, 1986), pp. 316–17, note 27.

53 Ruth Chang, Introduction to Ruth Chang, ed., *Incommensurability, Incomparability, and Practical Reason* (Cambridge, MA: Harvard University Press, 1997), p. 13.

54 Gadamer, *Truth and Method*, p. 365.

55 Charles Taylor, "Leading a Life," in Ruth Chang, ed., *Incommensurability, Incomparability, and Practical Reason* (Cambridge, MA: Harvard University Press, 1997), p. 179. Of course, there is a sense of "fit" where values have a fit in a value hierarchy. I hope it is clear from the context of the discussion that the fit I am considering is fit in a life, a fit concerned for time and place and not just value ranking.

56 Taylor, "Leading a Life," p. 179.

57 Ibid., pp. 180–1.

58 Ibid., p. 182.

59 Ibid.

60 Reverence does seem to be different from awe and wonder. I refer to reverence as an attitude because it does seem to be a more or less stable disposition as opposed to more occasional experiences of awe and wonder.

61 Richard J. Bernstein, *Beyond Objectivism and Relativism* (Philadelphia: University of Pennsylvania Press, 1983), p. 86.

62 T. K. Seung and Daniel Bonevac, "Plural Values and Indeterminate Rankings," *Ethics* 102 (1992): 799–813.

63 Chang, Introduction to *Incommensurability, Incomparability, and Practical Reason*, p. 12.

64 Gadamer, *Truth and Method*, p. 567.

65 Ibid., p. 568. See also Gerald Bruns's depiction of rhetoric as a "real-world construction of a provisional order of reason, a practical construction of what is reasonable in a world where randomness and contingency cannot be eliminated, at least not now, or not without great cost" (Gerald Bruns, "The Hermeneutical Anarchist," in Jeff Malpas, Ulrich Arnswald, and Jens Kertscher, eds., *Gadamer's Century* [Cambridge, MA: MIT Press, 2002], p. 51).

66 McDowell, "Deliberation and Moral Development," p. 27.

*Chapter 5: Structuring and Evaluating a Life*

1 See Susan Wolf, "Two Levels of Pluralism," *Ethics* 102 (1992): 785–98.

2 Hans-George Gadamer, *Truth and Method*, 2nd rev. ed., trans. Joel Weinsheimer

and Donald G. Marshall (New York: Continuum, 1989), pp. 66–7; emphasis in the original.

3 Charles Taylor, *Sources of the Self* (Cambridge, MA: Harvard University Press, 1989), p. 48; emphasis added.

4 John Dewey, *Experience and Education* (New York: Collier, 1938), p. 49.

5 Richard J. Bernstein, *The New Constellation: The Ethical-Political Horizons of Modernity/Postmodernity* (Cambridge, MA: MIT Press, 1991), p. 8. I have referred to a proper conception of well-being as being at the "core" of living well, but that is not the sort of substantial core Bernstein is questioning.

6 In Chapter 9 I criticize the postmodernist valorization of contradictory elements in lives. In a constellation, elements are juxtaposed and perhaps in tension, but that does not mean they are contradictory or that we should be content with contradictions. My desire for personal free time might be juxtaposed with my desire to earn a living, but that does not mean those desires contradict each other. They might contradict if my desires were for only free time and for only earning a living, but normally we do not understand our values in such extreme terms. There are times when I don't like going to work, and times when I get angry at myself for being lazy, but although I experience some tension, I know my desires are not mutually exclusive.

7 When I say "center of gravity" I do not mean to suggest some fixed entity at the center of things. Of course, there is a person at the center of her life. But a constellation is not a static thing. The stars are in motion, and as they move the center of gravity shifts. "Center of gravity" seems an apt analogy if we see the self not as something fixed but as something that develops through the experiences the individual undergoes.

8 For example, regarding the question of when a person is "fully informed," Griffin argues that a person — his example is a person who devotes time to counting blades of grass — whose desires are not formed "by appreciation of the nature of the object" is not fully informed (*Well-Being* [Oxford: Oxford University Press, Clarendon Press, 1986], p. 323, note 29). I am inclined to agree. But this shows the inadequacy of an end state such as "fully informed." Fully informed or not, the person could still be living a satisfying life. Griffin argues that blade counting does not make a life valuable. Again, I am inclined to agree. But here I'll recall the distinction I made earlier between a good life and a life experienced as good. Counting blades of grass is a waste of life, but that is not decisive so far as what the person experiences. Because of the lack of understanding a blade counter has, we have reason to try to inform him. But if our goal is his well-being, we cannot reduce that to an end state like "fully informed desires."

9 Charles Taylor, "Explanation and Practical Reasoning," in Martha C. Nussbaum and Amartya Sen, eds., *The Quality of Life* (Oxford: Oxford University Press, Clarendon Press, 1993), pp. 208–31.

10 In light of that, Dewey's idea of growth as the aim of education and a more or less open-ended process is problematic. We might aim for enabling people

to be capable of growth, but that is different than making growth the aim. I return to this issue later.

11    John Dewey, "Analysis of Reflective Thinking," in *The Essential Dewey*, vol. 2, Larry A. Hickman and Thomas M. Alexander, eds., *Ethics, Logic, Psychology* (Bloomington: Indiana University Press, 1998) pp. 138–40.

12    John Dewey, *Art as Experience* (New York: Perigree, 1934), p. 49.

13    Dewey, *Experience and Education*, p. 69. Dewey says, "A deadly and fanatic consistency is not our goal," but he also says ideas should combine into "a single steady trend toward a unified conclusion" (*How We Think* [Boston: D. C. Heath, 1910], p. 40). If I am being unfair to Dewey, we still should be wary of emphasizing "steady trends" at the expense of detours, diversions, and other adventures.

14    Gadamer, *Truth and Method*, p. 69.

15    Jonathan Haidt, *The Happiness Hypothesis* (New York: Basic Books, 2006), pp. 84–6.

16    Taylor, "Explanation and Practical Reasoning," p. 221.

17    Alasdair MacIntyre, *Whose Justice? Which Rationality?* (Notre Dame, IN: University of Notre Dame Press, 1988).

18    Dewey, *Experience and Education*, p. 36.

19    For Dewey, likely this would be a nonsensical idea, because "life means growth" (*Democracy and Education* [New York: Free Press, 1916], p. 51). While I tend to agree with Dewey that a person who closes off possibilities for growth is making a mistake, it is not unreasonable for a person to give growth little if any place among his central prudential values.

20    Gadamer, *Truth and Method*, p. 355; emphasis in the original. "Orientation to new experience" is a better way to think of the outcome of experience than ongoing "growth." It would be worthwhile that a person be open to growth even if actual growth is not an aim or achievement necessary for well-being.

      Gadamer's idea is not without its problems, too, though. What does it mean to say an experienced person is open to new experiences? If it is an empirical claim, then likely it is false; at least it is not too hard to imagine someone with a lot of experiences who still is closed-minded. Clearly, Gadamer is referring to a particular sort of experienced person, but then his claim is a tautology, like "a bachelor is an unmarried man." What his point can do is help us ponder the nature and value of openness and the sort of experiences that might lead to it. If experience does not guarantee openness, experience with the unpredictability and mystery of the world and of people tends to make people nondogmatic.

21    Gadamer, *Truth and Method*, p. 355.

22    John McDowell, "Deliberation and Moral Development in Aristotle's Ethics," in Stephen Engstrom and Jennifer Whiting, eds., *Aristotle, Kant, and the Stoics: Rethinking Happiness and Duty* (New York: Cambridge University Press, 1996), p. 26.

23  Martha Nussbaum, *Love's Knowledge* (Oxford: Oxford University Press, 1990),
    p. 148.


*Chapter 6: Perfectionism and Human Capabilities*

1  At the same time, though, serving expensive desires can be perfectly acceptable in some circumstances. See James Griffin, *Well-Being* (Oxford: Oxford
   University Press, Clarendon Press, 1986), pp. 48–9.
2  This is an ambiguous, controversial, and potentially dangerous claim.
   Particularly, how do we think about human beings who are unable to exercise
   characteristic human capabilities because they are brain-dead or have some
   other severe injury or disability? To forthrightly address the question of quality of life, we have to ask, "Is this person living a human life?" By making my
   claim about all people living a human life, I do not propose "No" can never
   be an appropriate answer to the question. I am saying all persons, regardless
   of their physical or mental state, deserve to have the quality of their lives
   evaluated according to the same criteria.
      However, if people are seriously impaired in some way, it does not follow
   that they cannot be living well. This is one reason I rejected "flourishing"
   as the standard for well-being. Using that standard, Richard Kraut argues
   that if people are sick, weak, mutilated, injured, or stunted, they cannot be
   flourishing and so cannot be doing well (*What Is Good and Why: The Ethics
   of Well-Being* [Cambridge, MA: Harvard University Press, 2007], p. 133). But
   that is too extreme. Of course people afflicted with such things likely would be
   better-off if they did not suffer from them; they still can live satisfying, productive lives, though. Raz argues that we face a difficult puzzle here because
   things we generally want to avoid — disability, illness, fear, suffering — still
   can be part of valuable activities, even being part of what makes the activities
   valuable. He uses the example of a legless pilot who learned to fly with arti-
   ficial limbs (*Ethics in the Public Domain*, rev. ed. [Oxford: Oxford University
   Press, Clarendon Press, 1994], pp. 17–19). The pilot thus accomplished something remarkable. Of course, it does not follow that we have no duty to help
   people avoid harm and to aid them when they are harmed.
3  Here and elsewhere I am thinking of "comprehensive" in a way different from Rawls (for example, John Rawls, *Political Liberalism* [New York:
   Columbia University Press, 1993] and *A Theory of Justice* [Cambridge,
   MA: Harvard University Press, 1971]). For Rawls, a comprehensive view
   of life and well-being emphasizes the basic religious and moral values that
   underlie and connect aspects of persons' lives. Thus, to offer a comprehensive view is to offer a view based on values that might not be widely shared.
   However, a view can be comprehensive in the sense of taking account of
   the full range of elements of human life without also proposing some particular comprehensive way these elements must be "packaged." It is in the

latter sense that Nussbaum's human capabilities (discussed shortly) are comprehensive.

4    Thomas M. Scanlon takes a similar view in "The Moral Basis of Interpersonal Comparisons," in Jon Elster and John E. Roemer, eds., *Interpersonal Comparisons of Well-Being* (New York: Cambridge University Press, 1991), pp. 39–40.

5    Martha Nussbaum, *Women and Human Development* (Cambridge: Cambridge University Press, 2000), pp. 78–80. Griffin offers his own list (*Well-Being*, p. 67). Although he does not offer a list of particular items, Raz endorses a similar "Basic-Capacities Principle" as the basis of our duties to others' welfare (*Ethics in the Public Domain*, pp. 16–17).

6    Richard J. Arneson, "Perfectionism and Politics," *Ethics* 111 (2000): 38. While perfectionists make this claim, it is not unique to them. There might be a number of ways that values might be independent of individuals' particular beliefs. I take it that what is unique to perfectionism is that it bases the independence of values in human nature. (Griffin concedes that there is a good point "buried" in perfectionism. See *Well-Being*, pp. 70–1.) In her "Aristotle, Politics, and Human Capabilities: A Response to Antony, Arneson, Charlesworth, and Mulgan," *Ethics* 111 (2000), Martha Nussbaum denies her theory is perfectionist "in any interesting sense," where perfectionism is a political theory "that advocates a comprehensive theory of the human good as giving a set of appropriate goals for politics" (p. 128). I think Nussbaum's position is more perfectionist than she supposes, but part of the difficulty here is that "perfectionism" can be used to describe a variety of positions. Hopefully, the perfectionism I advocate is interesting in its contrast to other theories of well-being, such as desire theory. In Chapters 7 and 8 I argue for perfectionism as a political theory.

7    Thomas Hurka, *Perfectionism* (New York: Oxford University Press, 1993), p. 56.

8    Ed Diener and Eunkook M. Suh, "Measuring Subjective Well-Being to Compare the Quality of Life of Cultures," in Diener and Suh, eds., *Culture and Subjective Well-Being* (Cambridge, MA: MIT Press, 2000), pp. 3–5. The typical assumption seems to be that all people are "different." However, the extent of differences can be exaggerated. For example, in addition to Nussbaum's argument in *Women and Human Development*, see Gene Outka and John P. Reeder Jr., eds., *Prospects for a Common Morality* (Princeton, NJ: Princeton University Press, 1993) and Fred Dallmayr, ed., *Border Crossings: Toward a Comparative Political Theory* (Lanham, MD: Lexington, 1999). In his introduction to that last volume, Dallmayr proposes that denying there are "essential or invariant differences between cultures does not amount to an endorsement of essential sameness and non-distinction" (p. 3). A human capabilities approach takes the sort of middle ground Dallmayr describes.

9    These capabilities need not be taken to define our humanity, nor are they the only basis for our solidarity as human beings: human beings have a bond simply as human beings. To focus exclusively on our differences, "viewing

... other people as 'another race of creatures, bound on other journeys,' is an expression of one's having suppressed or rejected, rather than imaginatively owned, one's own being human" (Cora Diamond, "The Importance of Being Human," in David Cockburn, ed., *Human Beings* [Cambridge: Cambridge University Press, 1991], p. 49). Regard for other people's "journeys" might be well motivated, but it can reflect limited insight into one's own self and soul, blindness to the mystery and other commonalities inherent to any human life.

10  The example and criticism are Charles Taylor's ("Understanding the Other: A Gadamerian View on Conceptual Schemes," in Jeff Malpas, Ulrich Arnswald, and Jens Kertscher, eds., *Gadamer's Century* [Cambridge, MA: MIT Press, 2002], p. 294).

11  Martha Nussbaum, "Aristotle, Politics, and Human Capabilities," p. 130.

12  Ibid.

13  Nussbaum acknowledges that in some cases public responsibility goes beyond securing capabilities to ensuring or encouraging functionings. She says, for example, "Of course I support mandatory functioning for children" (Nussbaum, "Aristotle, Politics, and Human Capabilities," p. 130).

14  Joseph Raz argues, "[I]t is the goal of all political action to enable individuals to pursue valid conceptions of the good and to discourage evil or empty ones" (Joseph Raz, *The Morality of Freedom* [Oxford: Oxford University Press, Clarendon Press, 1986], p. 133).

## Chapter 7: Perfectionism, Liberalism, and Political Deliberation

1  John Rawls's *Political Liberalism* (New York: Columbia University Press, 1993) will be my primary source for liberal theory.

2  Ibid., xviii.

3  I take my view to be similar to Joseph Raz's, as presented in *The Morality of Freedom* (Oxford: Oxford University Press, Clarendon Press, 1986) and *Ethics in the Public Domain*, rev. ed. (Oxford: Oxford University Press, Clarendon Press, 1994).

4  Thomas Hurka, *Perfectionism* (New York: Oxford University Press, 1993), p. 190.

5  Charles Taylor, *The Ethics of Authenticity* (Cambridge, MA: Harvard University Press, 199), p. 18. I am not sure how much liberalism can be blamed for this marginalization and inarticulacy. There could be a number of sources for the inarticulacy.

6  If we believe that the moral significance of some action is so great that that is a reason not to do it, it would seem that avoiding the action also would have great significance. So, why must we favor avoidance? See Raz, *Ethics in the Public Domain*, p. 103.

7  Raz gives a subtle analysis of political neutrality, arguing that it can take a

number of forms. His basic distinction, which I am using, is between neutrality and what Raz calls "the exclusion of ideals." See *The Morality of Freedom*, pp. 107–62.

8  It is not difficult to imagine how the preferences people express don't reflect their values, or the values they would have if they were better informed. However, similar to the point made before, one might argue that expressed preferences are the best we can do, politically speaking.

9  John Rawls introduces the notion of "overlapping consensus" in his *A Theory of Justice* (Cambridge, MA: Harvard University Press, 1971) and continues to develop it in *Political Liberalism*. Overlapping consensus might be a proper aim and standard for public reason and decisions. My argument then would be that the possible consensus is broader than Rawls supposes. See, for example, John P. Reeder Jr.'s argument, contrasting his view with Rawls's (and Rorty's), that "between traditions we can find common comprehensive and general reasons for common moral convictions" ("Foundations without Foundationalism," in Gene Outka and John P. Reeder Jr. eds. *Prospects for a Common Morality* [Princeton, NJ: Princeton University Press, 1993], p. 206).

10  See Raz, *The Morality of Freedom*, p. 120.

11  Rawls says, "[T]he right and good are complementary: no conception of justice can draw entirely upon one or the other, but must combine in a definite way" (*Political Liberalism*, p. 173). Clearly, I disagree with Rawls about the way the right and good are complementary.

12  Kent Greenawalt, *Private Consciences and Public Reasons* (New York: Oxford University Press, 1995), pp. 163–4.

13  Ibid., p. 164.

14  Kenneth A. Strike, "Perfectionism and Neutrality," in Randall Curren, ed., *Philosophy of Education 1999* (Urbana, IL: Philosophy of Education Society, 2000), p. 69.

15  Raz, *The Morality of Freedom*, p. 112.

16  Helen Longino, *Science as Social Knowledge* (Princeton, NJ: Princeton University Press, 1990).

17  Strike, "Perfectionism and Neutrality," p. 69.

18  Raz argues that pluralism, rather than neutrality or skepticism about value, provides the protection needed against imposition of particular ways of life. See *Ethics in the Public Domain* (e.g., p. 120) and *The Morality of Freedom*.

19  Raz argues, "[f]easibility or workability can only be a small part" of the justification for a theory of justice (*Ethics in the Public Domain*, p. 73). I do not disagree, but surely workability is a factor in a theory's favor.

20  Rawls, *Political Liberalism*, pp. 248–51.

21  David B. Wong, "Coping with Moral Conflict and Ambiguity," *Ethics* 102 (1992): 779.

22  Raz, *Ethics in the Public Domain*, p. 59.

23  Charles Larmore, *Patterns of Moral Complexity* (Cambridge: Cambridge University Press, 1987).

24  Ibid., p. 53.

25  Ibid.

26  Alasdair MacIntyre, *Whose Justice? Which Rationality?* (Notre Dame, IN: University of Notre Dame Press, 1988), p. 351.

27  Rawls insists that the attitudes parties are imagined to adopt in the original position are not intended as an account of moral psychology but should be looked upon as a role one steps into when deliberating on the principles of justice (*Political Liberalism*, pp. 27–8). I accept Rawls's argument about that. Nonetheless, if one is to play the role Rawls proposes, it must in some psychological sense be doable, be reasonable enough that a person is able to take on the role. So, when I criticize Rawls I am not criticizing him for an erroneous account of moral psychology but for his position that reasonable persons would be more inclined to adopt the role he describes than the alternative role I propose.

28  See Kraut's argument for the justification of modest or "strategic" anti-paternalism as opposed to "pure" anti-paternalism (Richard Kraut, *What Is Good and Why: The Ethics of Well-Being* [Cambridge, MA: Harvard University Press, pp. 234–8). Raz says, "According to Rawls, people care most about their ability to realize their own conceptions of the good" (*Ethics in the Public Domain*, p. 82), but replies, "I am inclined to say that they care most about realizing the sound conception of the good" (p. 82, note 57).

29  *Thus Spoke Zarathustra*, trans. R. J. Hollingdale (New York: Penguin Books, 1969), p. 74. Of course, Nietzsche doubted that many people were capable of that attitude.

30  Rawls, *Political Liberalism*, p. 217.

31  Kent Greenawalt, *Private Consciences and Public Reasons*, p. 77.

32  Amy Gutmann and Dennis Thompson, *Democracy and Disagreement* (Cambridge, MA: Harvard University Press, 1996). On relevant issues Gutmann and Thompson take a position similar to Rawls, so I do not think my shift to their arguments is problematic for my discussion. Part of the need for a shift is that Rawls simply does not do much to discuss the conduct of actual deliberation. This is the principal advantage Gutmann and Thompson see in their "deliberative" approach, compared with Rawls.

33  Gutmann and Thompson, *Democracy and Disagreement*, p. 64. I rely on the authors' account of the incident.

34  Ibid., p. 65.

35  Greenawalt, *Private Consciences and Public Reasons*, p. 40.

36  Ibid., p. 41.

37  Nel Noddings, "Education as a Public Good," in Anatole Anton, Milton Fisk, and Nancy Holstrom, eds., *Not for Sale: In Defense of Public Goods* (Boulder, CO: Westview Press, 2000), p. 286; emphasis in the original.

38  Will Kymlicka, "Liberal Individualism and Liberal Neutrality," *Ethics* 99 (1989): 901. One issue here concerns the dynamics of power, which are more complicated than Kymlicka's simple majority-versus-minority scheme

implies. I will set that issue aside. It does not subvert the basics of Kymlicka's concerns.

39 Ibid.


*Chapter 8: Judging Well-Being*

1 David Wong, "Coping with Moral Conflict and Ambiguity," *Ethics* 102 (1992): 776.

2 Larry Cuban, "Why Is It So Hard to Get 'Good' Schools?" in Larry Cuban and Dorothy Shipps, eds., *Reconstructing the Common Good in Education* (Stanford, CA: Stanford University Press, 2000), p. 167.

3 Wong, "Coping with Moral Conflict and Ambiguity," p. 778.

4 William E. Connolly, *Politics and Ambiguity* (Madison: University of Wisconsin Press, 1987).

5 See Richard J. Bernstein's chapter "Reconciliation/Rupture" in his *The New Constellation: The Ethical-Political Horizons of Modernity/Postmodernity* (Cambridge, MA: MIT Press, 1991), pp. 293–322, where he argues that we should live with the "both/and" of "reconciliation/rupture."

6 Raz, *The Morality of Freedom* (Oxford: Oxford University Press, Clarendon Press, 1994), p. 160.

7 Wong, "Coping with Moral Conflict and Ambiguity," p. 781.

8 Charles Taylor, "The Politics of Recognition," in Amy Gutmann, ed., *Multiculturalism and "The Politics of Recognition"* (Princeton, NJ: Princeton University Press, 1992), pp. 66–73.

9 John Dewey argues, "Attending to wrong-doing ought to be an incident rather than a principle" (*Moral Principles in Education* [Carbondale: Southern Illinois University Press, 1909], p. 16).

10 James Griffin, *Well-Being* (Oxford: Oxford University Press, Clarendon Press, 1986), p. 91.

11 Michael Stocker, *Plural and Conflicting Values* (Oxford: Oxford University Press, 1990), p. 200. This is the problem Taylor is concerned with when he advocates reverence.

12 Richard J. Arneson, "Perfectionism and Politics," *Ethics* 111 (2000): 55.

13 Martha Nussbaum, *Women and Human Development* (Cambridge: Cambridge University Press, 2000), p. 79.

14 Arneson, "Perfectionism and Politics," p. 55.

15 Martha Nussbaum, "Aristotle, Politics, and Human Capabilities: A Response to Antony, Arneson, Charlesworth, and Mulgan," *Ethics* 111 (2000): 129.

16 Christine M. Korsgaard, *Creating the Kingdom of Ends* (Cambridge: Cambridge University Press, 1996), p. 250.

17 Arneson, "Perfectionism and Politics," p. 48.

18 Korsgaard, *Creating the Kingdom of Ends*, p. 251.

19 Ibid., p. 258; emphasis in the original.

20  See John Rawls, *A Theory of Justice* (Cambridge, MA: Harvard University Press, 1971), pp. 504–12, and *Political Liberalism* (New York: Columbia University Press, 1993), p. 19.

21  Rawls, *A Theory of Justice*, p. 330.

22  Of course, Rawls does not deny the importance of particular, small-scale decisions about justice. Jon Elster discusses Rawls and other examples of what he calls "global" theories of justice in his "Local Justice and Interpersonal Comparisons" in Jon Elster and John E. Roemer, eds., *Interpersonal Comparisons of Well-Being* (New York: Cambridge University Press, 1991), pp. 98–126.

23  Elster offers and discusses a number of examples in his "Local Justice and Interpersonal Comparisons."

24  Ibid., p. 114. "Local justice" is Elster's term.

25  Ibid., pp. 119–20. In his paper, Elster gives a number of different examples of criteria relevant to distribution issues.

26  Henry S. Richardson, "The Problem of Liberalism and the Good," in R. Bruce Douglass, Gerald M. Mara, and Henry S. Richardson, eds., *Liberalism and the Good* (New York: Routledge, 1990), p. 21.

27  MacIntyre, *Whose Justice? Which Rationality?* (Notre Dame, IN: University of Notre Dame Press, 1988) pp. 387–8. Richardson's account of rational progress has much in common with MacIntyre's. Recall also Taylor's depiction of the process in Chapter 5.

28  Elster, "Local Justice and Interpersonal Comparisons," p. 125.

29  Thomas Scanlon, "The Moral Basis of Interpersonal Comparisons," in Elster and Roemer, eds., *Interpersonal Comparisons of Well-Being*, p. 36.

30  Nel Noddings, *Happiness and Education* (Cambridge: Cambridge University Press, 2003), p. 61.

31  L. W. Sumner, *Welfare, Happiness, and Ethics* (Oxford: Oxford University Press, 1996), p. 54.

32  Scanlon, "The Moral Basis of Interpersonal Comparisons," p. 25; emphasis in the original.

33  Nel Noddings, *The Challenge to Care in Schools* (New York: Teachers College Press, 1992) and *Caring: A Feminine Approach to Ethics* (Berkeley: University of California Press, 1984).

34  Noddings, *Happiness and Education*, p. 247.

35  But also consider Lee Yearley's argument that, for some conflicts in conceptions of well-being, "I cannot, without ceasing to be me, incarnate the excellences I face" ("Conflicts among Ideals of Human Flourishing," in Gene Outka and John P. Reeder Jr., eds., *Prospects for a Common Morality* [Princeton, NJ: Princeton University Press, 1993], p. 247). Yearley's example is a Westerner trying to become a Confucian.

36  Maurice Merleau-Ponty, *The Primacy of Perception*, James M. Edie, ed. [Evanston, IL: Northwestern University Press, 1964], p. 17. This is no mere imposition of one's own point of view. Similar to Gadamer (as we will see in

Chapter 9), Merleau-Ponty describes the experience involving a tension that "transcends itself" (p. 27).

For Gerald Bruns, the imperative is: "I want to tell you something I've seen, or heard, or realized, or come to understand (because it is news, about a world we share, or could) . . . It matters, there is a burden, because unless I can tell you what I know, there is a suggestion (and to myself as well) that I do *not* know. But I *do* — what I see is *that* (pointing to the object). But for that to communicate, you have to see it too" (Gerald Bruns, "The Hermeneutical Anarchist," in Jeff Malpas, Ulrich Arnswald, and Jens Kertscher, eds., *Gadamer's Century* [Cambridge, MA: MIT Press, 2002], pp. 70–1; emphasis in the original).

37 Gadamer, *Truth and Method*, 2nd rev. ed., trans. Joel Weinsheimer and Donald G. Marshall (New York: Continuum, 1989), p. 361.

38 Ibid., p. 299.

39 Scanlon, "The Moral Basis of Interpersonal Comparisons," p. 37.

40 Ignacio Ortuño-Ortin and John E. Roemer, "Deducing Interpersonal Comparisons from Local Expertise," in Elster and Roemer, eds., *Interpersonal Comparisons of Well-Being*, pp. 321–36.

41 Ibid., p. 324.

*Chapter 9: Seducing Souls*

1 Pierre Hadot, *Philosophy as a Way of Life*, Arnold I. Davidson, ed. (Oxford: Blackwell, 1995).

2 Ibid., p. 89; emphasis in the original. Hadot might be exaggerating when he says Socrates did not, and did not intend to, "teach." Gregory Vlastos advises we should look at Socrates's declarations of his ignorance as "complex ironies." There are things Socrates claims not to know, but also things he does claim to know. See Gregory Vlastos, *Socrates: Ironist and Moral Philosopher* (Ithaca, NY: Cornell University Press, 1991), p. 32.

3 I will focus on writing and reading here, but the points made would apply to other activities as well. I imagine many of us have also forgotten (if we ever knew) how to look at artwork, listen to music, and smell a spring rain.

4 See Michel Foucault, *Ethics*, chapters, "Self Writing" (pp. 207–22) and "The Ethics of the Concern for Self as a Practice of Freedom" (pp. 281–301) (*The Essential Works of Foucault, 1954–1984*, vol. 1, *Ethics*, Paul Rabinow, ed. [New York: New Press, 1997]).

5 David Schaafsma, "Performing the Self: Constructing Written and Curricular Fictions," in Thomas S. Popkewitz and Marie Brennan, eds., *Foucault's Challenge: Discourse, Knowledge, and Power in Education* (New York: Teachers College Press, 1998), p. 264.

6 Hadot, *Philosophy as a Way of Life*, pp. 210–11.

7 Ibid., p. 211.

8 Charles Taylor, *The Ethics of Authenticity* (Cambridge, MA: Harvard University

Press, 1991), p. 89. See also his *Sources of the Self* (Cambridge, MA: Harvard University Press, 1989).

9   Foucault, *Ethics*, pp. 233–4.

10  Hadot, *Philosophy as a Way of Life*, p. 212.

11  Quoted in Martha Nussbaum, *Love's Knowledge* (Oxford: Oxford University Press, 1990), p. 230.

12  Zora Neale Hurston, *Their Eyes Were Watching God* (New York: Harper and Row, 1937), pp. 183–4.

13  Nussbaum addresses this issue in several essays in *Love's Knowledge*.

14  Hadot, *Philosophy as a Way of Life*, p. 109; emphasis in the original. Generalizing to all works of art, Hans-Georg Gadamer makes a similar point: "The consciousness of art — the aesthetic consciousness — is always secondary to the immediate truth-claim that proceeds from the work of art itself. To this extent, when we judge a work of art on the basis of its aesthetic quality, something that is really much more intimately familiar to us is alienated" (*Philosophical Hermeneutics*, trans. David E. Linge [Berkeley: University of California Press, 1976], p. 5).

15  Hadot, *Philosophy as a Way of Life*, p. 91.

16  David Schaafsma, "Performing the Self: Constructing Written and Curricular Fictions," in Thomas S. Popkewitz and Marie Brennan, eds., *Foucault's Challenge: Discourse, Knowledge, and Power in Education* (New York: Teachers College Press, 1998), p. 264.

17  David Blacker, "Intellectuals at Work and in Power: Toward a Foucaultian Research Ethic," in Thomas S. Popkewitz and Marie Brennan, eds., *Foucault's Challenge: Discourse, Knowledge, and Power in Education* (New York: Teachers College Press, 1998), p. 358.

18  McDowell uses this language in his "Towards Rehabilitating Objectivity" in Robert B. Brandom, ed., *Rorty and His Critics* (Malden, MA: Blackwell, 2000), pp. 109–23.

19  Thomas McCarthy, *Ideals and Illusions: On Reconstruction and Deconstruction in Contemporary Critical Theory* (Cambridge, MA: MIT Press, 1991), p. 33.

20  Hadot, *Philosophy as a Way of Life*, p. 211.

21  Maurice Merleau-Ponty, *The Primacy of Perception*, James M. Edie, ed. (Evanston, IL: Northwestern University Press, 1964). p. 167.

22  Ibid., p. 164; emphasis in the original.

23  In her *Happiness and Education* (Cambridge: Cambridge University Press, 2003) and *Educating for Intelligent Belief or Unbelief* (New York: Teachers College Press, 1993) Nel Noddings gives numerous examples of relevant questions.

24  Hans-Georg Gadamer, *Truth and Method*, 2nd rev. ed., trans. Joel Weinsheimer and Donald G. Marshall (New York: Continuum, 1989), p. 363.

25  Ibid., p. 362.

26  Ibid.

27  Ibid., p. 365.

28  Ibid.

29  Martin Heidegger, *Basic Writings*, David Krell, ed. (New York: Harper and Row, 1977), p. 299.

30  Jerome S. Bruner argues, "any subject can be taught effectively in some intellectually honest form to any child at any stage of development" (*The Process of Education* [New York: Random House, Vintage, 1960], p. 33). Of course, Bruner is not saying educators should ignore students' readiness for learning; just the opposite. But just because some concept is abstract, that does not mean understanding it must be deferred until students mature. "Abstract" concepts can start to be learned through "concrete" ideas and activities.

John Dewey argues that "abstract" and "concrete" tend to be misunderstood. (See his chapter "Concrete and Abstract Thinking," in *How We Think* [Boston: D. C. Heath, 1910], pp. 135–44.) A particular thing can be concrete or abstract depending on circumstances. Dewey argues, "Concrete denotes a meaning definitely marked off from other meanings so that it is readily apprehended by itself" (p. 136). So, must we assume that young people cannot understand a notion such as justice, which might be deemed "abstract"? If Dewey is correct, the problem would not be in the nature of the idea but in students lacking experience in using it, dealing with examples of it so that it can be "readily apprehended."

31  For example, see Gareth Matthews, *Dialogues with Children* (Cambridge, MA: Harvard University Press, 1984), and Robert Coles, *The Moral Life of Children* (Boston: Atlantic Monthly Press, 1986) and *The Spiritual Life of Children* (Boston: Houghton Mifflin, 1990).

32  John Dewey emphasizes immaturity as a power rather than as a deficit; it implies the power to grow. See Dewey, *Democracy and Education* (New York: Free Press, 1916), pp. 41–2 and *passim*.

33  Gadamer, *Truth and Method*, p. 167.

34  Ibid., p. 125.

35  John Dewey, *Art as Experience* (New York: Perigree, 1934), pp. 55–6; emphasis in the original.

36  Gadamer, *Truth and Method*, p. 366.

37  Ibid., p. 368.

38  Perhaps many people would not see the questionability in this question.

39  Gadamer, *Truth and Method*, p. 464.

40  Ibid., p. 379.

41  Joseph Raz argues that proper caution does not require we hold back on truth claims, that we treat our beliefs only as "beliefs" no more justified than others' beliefs. See Raz, *Ethics in the Public Domain*, rev. ed. (Oxford: Oxford University Press, Clarendon Press, 1994), p. 90 and *passim*.

42  Hadot, *Philosophy as a Way of Life*, p. 92.

43  Gadamer proposes, "Every emotional influence occurring through speech is in a certain sense . . . a manipulation," and that Habermas's view "that rhetoric contains a coercive character and must be circumvented in the interest

of coercion-free rational dialogue seems to me to be shockingly unrealistic"
(Gadamer, "Reply to My Critics," in Gayle L. Ormiston and Alan D. Schrift,
eds., *The Hermeneutic Tradition* [Albany: State University of New York Press,
1990], p. 292).

44  Hadot, *Philosophy as a Way of Life*, pp. 149–52.

45  Ibid., p. 154.

46  Ibid., p. 92.

47  Georgia Warnke (*Gadamer: Hermeneutics, Tradition and Reason* [Stanford:
Stanford University Press, 1987], p. 170) describes fusion of horizons this way:
"Whether [participants] conclude by agreeing or disagreeing in a substan-
tive sense, their positions are now informed by all the other positions. They
are able to see the worth of different considerations, incorporate different
examples and defend themselves against different criticisms. In this way their
views acquire a greater warrant; they are less blind and one-sided and, to this
extent, more rational than they previously were."

48  Gadamer, *Truth and Method*, p. 365. Foucault writes about "technologies of
the self" (Foucault, *Ethics*, pp. 223–51). The various schools of classical therapeutic philosophy did develop particular, typically very prescriptive, strategies
and activities. (See also Martha Nussbaum, *The Therapy of Desire* [Princeton,
NJ: Princeton University Press, 1994].) There could be helpful tricks for teachers to try, but they do not add up to a "technology" for well-being.

49  Again, I do not want to exaggerate my differences with Dewey. Of course, he
too decries the sort of narrow experience I describe (if he would even call it
an experience). He might even deny such an experience is created in the sense
he has in mind, because a person so predisposed in their perceptions could be
said to reproduce a previous experience rather than create one. Nonetheless, I
think Dewey overemphasizes the active aspects of "taking in" compared with
the passive.

50  Gadamer, *Truth and Method*, p. 367.

*Epilogue*

1  Pierre Hadot, *Philosophy as a Way of Life*. Arnold I. Davidson, ed. (Oxford:
Blackwell, 1995).

2  Hans-Georg Gadamer, *Reason in the Age of Science*, trans. Frederick G.
Lawrence (Cambridge, MA: MIT Press, 1981), p. 149. Gadamer believes
human beings have a natural inclination toward philosophy, toward the desire
to know.

3  Charles Taylor, *The Ethics of Authenticity* (Cambridge, MA: Harvard University
Press, 1991), p. 73.

4  Martha Nussbaum, *Love's Knowledge* (New York: Oxford University Press,
1990), p. 148.

5  Hadot, *Philosophy as a Way of Life*, pp. 266–7.

6   Ibid., p. 268.

7   Ibid., p. 265.

8   John McDowell, *Mind and World* (Cambridge, MA: Harvard University Press, 1996).

9   Charles Taylor, *Sources of the Self* (Cambridge, MA: Harvard University Press, 1989), p. 520.

# Works Cited

Ambrose, Stephen E. *D-Day*. New York: Simon and Schuster, 1994.

Anton, Anatole, Milton Fisk, and Nancy Holstrom, eds. *Not for Sale: In Defense of Public Goods*. Boulder, CO: Westview Press, 2000.

Aristotle. *Nicomachean Ethics*. Trans. J. A. K. Thomson. New York: Penguin Books, 1953.

Arneson, Richard J. "Perfectionism and Politics." *Ethics* 111 (2000): 37–63.

Audi, Robert. "Moral Judgment and Reasons for Action." In *Ethics and Practical Reason*. Eds. Garrett Cullity and Berys Gaut. Oxford: Oxford University Press, 1997, Clarendon Press, pp. 125–59.

Barber, Benjamin. *Strong Democracy*. Berkeley: University of California Press, 1984.

Benson, Jackson J. *John Steinbeck, Writer*. New York: Penguin, 1984.

Bentham, Jeremy. "An Introduction to the Principles of Morals and Legislation." In *The Utilitarians*. Garden City, NY: Anchor Books, 1973, pp. 7–398.

Berliner, David C. "Our Impoverished View of Educational Reform." *TCRecord*, August 2, 2005. Available online at www.tcrecord.org/content.asp?contentid=12106 (accessed on March 7, 2010).

Bernstein, Richard J. *The Restructuring of Social and Political Theory*. Philadelphia: University of Pennsylvania Press, 1976.

——*Beyond Objectivism and Relativism*. Philadelphia: University of Pennsylvania Press, 1983.

——*The New Constellation: The Ethical-Political Horizons of Modernity/Postmodernity*. Cambridge, MA: MIT Press, 1991.

Blacker, David. "Intellectuals at Work and in Power: Toward a Foucaultian Research Ethic." In *Foucault's Challenge: Discourse, Knowledge, and Power in Education*. Eds. Thomas S. Popkewitz and Marie Brennan. New York: Teachers College Press, 1998, pp. 348–67.

Brandom, Robert B., ed. *Rorty and His Critics*. Malden, MA: Blackwell, 2000.

Bredo, Eric and Walter Feinberg, eds. *Knowledge and Values in Social and Educational Research*. Philadelphia: Temple University Press, 1982.

Bruner, Jerome S. *The Process of Education*. New York: Random House, Vintage, 1960.

Bruns, Gerald. "The Hermeneutical Anarchist." In *Gadamer's Century*. Eds. Jeff Malpas, Ulrich Arnswald, and Jens Kertscher. Cambridge, MA: MIT Press, 2002, pp. 45–76.

Cavell, Stanley. *The Claim of Reason*. New York: Oxford University Press, 1979.

Chang, Ruth. Introduction to *Incommensurability, Incomparability, and Practical Reason*. Ed. Ruth Chang. Cambridge, MA: Harvard University Press, 1997, pp. 1–34.

Chang, Ruth, ed. *Incommensurability, Incomparability, and Practical Reason*. Cambridge, MA: Harvard University Press, 1997.

Chisholm, Roderick M. "Gadamer and Realism: Reaching an Understanding." In *The Philosophy of Hans-Georg Gadamer*. Ed. Lewis Edwin Hahn. Chicago: Open Court, 1997, pp. 99–108.

Cockburn, David, ed. *Human Beings*. Cambridge: Cambridge University Press, 1991.

Coles, Robert. *The Moral Life of Children*. Boston: Atlantic Monthly Press, 1986.

——*The Spiritual Life of Children*. Boston: Houghton Mifflin, 1990.

Connolly, William E. *Politics and Ambiguity*. Madison: University of Wisconsin Press, 1987.

Crisp, Roger and Brad Hooker, eds. *Well-Being and Morality: Essays in Honour of James Griffin*. Oxford: Oxford University Press, Clarendon Press, 2000.

Cuban, Larry. "Why Is It So Hard to Get 'Good' Schools?" In *Reconstructing the Common Good in Education*. Eds. Larry Cuban and Dorothy Shipps. Stanford, CA: Stanford University Press, 2000, pp. 148–69.

Cuban, Larry and Dorothy Shipps, eds. *Reconstructing the Common Good in Education*. Stanford, CA: Stanford University Press, 2000.

Cullity, Garret and Berys Gaut, eds. *Ethics and Practical Reason*. Oxford: Oxford University Press, Clarendon Press, 1997.

Dallmayr, Fred, ed. *Border Crossings: Toward a Comparative Political Theory*. Lanham, MD: Lexington, 1999.

Dancy, Jonathan. "Recognition and Reaction." In *Well-Being and Morality: Essays in Honour of James Griffin*. Eds. Roger Crisp and Brad Hooker. Oxford: Oxford University Press, Clarendon Press, 2000, pp. 39–52.

Dewey, John. *Moral Principles in Education*. Carbondale: Southern Illinois University Press, 1909.

——*How We Think*. Boston: D. C. Heath, 1910.

——*Democracy and Education*. New York: Free Press, 1916.

——*Human Nature and Conduct*. Carbondale: Southern Illinois University Press, 1922.

——*Experience and Nature*. Chicago: Open Court, 1926.

——*The Quest for Certainty*. New York: Perigree, 1929.

——*Art as Experience*. New York: Perigree, 1934.

——*Experience and Education*. New York: Collier, 1938.

——*Philosophy of Education*. Ames, IA: Littlefield, Adams, 1956. Originally published as *Problems of Men* (Philosophical Library, 1946).

——"Analysis of Reflective Thinking." In *The Essential Dewey*, vol. 2, *Ethics, Logic, Psychology*. Eds. Larry A. Hickman and Thomas M. Alexander. Bloomington: Indiana University Press, 1998, pp. 137–44.

——"Moral Judgment and Knowledge." In *The Essential Dewey*, vol. 2, *Ethics, Logic, Psychology*. Eds. Larry A. Hickman and Thomas M. Alexander. Bloomington: Indiana University Press, 1998, pp. 328–40.

Dewey, John and James Tufts. *Ethics*. New York: Henry Holt, 1909.

Diamond, Cora. "The Importance of Being Human." In *Human Beings*. Ed. David Cockburn. Cambridge: Cambridge University Press, 1991, pp. 35–62.

Diener, Ed and Eunkook M. Suh. "Measuring Subjective Well-Being to Compare the Quality of Life of Cultures." In *Culture and Subjective Well-Being*. Eds. Ed Diener and Eunkook M. Suh. Cambridge, MA: MIT Press, 2000, pp. 3–12.

Diener, Ed and Eunkook M. Suh, eds. *Culture and Subjective Well-Being*. Cambridge, MA: MIT Press, 2000.

Douglass, R. Bruce, Gerald M. Mara, and Henry S. Richardson, eds. *Liberalism and the Good*. New York: Routledge, 1990.

Elster, Jon. "Local Justice and Interpersonal Comparisons." In *Interpersonal Comparisons of Well-Being*. Eds. Jon Elster and John E. Roemer. New York: Cambridge University Press, 1991, pp. 98–126.

Elster, Jon and John E. Roemer, eds. *Interpersonal Comparisons of Well-Being*. New York: Cambridge University Press, 1991.

Engstrom, Stephen and Jennifer Whiting, eds. *Aristotle, Kant, and the Stoics: Rethinking Happiness and Duty*. New York: Cambridge University Press, 1996.

Foote, Donna. "Lessons from Locke." *Newsweek*, August 11, 2008, p. 47.

Foucault, Michel. *The Essential Works of Foucault, 1954–1984*, vol. 1, *Ethics*. Ed. Paul Rabinow. New York: New Press, 1997.

Gadamer, Hans-Georg. *Philosophical Hermeneutics*. Trans. David E. Linge. Berkeley: University of California Press, 1976.

——*Reason in the Age of Science*. Trans. Frederick G. Lawrence. Cambridge, MA: MIT Press, 1981.

——*Truth and Method*, 2nd rev. ed. Trans. Joel Weinsheimer and Donald G. Marshall. New York: Continuum, 1989.

——"Reply to My Critics." In *The Hermeneutic Tradition*. Eds. Gayle L. Ormiston and Alan D. Schrift. Albany: State University of New York Press, 1990, pp. 273–97.

——"Reply to Roderick M. Chisholm." In *The Philosophy of Hans-Georg Gadamer*. Ed. Lewis Edwin Hahn. Chicago: Open Court, 1997, pp. 109–10.

Grandin, Temple. *Thinking in Pictures: My Life with Autism*. New York: Random House, Vintage, 2006.

Greenawalt, Kent. *Private Consciences and Public Reasons*. New York: Oxford University Press, 1995.

Griffin, James. *Well-Being*. Oxford: Oxford University Press, Clarendon Press, 1986.

———"Recognition and Reaction." In *Well-Being and Morality: Essays in Honour of James Griffin*. Eds. Roger Crisp and Brad Hooker. Oxford: Oxford University Press, Clarendon Press, 2000, pp. 289–96.

———"The Supervenience of the Evaluative on the Natural." In *Well-Being and Morality: Essays in Honour of James Griffin*. Eds. Roger Crisp and Brad Hooker. Oxford: Oxford University Press, Clarendon Press, 2000, pp. 296–303.

Gutmann, Amy, ed. *Multiculturalism and "The Politics of Recognition."* Princeton, NJ: Princeton University Press, 1992.

Gutmann, Amy and Dennis Thompson. *Democracy and Disagreement*. Cambridge, MA: Harvard University Press, 1996.

Hadot, Pierre. *Philosophy as a Way of Life*. Ed. Arnold I. Davidson. Oxford: Blackwell, 1995.

Hahn, Lewis Edwin, ed. *The Philosophy of Hans-Georg Gadamer*. Chicago: Open Court, 1997.

Haidt, Jonathan. *The Happiness Hypothesis*. New York: Basic Books, 2006.

Heidegger, Martin. *Basic Writings*. Ed. David Krell. New York: Harper and Row, 1977.

Heinaman, Robert, ed. *Aristotle and Moral Realism*. Boulder, CO: Westview Press, 1995.

Hickman, Larry A. and Thomas M. Alexander, eds. *The Essential Dewey*, vol. 2, *Ethics, Logic, Psychology*. Bloomington: Indiana University Press, 1998.

Hurka, Thomas. *Perfectionism*. New York: Oxford University Press, 1993.

Hurston, Zora Neale. *Their Eyes Were Watching God*. New York: Harper and Row, 1937.

Kahneman, Daniel, Ed Diener, and Norbert Schwarz, eds. *Well-Being: The Foundations of Hedonic Psychology*. New York: Russell Sage Foundation, 1999.

Kant, Immanuel. *Kant's Ethical Philosophy*. Trans. James W. Ellington. Indianapolis, IN: Hackett, 1983.

Kekes, John. *The Morality of Pluralism*. Princeton, NJ: Princeton University Press, 1993.

Kellert, Stephen R. and Timothy J. Farnham, eds. *The Good in Nature and Humanity*. Washington, DC: Island Press, 2002.

Kim, Jaegwon. *Supervenience and Mind*. Cambridge: Cambridge University Press, 1993.

Klein, Gary. *Sources of Power: How People Make Decisions*. Cambridge, MA: MIT Press, 1998.

Korsgaard, Christine M. *Creating the Kingdom of Ends*. Cambridge: Cambridge University Press, 1996.

Kraut, Richard. *What Is Good and Why: The Ethics of Well-Being*. Cambridge, MA: Harvard University Press, 2007.

Kristjánsson, Kristján. "'Emotional Intelligence' in the Classroom? An Aristotelian Critique." *Educational Theory* 56 (2006): 39–56.

Kuhn, Thomas. *The Structure of Scientific Revolutions*, 2nd ed. Chicago: University of Chicago Press, 1970.

Kymlicka, Will. "Liberal Individualism and Liberal Neutrality." *Ethics* 99 (1989): 883–905.

Larmore, Charles. *Patterns of Moral Complexity*. Cambridge: Cambridge University Press, 1987.

Longino, Helen E. *Science as Social Knowledge*. Princeton, NJ: Princeton University Press, 1990.

Lutz, Catherine. *Unnatural Emotions*. Chicago: University of Chicago Press, 1988.

MacIntyre, Alasdair. *Whose Justice? Which Rationality?* Notre Dame, IN: University of Notre Dame Press, 1988.

Malpas, Jeff, Ulrich Arnswald, and Jens Kertscher, eds. *Gadamer's Century*. Cambridge, MA: MIT Press, 2002.

Matthews, Gareth B. *Dialogues with Children*. Cambridge, MA: Harvard University Press, 1984.

McCarthy, Thomas. *Ideals and Illusions: On Reconstruction and Deconstruction in Contemporary Critical Theory*. Cambridge, MA: MIT Press, 1991.

McDowell, John. "Eudaimonism and Realism in Aristotle's Ethics." In *Aristotle and Moral Realism*. Ed. Robert Heinaman. Boulder, CO: Westview Press, 1995, pp. 201–18.

——"Deliberation and Moral Development in Aristotle's Ethics." In *Aristotle, Kant, and the Stoics: Rethinking Happiness and Duty*. Eds. Stephen Engstrom and Jennifer Whiting. New York: Cambridge University Press, 1996, pp. 19–35.

——*Mind and World*. Cambridge, MA: Harvard University Press, 1996.

——*Mind, Value, and Reality*. Cambridge, MA: Harvard University Press, 1998.

——"Towards Rehabilitating Objectivity." In *Rorty and His Critics*. Ed. Robert B. Brandom. Malden, MA: Blackwell, 2000, pp. 109–23.

——"Gadamer and Davidson on Understanding and Relativism." In *Gadamer's Century*. Eds. Jeff Malpas, Ulrich Arnswald, and Jens Kertscher. Cambridge, MA: MIT Press, 2002, pp. 173–93.

McMahon, Darrin M. *Happiness: A History*. New York: Atlantic Monthly Press, 2006.

Meier, Deborah. *The Power of Their Ideas*. Boston: Beacon Press, 1995.

Meier, Deborah and George Wood, eds. *Many Children Left Behind*. Boston: Beacon Press, 2004.

Merleau-Ponty, Maurice. *The Primacy of Perception*. Ed. James M. Edie. Evanston, IL: Northwestern University Press, 1964.

The National Commission on Excellence in Education. *A Nation at Risk*. Washington, DC: US Government Printing Office, 1983.

Nietzsche, Friedrich. *Twilight of the Idols*. Trans. R. J. Hollingdale. New York: Penguin Books, 1968.

——*Thus Spoke Zarathustra*. Trans. R. J. Hollingdale. New York: Penguin Books, 1969.

——*The Gay Science*. Trans. Walter Kaufmann. New York: Vintage Books, 1974.

Noddings, Nel. *Caring: A Feminine Approach to Ethics*. Berkeley: University of California Press, 1984.

——*The Challenge to Care in Schools*. New York: Teachers College Press, 1992.

——*Educating for Intelligent Belief or Unbelief*. New York: Teachers College Press, 1993.

——"Education as a Public Good." In *Not for Sale: In Defense of Public Goods*. Eds. Anatole Anton, Milton Fisk, and Nancy Holmstrom. Boulder, CO: Westview Press, 2000, pp. 279–94.

——*Happiness and Education*. New York: Cambridge University Press, 2003.

Nussbaum, Martha C. *The Fragility of Goodness*. Cambridge: Cambridge University Press, 1986.

——*Love's Knowledge*. Oxford: Oxford University Press, 1990.

——*The Therapy of Desire*. Princeton, NJ: Princeton University Press, 1994.

——*Cultivating Humanity*. Cambridge, MA: Harvard University Press, 1997.

——"Aristotle, Politics, and Human Capabilities: A Response to Antony, Arneson, Charlesworth, and Mulgan." *Ethics* 111 (2000): 102–40.

——*Women and Human Development*. Cambridge: Cambridge University Press, 2000.

——*Upheavals of Thought*. Cambridge: Cambridge University Press, 2001.

Nussbaum, Martha C. and Amartya Sen, eds. *The Quality of Life*. Oxford: Oxford University Press, Clarendon Press, 1993.

Ormiston, Gayle L. and Alan D. Schrift, eds. *The Hermeneutic Tradition*. Albany: State University of New York Press, 1990.

Ortuño-Ortin, Ignacio and John E. Roemer. "Deducing Interpersonal Comparisons from Local Expertise." In *Interpersonal Comparisons of Well-Being*. Eds. Jon Elster and John E. Roemer. New York: Cambridge University Press, 1991, pp. 321–36.

Outka, Gene and John P. Reeder Jr., eds. *Prospects for a Common Morality*. Princeton, NJ: Princeton University Press, 1993.

Plato. *The Republic*. Trans. Benjamin Jowett. Buffalo, NY: Prometheus Books, 1986.

Popkewitz, Thomas S. and Marie Brennan, eds. *Foucault's Challenge: Discourse, Knowledge, and Power in Education*. New York: Teachers College Press, 1998.

Rawls, John. *A Theory of Justice*. Cambridge, MA: Harvard University Press, 1971.

——*Political Liberalism*. New York: Columbia University Press, 1993.

Raz, Joseph. *The Morality of Freedom*. Oxford: Oxford University Press, Clarendon Press, 1986.

——*Ethics in the Public Domain*, rev. ed. Oxford: Oxford University Press, Clarendon Press, 1994.

Reeder, John P., Jr. "Foundations without Foundationalism." In *Prospects for a Common Morality*. Eds. Gene Outka and John P. Reeder Jr. Princeton, NJ: Princeton University Press, 1993, pp. 191–214.

Richardson, Henry S. "The Problem of Liberalism and the Good." In *Liberalism and the Good*. Eds. R. Bruce Douglass, Gerald M. Mara, and Henry S. Richardson. New York: Routledge, 1990, pp. 1–28.

Rorty, Richard. *Contingency, Irony, and Solidarity*. Cambridge: Cambridge University Press, 1989.

Scanlon, Thomas M. "The Moral Basis of Interpersonal Comparisons." In *Interpersonal Comparisons of Well-Being*. Eds. Jon Elster and John E. Roemer. New York: Cambridge University Press, 1991, pp. 17–44.

Schaafsma, David. "Performing the Self: Constructing Written and Curricular Fictions." In *Foucault's Challenge: Discourse, Knowledge, and Power in Education*. Eds. Thomas S. Popkewitz and Marie Brennan. New York: Teachers College Press, 1998, pp. 255–77.

Seung, T. K. and Daniel Bonevac. "Plural Values and Indeterminate Rankings." *Ethics* 102 (1992): 799–813.

Sher, George. *Beyond Neutrality*. Cambridge: Cambridge University Press, 1997.

Smith, Michael. "Does the Evaluative Supervene on the Natural?" In *Well-Being and Morality: Essays in Honour of James Griffin*. Eds. Roger Crisp and Brad Hooker. Oxford: Oxford University Press, Clarendon Press, 2000, pp. 91–114.

Stocker, Michael. *Plural and Conflicting Values*. New York: Oxford University Press, 1990.

——"Abstract and Concrete Value: Plurality, Conflict, and Maximization." In *Incommensurability, Incomparability, and Practical Reason*. Ed. Ruth Chang. Cambridge, MA: Harvard University Press, 1997, pp. 196–214.

Strike, Kenneth A. "Perfectionism and Neutrality." In *Philosophy of Education 1999*. Ed. Randall Curren. Urbana, IL: Philosophy of Education Society, 2000, pp. 66–9.

Sumner, L. W. *Welfare, Happiness, and Ethics*. Oxford: Oxford University Press, 1996.

Taylor, Charles. "Interpretation and the Sciences of Man." Reprinted in *Knowledge and Values in Social and Educational Research*. Eds. Eric Bredo and Walter Feinberg. Philadelphia: Temple University Press, 1982, pp. 153–86.

——*Sources of the Self*. Cambridge, MA: Harvard University Press, 1989.

——*The Ethics of Authenticity*. Cambridge, MA: Harvard University Press, 1991.

——"The Politics of Recognition." In *Multiculturalism and "The Politics of Recognition."* Ed. Amy Gutmann. Princeton, NJ: Princeton University Press, 1992, pp. 25–73.

——"Explanation and Practical Reasoning." In *The Quality of Life*. Eds. Martha C. Nussbaum and Amartya Sen. Oxford: Oxford University Press, Clarendon Press, 1993, pp. 208–31.

——"Leading a Life." In *Incommensurability, Incomparability, and Practical*

*Reason.* Ed. Ruth Chang. Cambridge, MA: Harvard University Press, 1997, pp. 170–83.

——"Understanding the Other: A Gadamerian View on Conceptual Schemes." In *Gadamer's Century.* Eds. Jeff Malpas, Ulrich Arnswald, and Jens Kertscher. Cambridge, MA: MIT Press, 2002, pp. 279–98.

Vlastos, Gregory. *Socrates: Ironist and Moral Philosopher.* Ithaca, NY: Cornell University Press, 1991.

Warnke, Georgia. *Gadamer: Hermeneutics, Tradition and Reason.* Stanford, CA: Stanford University Press, 1987.

White, John. *Education and the Good Life.* New York: Teachers College Press, 1991.

Wolf, Susan. "Two Levels of Pluralism." *Ethics* 102 (1992): 785–98.

Wong, David B. "Coping with Moral Conflict and Ambiguity." *Ethics* 102 (1992): 763–84.

Yearley, Lee H. "Conflicts among Ideals of Human Flourishing." In *Prospects for a Common Morality.* Eds. Gene Outka and John P. Reeder Jr. Princeton, NJ: Princeton University Press, 1993, pp. 233–53.

# Index

241